Pro SQL Server 2008 Policy-Based Management

Ken Simmons

Colin Stasiuk

Jorge Segarra

Apress®

PRO SQL SERVER 2008 POLICY-BASED MANAGEMENT

ISBN-13 (pbk): 978-1-4302-2910-0

ISBN-13 (electronic): 978-1-4302-2911-7

Printed and bound in the United States of America 9 8 7 6 5 4 3 2 1

Trademarked names may appear in this book. Rather than use a trademark symbol with every occurrence of a trademarked name, we use the names only in an editorial fashion and to the benefit of the trademark owner, with no intention of infringement of the trademark.

President and Publisher: Paul Manning
Lead Editor: Jonathan Gennick
Technical Reviewer: Thomas LaRock
Editorial Board: Clay Andres, Steve Anglin, Mark Beckner, Ewan Buckingham, Gary Cornell, Jonathan Gennick, Jonathan Hassell, Michelle Lowman, Matthew Moodie, Duncan Parkes, Jeffrey Pepper, Frank Pohlmann, Douglas Pundick, Ben Renow-Clarke, Dominic Shakeshaft, Matt Wade, Tom Welsh
Coordinating Editor: Kelly Moritz
Copy Editor: Marilyn Smith
Compositor: Bytheway Publishing Services
Indexer: John Collin
Artist: April Milne
Cover Designer: Anna Ishchenko

Distributed to the book trade worldwide by Springer-Verlag New York, Inc., 233 Spring Street, 6th Floor, New York, NY 10013. Phone 1-800-SPRINGER, fax 201-348-4505, e-mail **orders-ny@springer-sbm.com**, or visit **www.springeronline.com**.

For information on translations, please e-mail **rights@apress.com**, or visit **www.apress.com**.

Apress and friends of ED books may be purchased in bulk for academic, corporate, or promotional use. eBook versions and licenses are also available for most titles. For more information, reference our Special Bulk Sales–eBook Licensing web page at **www.apress.com/info/bulksales**.

The source code for this book is available to readers at **www.apress.com**. You will need to answer questions pertaining to this book in order to successfully download the code.

To my wife Susan and son Nathan.

– Ken Simmons

For Robbie and Lana, who always put a smile on my face, and for Heather, whose policies always keep me in check.

– Colin Stasiuk

I'd like to dedicate this book to my wife, Jessica. Without your love, understanding, and support, I wouldn't have been able to do this. I love you always and forever.

– Jorge Segarra

Contents at a Glance

Contents

About the Authors

■ **Ken Simmons** is a database administrator, developer, and Microsoft SQL Server MVP. His other books on SQL Server include *SQL Server 2008 Administration* (Apress, 2009) and *Pro SQL Server 2008 Mirroring* (Apress, 2009). He has been working in the IT industry since 2000, and currently holds certifications for MCP, MCAD, MCSD, MCDBA, and MCTS for SQL Server 2005.

Ken is active in the online community, and often participates in the SQL Server forums on MSDN and SQLServerCentral.com. He enjoys sharing tips by writing articles for **http://SQLServerCentral.com** and **http://MSSQLTips.com**. When he is not working, Ken enjoys traveling with his wife Susan and son Nathan, and he can often be found on a cruise ship, at a Disney resort, or at the beach in his hometown of Pensacola, Florida.

■ **Colin Stasiuk** is a database administrator and owner of Benchmark IT Consulting, based in Edmonton, Alberta, Canada. He has worked with SQL Server since 1996, and currently holds certifications for MCP, MCTS, and MCITP for Database Administration and Development. Colin is also the president of EDMPASS, the Edmonton-based chapter of the Professional Association for SQL Server (PASS), and his blog **http://BenchmarkITConsulting.com** is syndicated at **http://SQLServerPedia.com**.

Colin (like any good Canadian boy) is an avid hockey fan, and enjoys spending quality time with his wife Heather, son Robbie, and daughter Lana.

■ **Jorge Segarra** is a database and system administrator for University Community Hospital in Tampa, Florida. He has been administering SQL Server for more than five years, and holds certifications for MCP and MCTS.

Jorge is very active in the online community and can be found on Twitter under the handle SQLChicken and at his blog **http://Sqlchicken.com**. He is also a founding member (or hypervisor) for the PASS Virtualization Virtual Chapter and a general volunteer for PASS. On the local level, he is a member of the Tampa SQL Server User Group as well as the Tampa Bay SQL Server Business Intelligence User Group. Jorge also enjoys traveling to various local user groups and events to present on all things SQL Server. When not being a total geek, Jorge enjoys spending time at home with his wife Jessica.

About the Technical Reviewers

 **Thomas LaRock** is a seasoned IT professional with more than a decade of technical and management experience. Currently serving as a database administration manager with ING Investment Management, Thomas has progressed through several roles at ING, including programmer, analyst, and database administrator. Prior to ING, he worked with several software and consulting companies, at customer sites in the United States and abroad. Thomas holds an MS degree in Mathematics from Washington State University. He is a member of the Usability Professional's Association and Quest's Association of SQL Server Experts, and currently serves on the Board of Directors for the Professional Association for SQL Server (PASS). Thomas is a Microsoft SQL Server MVP.

Acknowledgments

First of all, I would like to thank Jonathan Gennick for giving me an opportunity to write this book. He, along with everyone else at Apress, has been really supportive and easy to work with throughout this process. I want to thank Colin Stasiuk and Jorge Segarra for coauthoring the book with me. They both bring a lot of knowlege and experience to the table, and the book would not have been what it is without them. I was also lucky to get Thomas LaRock as a technical editor. He was able to offer valuable information and suggestions throughout the book, despite the fact that he was in the process of publishing his own book.

Ken Simmons

I want to thanks Ken Simmons for approaching me to coauthor with him and Jorge. He knew this was the first time I would be authoring a technical book and was very patient with all my questions. He was always more than willing to offer sound advice and to lend a hand in anything that would improve the overall quality of the book. Thanks as well to Thomas LaRock, whose comments and suggestions were key in improving the quality of both my chapters and my technical writing skills. Hopefully, I've now learned to "punch harder," as he would put it. Finally, I want to thank Apress for giving me the chance to take on this new challenge. Jonathan, Kelly, and Marilyn have all been very supportive and helpful throughout the process.

Colin Stasiuk

First and foremost, I'd like to thank Ken Simmons and Colin Stasiuk for inviting me to be a part of this project. You guys rock! To Kelly Moritz, Jonathan Gennick, Thomas LaRock, Marilyn Smith, and everyone at Apress, thank you all for all your tireless efforts. Without your patience and guidance, none of this would be possible. And thank you to the wonderful SQL Server community! Being able to interact with people from all over the world and share knowledge, experience, and enthusiasm has been amazing.

Jorge Segarra

Introduction

Pro SQL Server 2008 Policy-Based Management is critical for database administrators seeking in-depth knowledge on administering servers using the new Policy-Based Management features introduced in SQL Server 2008. Policy-Based Management allows you to take control of your environment by managing your servers by intent. Policy-Based Management is a key component in any infrastructure where you want to maintain standards and consistency across one or more SQL Server systems.

This book covers the full spectrum of Policy-Based Management, taking you from the planning phase through the implementation to the maintenance phase and beyond. It is for database administrators getting ready to move to SQL Server 2008 or anyone who wants to learn the ins and outs of Policy-Based Management to implement standards across the organization.

How This Book Is Structured

This book introduces you to the basic concepts of Policy-Based Management as well as covering the advanced topics you need to know in order to enforce consistent rules across your organization. Here is a quick rundown of what you'll learn:

- Chapter 1 provides an overview of Policy-Based Management. It introduces many of the terms and concepts you'll encounter throughout the rest of the book.
- Chapter 2 covers the many different options for creating conditions and policies, including how to categorize policies to ease administration.
- Chapter 3 explains the different evaluation modes and walks you through the steps for evaluating and scheduling policies.
- Chapter 4 shows you how you can extend the evaluation features offered in Policy-Based Management by using PowerShell.
- Chapter 5 covers everything you need to know in order to receive an alert when a policy fails. Topics include setting up Database Mail, creating an operator, and creating alerts on the appropriate conditions.
- Chapter 6 describes the tables, stored procedures, and system views in the `msdb` database where the Policy-Based Management information is stored, as well as the roles and permissions required to use Policy-Based Management.
- Chapter 7 shows you how you can take advantage of the Enterprise Policy Management Framework as a central reporting tool for Policy-Based Management.
- Chapter 8 provides you with some practical uses for Policy-Based Management. It discusses how to use a combination of Microsoft best practice policies and custom policies.

- Chapter 9 addresses how you can use Policy-Based Management to meet the compliance needs of your organization.
- Chapter 10 discusses the various resources you have to help you continue learning Policy-Based Management, as well as the support options you have if you need further assistance.

Prerequisites

Policy-Based Management was introduced in SQL Server 2008, so you will need to have at least one instance of SQL Server 2008 installed. We also cover Central Management Servers in this book, which require SQL Server 2008 as well. However, once you have installed an instance of SQL Server 2008, both Policy-Based Management and Central Management Servers will work with prior versions of SQL Server. You can download SQL Server 2008 Express with Advanced Services at no cost, from `www.microsoft.com/downloads/details.aspx?FamilyID=b5d1b8c3-fda5-4508-b0d0-1311d670e336&displaylang=en`.

In addition, the sample databases are no longer provided as a part of the SQL Server 2008 installation. A set of sample databases you can use for testing purposes can be obtained from the CodePlex web site at `www.codeplex.com/MSFTDBProdSamples`. Download the SQL Server 2008 Product Sample Databases from this web site and follow the installation instructions.

Contacting the Authors

You can contact this book's authors as follows:

- Send e-mail to Ken Simmons at `KenSimmonsii@gmail.com`, or visit his blog at `http://cybersql.blogspot.com`.

- Send e-mail to Colin Stasiuk at `ColinStasiuk@BenchmarkITConsulting.com`, or visit his blog at `http://benchmarkitconsulting.com`.

- Send e-mail to Jorge Segarra at `Jorge@sqlchicken.com`, or visit his blog at `http://sqlchicken.com`.

Please include the book title in any e-mail messages to the authors to help them identify questions or comments about the book.

CHAPTER 1

Introduction to Policy-Based Management

Have you ever had to manage multiple SQL Server systems and wished you could check on settings in a centralized, easy, consistent, and perhaps even automated manner? With the release SQL Server 2008, database administrators now have this ability, thanks to the introduction of a feature called Policy-Based Management.

In this chapter, we will explain what Policy-Based Management is and why you should use it in your environment. You will be introduced to the terms and concepts you need to be familiar with to take advantage of Policy-Based Management, as described in this book.

What Is Policy-Based Management?

Policy-Based Management is a new feature in SQL Server 2008 that allows you to define and implement policies across your SQL Server infrastructure. Policy-Based Management works in a manner similar to Active Directory's Group Policies, a feature of Microsoft Windows NT-based operating systems. Group Policy offers centralized management and configuration of systems, applications, and users via administrator- or system-controlled policies, which can then be applied at various levels of the managed directory structure.

Policy-Based Management adheres to those same principles as Group Policy, in that you can apply a policy against a target (such as a database, table, or stored procedure) and evaluate whether the target complies with your policy. If your target does not adhere to your policy, you can either enforce compliance with that policy or trigger an alert to let an administrator know about the policy violation. You can set up your policy to actively deny any nonconforming actions, or choose to simply log such actions, so that an administrator can address them later.

Policy-Based Management is a system for managing one or more instances of SQL Server 2008. Through the creation, management, and deployment of policies, you are able to apply your own custom-defined standards across an entire SQL Server enterprise.

Why Use Policy-Based Management?

Due to the recent economic downturn, businesses are trying to cut costs now more than ever. One common short-term solution is to reduce head count and make the most of the existing workforce. This means that many workers are forced to balance more and more responsibilities. Another trend that affects database administrators (DBAs) is the increasing scalability of hardware. So, DBAs who used to

1

manage ten databases may now be expected to manage hundreds. Now more than ever, DBAs need a way to manage their servers without having to babysit each one individually.

As a DBA, it falls on you to protect the integrity of the environment you manage by making sure that standards are in place. By *standards*, we mean the standardization rules you, as the DBA, create to enforce in your environment. For example, you may create a standard that states any database that is in full recovery mode *must* have transaction log backups every hour on the hour. Instead of just having the standard on paper and hoping this practice is followed, you can use Policy-Based Management as a means to proactively monitor and enforce this as a policy in your SQL Server environment. Using Policy-Based Management allows you manage by intent.

In previous versions of SQL Server, in order to find out when your last backup occurred, you would need to manually connect to each instance and check each database individually for its backup dates. An instance might have dozens, or even hundreds, of databases on it. That is a lot of manual labor! Using a policy, you can instantly check the last backup dates of every database on an instance—or even better, every database on every server—in just a few clicks. Just imagine—your morning backup-check routine, which previously took an hour, is now reduced to just a few minutes! That's a nice return on investment.

As a DBA, you also need to protect against unauthorized configuration changes on your system. For example, suppose you configured an advanced setting like Max Degree of Parallelism on a server. One day, a junior DBA or a vendor decides to flip it back to the default value of 0. Do you have any way of knowing when someone does this? Typically, you won't be aware of that change until users start to complain that the production environment is not running as it should, and you need to track down the problem. With Policy-Based Management, you can do routine configuration checks and make sure your database servers are configured the way you want them to be.

Policy-Based Management also offers the ability to enforce best practice standards against your databases. In addition to being able to create custom policies, you can use the SQL Server best practice policies that Microsoft has bundled with the default installation. Often, finding best practices can be quite a chore, since everyone seems to have an opinion on what they should be. Now, with Policy-Based Management, you get tried-and-true best practices straight from the source.

Policy-Based Management Requirements

Many of the new features in SQL Server 2008, such as Resource Governor, SQL Server Audit, and backup compression, require you to have either the Enterprise or Developer edition. This is not the case with Policy-Based Management. You can configure Policy-Based Management in your environment with any edition of SQL Server 2008, including Express (although with the Express edition, you are unable to create a Central Management Server).

Once your SQL Server 2008 instance is installed, you can evaluate policies against any SQL Server in your environment, as long as you have proper permissions to access each server. In fact, your SQL Servers do not even need to be running SQL Server 2008 to be evaluated by a policy; you can run policy evaluations against older versions of SQL Server as well.

■ **Note**: Some policies may not work on previous versions of SQL Server because of feature differences. For instance, since database mirroring was not available in SQL Server 2000, any policy trying to evaluate against that feature on a SQL Server 2000 instance will fail.

Policy-Based Management Components

When you look at the Policy Management node in SQL Server Management Studio, you will see three folders: Policies, Conditions, and Facets, as shown in Figure 1-1. The folder structure forms a sort of hierarchy of the objects required to use Policy-Based Management. Facets are required in order to create conditions, and conditions are required in order to create policies. Additionally, policies are applied to the targets you specify.

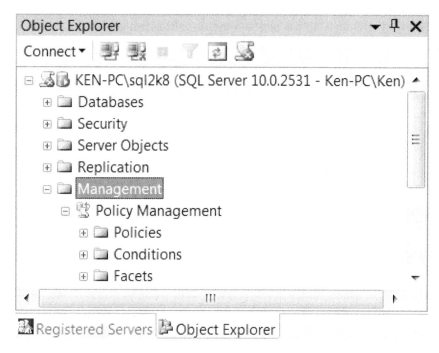

Figure 1-1. Policy Management node in SQL Server 2008

Let's take a closer look at each of the components that make up Policy-Based Management.

Targets

Targets are the objects that are managed by a policy. Targets can refer to many objects: servers, databases, instances, stored procedures, and so on. Policies can contain multiple targets. The available targets change depending on the context of the policy.

Facets

A *facet* is a group of logical properties that are related to each other within the context of the specified target. SQL Server 2008 exposes 74 facets, each with one or more properties. This allows you to leverage hundreds of properties in order to create policies.

You can display the properties of a facet by expanding the Facets folder and double-clicking a facet. For example, the Database facet exposes many properties, such as configuration checks for autoclose, autoshrink, compatibility level, and last backup date. You can see all the properties exposed by the selected facet on the General page of the Facet Properties dialog box, as shown in the example in Figure 1-2. In addition, you can select the Dependent Policies page to view the policies using this facet, and the Dependent Conditions page to view the conditions using this facet.

▪ **Note**: Facets are read-only. Also, as of SQL Server 2008, you cannot create your own custom facets.

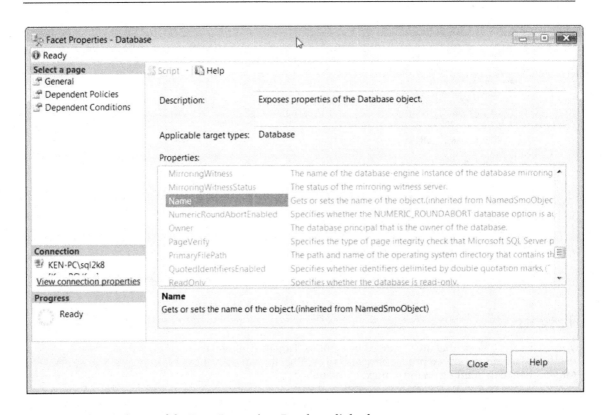

Figure 1-2. General page of the Facet Properties - Database dialog box

Conditions

A *condition* is a specified required state for the policy or facet being evaluated. Basically, a policy checks the condition of a target. If the target does not comply with the specified condition, the policy fails. A policy can evaluate only one condition, but you can evaluate one or more properties within a single condition.

You can display a condition by expanding the Conditions folder and double-clicking the condition. Figure 1-3 shows an example of a condition that uses multiple expressions. The Description page will show the description of the condition, if one has been provided. You can see any policies that depend on this condition by selecting the Dependent Policies page. Chapter 2 describes how to create conditions.

■ **Note**: You will not have any conditions unless you have previously imported a policy or manually created a condition.

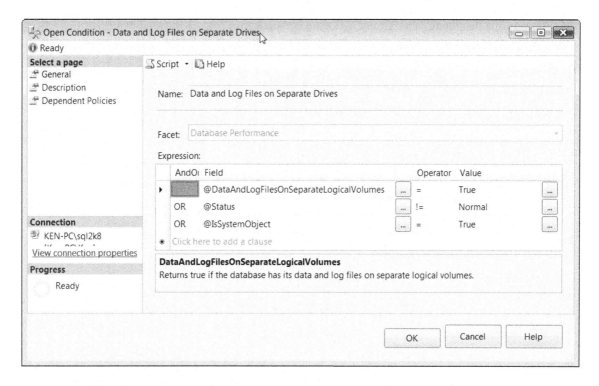

Figure 1-3. Open Condition dialog box

Policies

A *policy* is a complete package that includes conditions, facets, targets, evaluation modes, and server restrictions (evaluation modes and server restrictions are discussed in the next section).

Policies are stored within the `msdb` system database when you create them, but you can export and store them in XML format as well. This portability allows administrators to easily share and compare custom policies.

You can display a policy by expanding the Policies folder and double-clicking the policy. Figure 1-4 shows an example of a complete policy. Unlike with conditions, the Description page of the dialog box contains a few other valuable options you can use when managing policies. We will discuss creating policies in Chapter 2.

■ **Note**: You will not have any policies unless you have previously imported or manually created one.

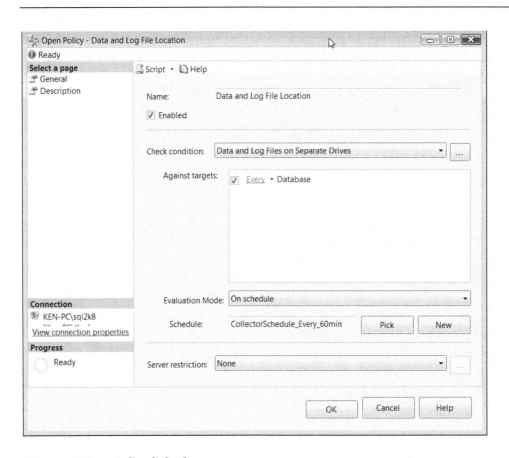

Figure 1-4. Open Policy dialog box

Policy Behavior

In addition to the components used with Policy-Based Management, evaluation modes and server restrictions can affect the behavior of a given policy.

Evaluation Modes

Policy-Based Management has four distinct modes in which a policy may be set to execute. These modes determine how the policy will be enforced against the previously defined targets. The following evaluation modes may be available, depending on the facet being evaluated in the policy:

- *On Demand*: This mode specifies that the policy will be run manually. By default, because this policy is meant as an ad hoc check, it will be set to disabled automatically. Even though the policy is created as disabled, you can still evaluate it at any time.

- *On Schedule*: Selecting this mode allows you to schedule the policy to be evaluated at any time. By default, you are able to choose from an existing schedule or create a new one to fit your needs. Creating custom schedules allows you to specify items such as recurrence options, frequency by day, frequency by time, and even how long the policy schedule will run (for example, run this job for the next two weeks).

- *On Change: Log Only*: Selecting this mode evaluates if the event occurring is attempting to make a change on a target specified within the policy. If the event violates the policy, the event will complete, and the results of the policy violation will then be logged to the event log, as well as to the msdb system database. This method is useful if you wish to evaluate the number of occurrences happening on a specific system and use this information to report to management. Having this sort of information can help administrators show the effectiveness of Policy-Based Management without actively affecting current production transactions negatively.

- *On Change: Prevent*: Much like the previous option, this method evaluates the policy based on an event making a change on a target specified within the policy. But unlike the log only option, the prevent option will actively roll back any transaction that violates the policy in place. This method is a proactive approach to controlling your environment, as you can select to enable the policy.

Figure 1-5 shows an example of a policy with multiple targets and the various evaluation modes available for it. We will discuss selecting these modes in Chapter 2, and cover evaluating policies in Chapter 3.

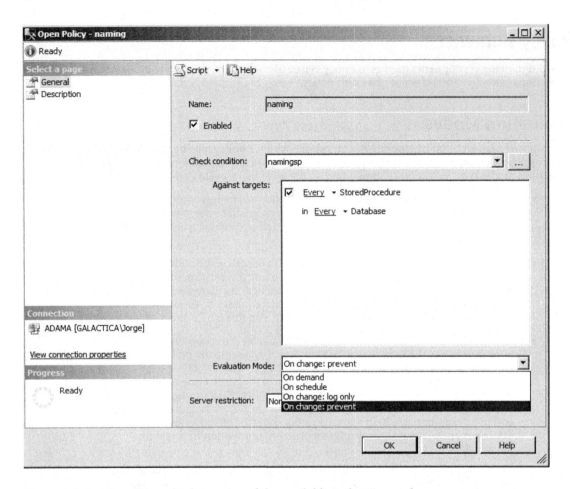

Figure 1-5. A policy with multiple targets and the available evaluation modes

Server Restrictions

Along with targets and facets, server restrictions are another way to control how a policy is evaluated. A server restriction is nothing more than a condition you can use to exclude servers from a policy by using the Server facet.

For instance, you can create a server restriction that limits the policy to evaluate against only SQL Server 2008 servers that are Standard or Enterprise edition. When you apply that policy, SQL Server will not attempt to evaluate that policy against any instance that is not one of those editions.

Policy Management

SQL Server 2008 provides some features that make managing and evaluating policies much easier. You can use categories to help you group and identify like policies, and you can use a Central Management Server to execute those policies across your organization.

Categories

Categories are a logical grouping of one or more policies that help you manage policy enforcement. For example, you can create a set of policies that are intended to be run against only test or development environments. When you create a policy, you are able to assign it to a specific category from the Description page of the Create Policy dialog box, as described in Chapter 2.

To display the categories, right-click the Policy Management node and select Manage Categories from the context menu. Figure 1-6 shows the Manage Policy Categories dialog box.

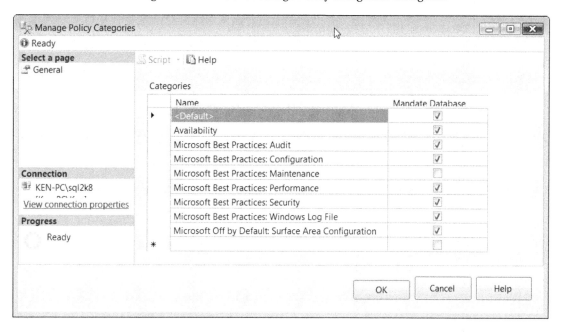

Figure 1-6. *Manage Policy Categories dialog box*

Central Management Servers

Technically speaking, a Central Management Server is not part of Policy-Based Management. However, this feature becomes extremely important in leveraging the power of policies against your whole SQL Server environment.

In SQL Server 2008, you can specify a single instance of SQL Server 2008 (Standard edition or higher) to be the Central Management Server. The Central Management Server stores a list of registered instances that can then be organized into one or more Central Management Server groups. You can view the Central Management Servers from the Registered Servers window of SQL Server Management Studio, as shown in Figure 1-7.

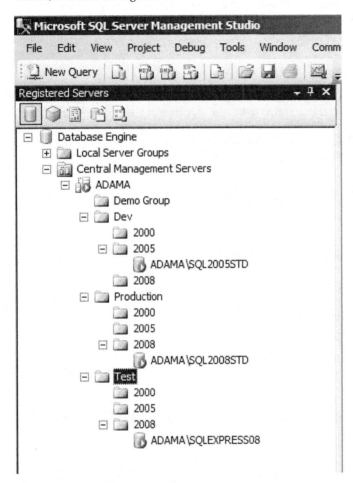

Figure 1-7. *A Central Management Server with custom groups*

We will discuss creating Central Management Servers, as well as using them to evaluate policies, in Chapter 3.

Enterprise Policy Management Framework

In addition to being able to query system tables and views, which we will cover in Chapter 6, you can use third-party open source projects to view the state and health of your policies in a graphical and automated manner. One popular project is Enterprise Policy Management Framework (available at `http://epmframework.codeplex.com/`), written by Lara Rubbelke. Here is a description of this project from Lara's blog (`http://sqlblog.com/blogs/lara_rubbelke/archive/2009/06/13/automating-sql-server-2005-2000-policy-evaluation.aspx`):

> *For those who are not familiar with the tool, the Enterprise Policy Management Framework is a reporting solution on the state of the SQL Server enterprise against a desired state defined in a policy. The key capabilities are to extend Policy-Based Management to all SQL Server instances in the enterprise, including SQL Server 2000 and SQL Server 2005. The EPM Framework will automate a scheduled evaluation of a set of policies against a group of servers, and provide reports for DBAs to understand where they have instances and database objects which are not complying with an organization's defined standards.*

Alerts

Once you set up your policies, you don't need to constantly check your servers to make sure they are compliant. Instead, you can use SQL Server Agent alerts in conjunction with Policy-Based Management to receive notifications automatically, or even to run a job, when a policy has been violated. We will walk you through the process of configuring alerts in Chapter 5.

Summary

This chapter laid the foundation for the remainder of the book by providing a brief introduction to the topics and concepts we will be covering throughout. First, we discussed what Policy-Based Management is and how you can use it to be more productive in your environment. Next, we covered the components that make up Policy-Based Management, including targets, facets, conditions, and policies. Then we talked about evaluation modes and server restrictions, which can affect the behavior of a policy. Finally, we covered the techniques available to help you manage and evaluate policies. In the next chapter, we will start digging into some of the topics covered in this chapter and show you how to create policies in your environment.

CHAPTER 2

■ ■ ■

Creating Policies

Before you can apply and enforce policies, you need to create them, because no policies are implemented by default in SQL Server 2008. You can create a policy in several ways, such as manually from scratch, using Transact SQL (T-SQL), exporting a policy based on your current SQL Server configuration, or even importing one of Microsoft's policies based on best practices. In addition, by using advanced conditions when creating a policy, you will see that there is almost no limit to the types of policies you can create for your environment. As you start creating policies, you will also find it helpful to create categories, which allow you group and manage similar policies.

Manually Creating Policies

In order to explain all the components that make up a policy and show you how they interact with each other, we will start by creating a new policy from scratch. To manually create a policy you must first create a condition, and then you will be able to create a policy that uses that condition. Once you have created a policy, you can place it in the appropriate category and apply it to one or more targets. This section will walk through the steps required to create a policy that checks to see if all of the databases on a server are using the full recovery model.

Creating a Condition

Let's start by creating a condition that will be used in a policy. In this example, we will create a condition that checks to see if a database is using the full recovery model.

To create a new condition, right-click the Conditions folder and select New Condition. (The Conditions folder is located under Policy Management in the Management node of Object Explorer in SQL Server Management Studio.) This will bring you to the Create New Condition dialog box, as shown in Figure 2-1.

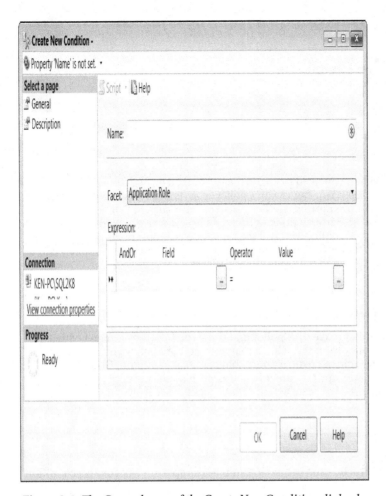

Figure 2-1. *The General page of the Create New Condition dialog box*

Create the new condition by entering the following information:

- *Name*: In the Name field, enter **Full Recovery Model**. Notice that the dialog box title is now Create New Condition – Full Recovery Model, and the error displayed under the title bar changes from saying that the name is not set to saying that the expression is not set.

- *Facet*: Before you set the expression, change the Facet field to Database Maintenance by selecting it from the drop-down list.

- *Expression*: Click the cell in the Field column and select @RecoveryModel from the drop-down list. Leave the equal sign (=) in the Operator column. You can see all the available operators by clicking the drop-down list. Click the drop-down list in the Value column and select Full. Notice that the Value column changes to reflect the values that are appropriate for the property that has been selected in the Field column. For example, if you changed the field to @LastBackupDate, a calendar control would be displayed in the Value drop-down list. You can also enter multiple expressions using AND/OR logic by selecting the next row and entering the appropriate information. Clicking one of the ellipsis buttons opens the Advanced Edit dialog box, which we will explain in detail in the section "Creating Advanced Conditions" later in this chapter.

Once you've entered all the information correctly, the errors are removed from the top of the dialog box, and the status changes to Ready, as shown in Figure 2-2.

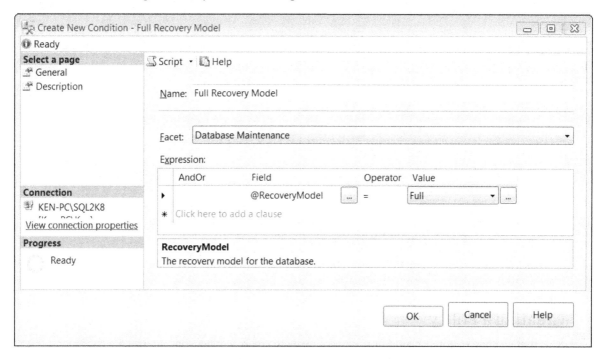

Figure 2-2. Completed General page of the Create New Condition dialog box

Optionally, you can provide a description by selecting the Description page from the list on the left and entering it in the text box provided. Select the Description page and type a brief description, such as **Condition to check to make sure a database recovery model is set to Full**, as shown in Figure 2-3.

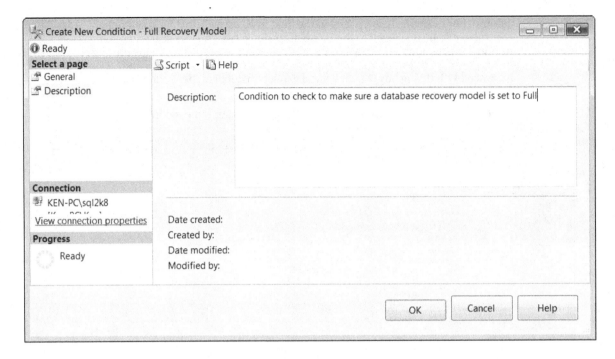

Figure 2-3. Description page of the Create New Condition dialog box

Click OK to finish creating the condition. You should now see the new condition under the Conditions folder under Policy Management.

Creating a Policy

Now that you have created a condition, you are ready to create a policy that can use the condition.

To create a new policy, right-click the Policies folder and select New Policy. (The Policies folder is located under Policy Management in the Management node of Object Explorer in SQL Server Management Studio.) You will see the Create New Policy dialog box, as shown in Figure 2-4.

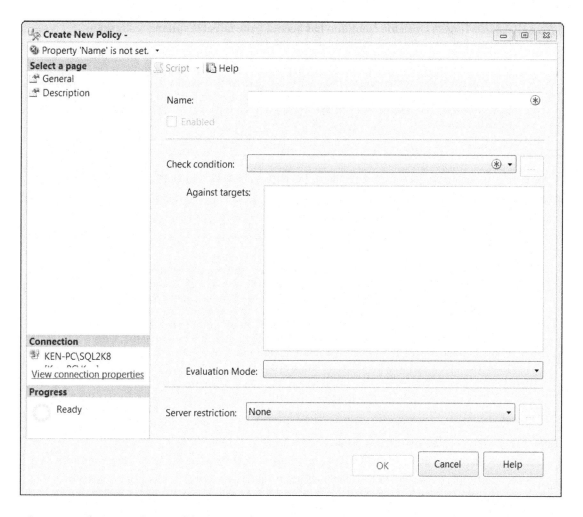

Figure 2-4. *The General page of the Create New Policy dialog box*

Create the new policy by entering the following information:

- *Name*: In the Name field, enter **Full Database Recovery Model**. Notice the title of the dialog box is now Create New Policy – Full Database Recovery Model, and the error displayed now indicates that the condition is not set instead of the name.

- *Check Condition*: Set the Check Condition option by clicking the drop-down list and selecting Full Recovery Model. If this is your first time using Policy-Based Management, it should be the only item you are allowed to select. If you have existing conditions, you will find them listed in alphabetical order, grouped by the facet to which they belong. Once you have selected the condition, you can click the ellipsis next to the drop-down list to edit or review the condition directly from the policy.

- *Against Targets*: Once the condition has been set, the target is automatically set to Every Database, which is the default behavior. However, you can exclude databases by clicking the drop-down menu next to Every (shown later in Figure 2-6) and selecting New Condition. This will allow you to create a condition you can use to exclude certain databases based on given properties exposed in the Database facet. For example, you may want to create a condition that will exclude read-only databases from a policy that verifies all databases are using the full recovery model.

■ **Note** A target is not always going to be a database. The targets change based on the context of the check condition. For example, if you were creating a policy to enforce a standard naming convention for new tables using the Tables facet, the Against Targets drop-down list would show All Tables.

- Evaluation Mode: Use this drop-down list to select the evaluation mode. Valid evaluation modes are On Demand, On Change: Prevent, On Change: Log Only, and On Schedule. For this example, we will use On Demand. Selecting On Schedule will enable you to either assign an existing schedule to run the policy or create a new one. Also, selecting On Schedule will allow you to enable the policy by selecting the Enabled check box located directly under the policy name. Only enabled policies will be run by the scheduled job that will be created to check the policies.

■ **Note** The evaluation modes displayed in the drop-down list depend on the facet you are using in the condition. All facets support On Change and On Schedule, but On Change: Prevent relies on the facet being able to use Data Definition Language (DDL) triggers to roll back the transaction. On Change: Log Only relies on the ability of the facet change to be captured by an event.

- *Server Restriction*: You can create a condition to exclude servers from the policy by using the Server facet. For example, you could create a condition that evaluates the policy only on SQL Servers that are running the Enterprise or Standard Edition. For this example, we will not be using a server restriction.

Select the Description page, as shown in Figure 2-5, to configure the remaining options.

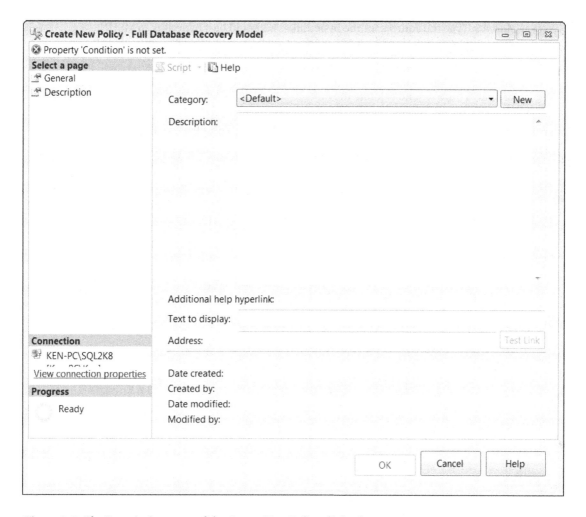

Figure 2-5. The Description page of the Create New Policy dialog box

The Description page of the Create New Policy dialog box includes the following options:

- *Category*: For this example, we will leave the category set to Default. To change the category, you can click the drop-down menu and select a defined category or click the New button to create a new category. We will show you how to manage categories later in this chapter, in the section "Managing Categories."

- *Description*: Optionally, you can supply a description. Enter a brief description in the text box, such as **Policy to make sure a database recovery model is set to Full**.

- *Text to Display*: Type the text that will be displayed as a hyperlink when the policy has been violated. For this example, enter **Choosing a Recovery Model**.

- *Address*: Type the address for the hyperlink. This could be a hyperlink to MSDN
    explaining why you should use the policy or even to an internal web site that lists
    the standards for the organization. For this example, type
    http://msdn.microsoft.com/en-us/library/ms175987.aspx, which will take you to
    an article on MSDN about choosing a recovery model. Click the Test Link button
    to open a browser and validate the link.

Once you have entered all of the information correctly, the errors are removed from the top of the
dialog box, and the status changes to Ready. Figure 2-6 shows the completed policy.

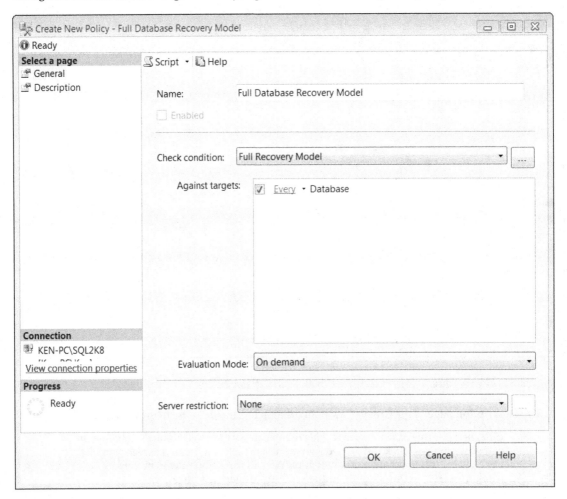

Figure 2-6. Completed Create New Policy dialog box

Click OK to finish creating the policy. You should now see the new policy under the Policies folder
under Policy Management.

That's all there is to manually creating a policy. Since Microsoft provides predefined policies, you may never need to manually create a policy, but it is the best way to become familiar with the available options.

Note that policies are stored in the **msdb** database. After you have created a new policy, you should make sure that the **msdb** is backed up. We will explain more about where the policies are stored in Chapter 6.

Viewing Dependent Policies

Once you create and save a condition, the next time you open it, you will see a new page called Dependent Policies. The Dependent Policies page shows all of the policies that depend on a given condition. If you open the Full Recovery Model condition we just created and select the Dependent Policies page, you will see that the Full Database Recovery Model policy is dependent on that condition, as shown in Figure 2-7. If there were multiple policies dependent on this condition, they would be displayed here as well.

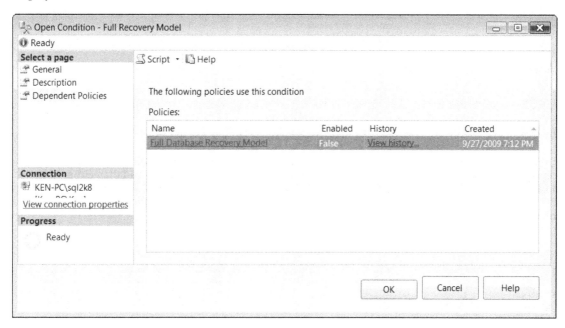

Figure 2-7. Dependent Policies page of the Open Condition dialog box

The Name and History columns are both hyperlinks. You can click the policy name to display the Open Policy dialog box, where you can manage the policy. For example, if you want to see why a policy is using this condition, you can easily launch the policy from the Dependent Policies page. You can click the View History link in the History column to display the Log File Viewer (see Figure 2-8), which displays the execution history for the selected policy. We will discuss how to execute policies in Chapter 3.

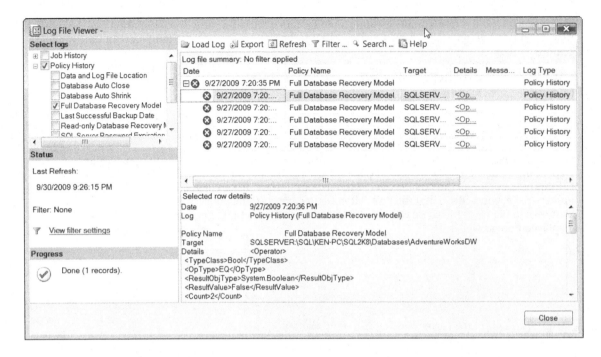

Figure 2-8. Log File Viewer showing the Full Database Recovery Model policy execution history

The Dependent Policies page is extremely useful if you want to delete a condition. Before you delete the condition, you first need to determine all the policies that use the condition, and then either delete those policies or define a different condition for them. If you try to delete a condition that has dependent policies, you will receive an error message stating that you cannot delete a condition referenced by a policy, as shown in Figure 2-9.

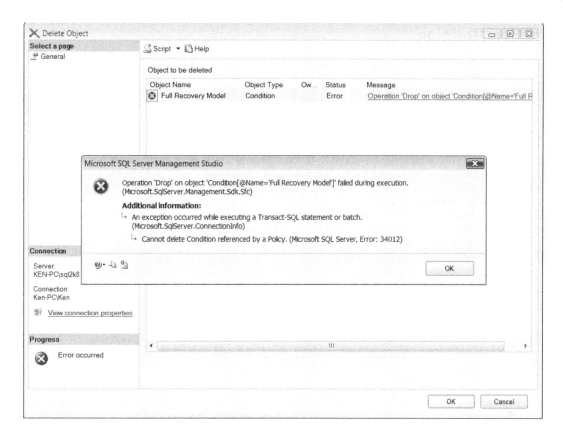

Figure 2-9. *Delete object error given when removing a referenced condition*

Alternatively, you can run the query in Listing 2-1 to determine all the policies that depend on a given condition. You will need to replace the condition name in the **WHERE** clause with the condition you would like to evaluate.

Listing 2-1. Query to determine policies that depend on a condition

```
SELECT Policy.name PolicyName,
               Policy.description PolicyDscr
FROM msdb.dbo.syspolicy_conditions Condition INNER JOIN
     msdb.dbo.syspolicy_policies Policy
        ON Condition.condition_id = Policy.condition_id
WHERE Condition.name = 'Full Recovery Model'
```

Importing Policies

You can import predefined policies that correspond with Best Practice Analyzer rules and default settings in the Surface Area Configuration tool. Microsoft provides these policies in the form of XML files as a part of the normal installation process. The XML files are located in the Policies folder in the Tools directory where you installed SQL Server.

Importing a predefined policy has several advantages. It not only creates the policy, but also sets all the required conditions. You know that the policy is based on Microsoft best practices and has been tested by someone other than yourself. However, you are not limited to importing predefined policies created by Microsoft; you can import any valid XML file that contains the necessary information to create a policy. By importing and exporting policies, you can easily apply custom policies throughout your organization. This section will walk through the steps required to import a policy. We will cover exporting policies in the next section.

For this example, we will import a policy that checks to make sure the data and log files are not stored on the same drive. To begin, right-click the Policies folder located under the Policy Management node in SQL Server Management Studio, and then select Import Policy from the context menu. This will open the Import dialog box, as shown in Figure 2-10.

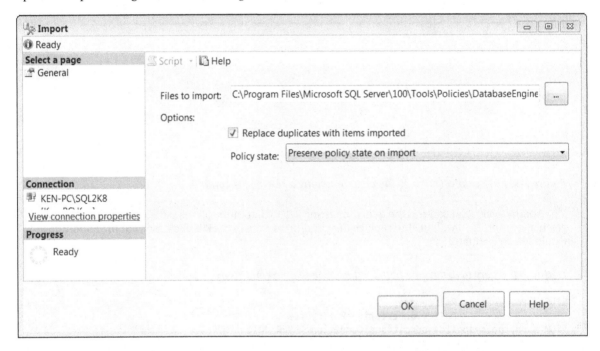

Figure 2-10. Import dialog box

Next to the Files to Import field, click the ellipsis button to open the Select Policy dialog box. Navigate to the C:\Program Files\Microsoft SQL Server\100\Tools\Policies\DatabaseEngine\1033\ directory and select the Data and Log File Location.xml file, as shown in Figure 2-11. (If you made custom installation changes, your files may be in a different directory.)

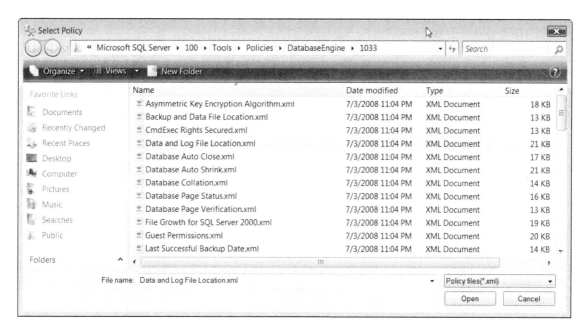

Figure 2-11. Select Policy dialog box

In the Select Policy dialog box, you can select multiple policies to import. Once you have selected all the policies you would like to import, click Open to return to the Import dialog box.

Select the Replace Duplicates with Items Imported check box to overwrite any policies and conditions that have the same name of the policy you are importing. Replacing an existing policy will not overwrite the history for the previous policy with the same name.

You can choose to preserve the state of the policy being imported, enable the policy on import, or, disable the policy on import. For example, setting the policy state is useful if you want to make sure a policy is disabled after you import it, even if the state was enabled when the policy was exported. In fact, it is a good idea to always make sure the policy is disabled until you are familiar with what the policy actually does. For this example, select Preserve Policy State on Import. Finally, click OK to import the policy.

You can now see the new policy and the conditions that were created under the Policy Management node in SQL Server Management Studio. The new policy is called Data and Log File Location (see Figure 2-12). The policy uses two conditions: one that checks to make sure the files are on separate logical drives (called Data and Log Files on Separate Drives) and one that places a server restriction on the policy (called Enterprise or Standard Edition). As you can see in Figure 2-12, you can use a condition as a check condition or a server restriction. By placing a server restriction on the policy, it will be evaluated against only servers that meet the condition defined for the restriction.

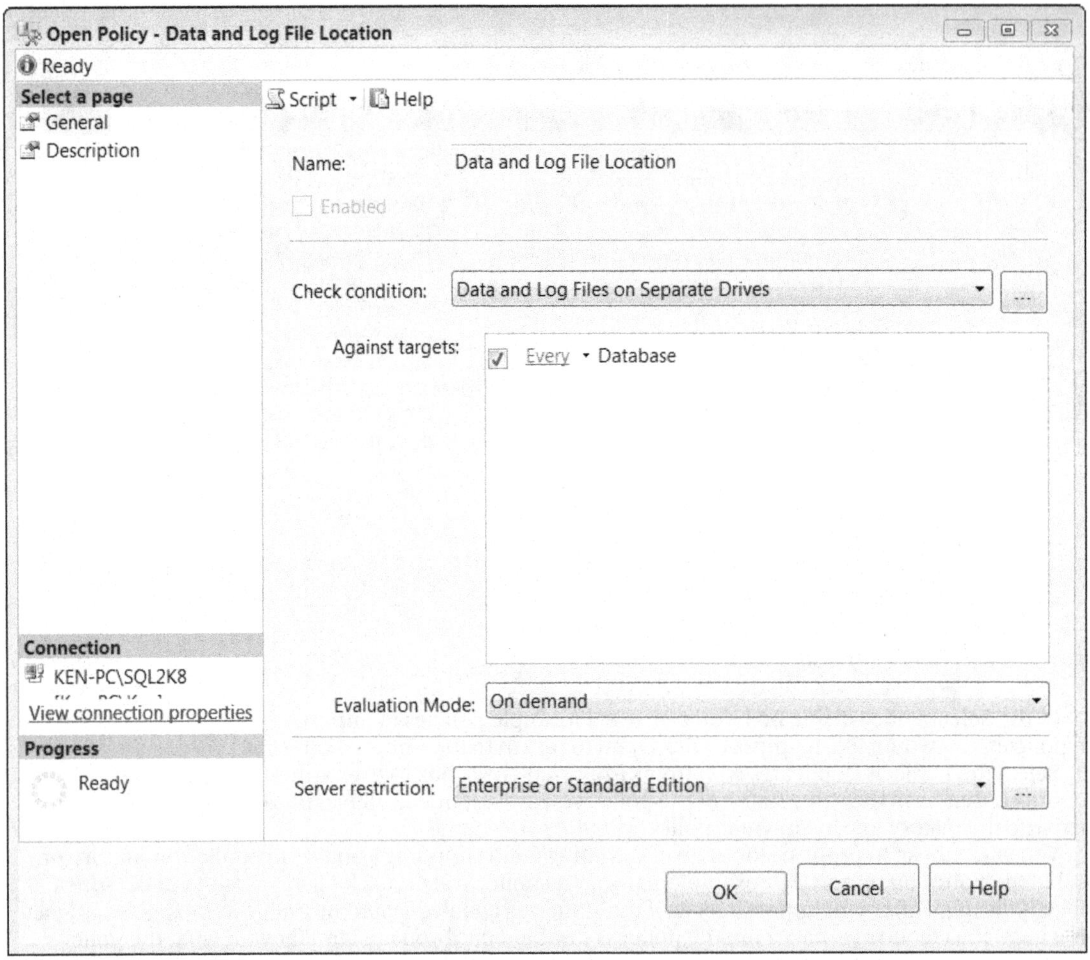

Figure 2-12. General page of the Open Policy dialog box

Figure 2-12 shows the general options that were automatically applied when you imported the policy. All the category, description, and hyperlink information is also prepopulated with the policy, as shown in Figure 2-13, making it easy to reference the documentation as to why this policy should be implemented.

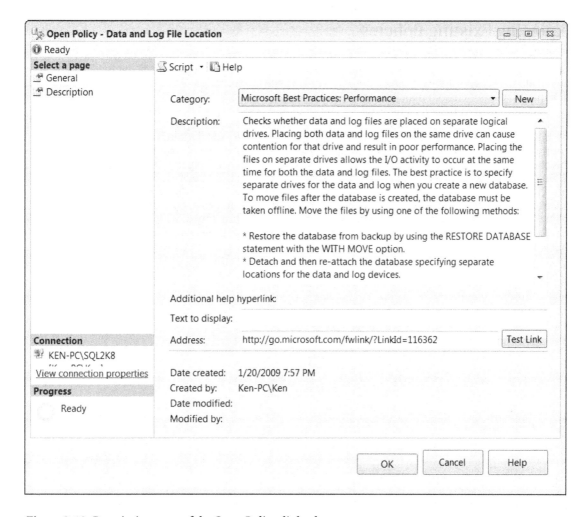

Figure 2-13. Description page of the Open Policy dialog box

As you can see, importing a predefined policy is an easy way to make sure your servers are using Microsoft best practices or standards that you have implemented within your organization. However, in the real world, you may find it hard, if not impossible, to align all of your applications with these best practice policies.

Exporting Policies

Just as you can import policies using XML files, you can export policies to create XML files as well. You can then use those XML files to import policies on other SQL Server systems. There are two ways to export a policy: exporting an existing policy and exporting the current state of a facet.

Exporting Existing Policies

It is extremely easy to export any policy you have already created to an XML file so you can distribute that policy throughout your organization. While you can back up the **msdb** database to save a copy of all of your policies, exporting a policy to an XML file is another good way to make sure you have a backup of all of your custom policies.

To export an existing policy, right-click that policy and select Export Policy from the context menu. This will open the Export Policy dialog box, which allows you to name and save your policy.

Just as you can import multiple policies at once, you can also export multiple policies. In order to export multiple policies, however, you must use the Object Explorer Details window. (You can open the Object Explorer Details window from the View menu in SQL Server Management Studio or by pressing F7.) In Object Explorer, select the policies you would like to export, as shown in Figure 2-14, and then right-click a policy and select Export Policy from the context menu. In the dialog box that appears when you are exporting multiple policies, you can specify only the location where you want to export the policies; you cannot enter names for them. If you browse to the directory to which you just exported the policies, you will see that each policy is created with a separate XML file using the original name of the policy.

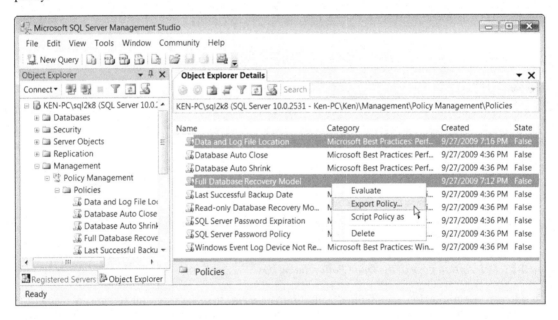

Figure 2-14. *Exporting multiple policies using Object Explorer*

After you have saved a policy to an XML file, you can open and review the policy in any XML editor. Listing 2-2 shows the XML generated by exporting the Full Database Recovery Model policy we created earlier in this chapter.

Listing 2-2. XML output generated by the Full Database Recovery Model policy

```xml
<model>
<identity>
 <name>urn:uuid:96fe1236-abf6-4a57-b54d-e9baab394fd1</name>
 <baseURI>http://documentcollection/</baseURI>
 </identity>
<definitions>
<document>
<docinfo>
<aliases>
 <alias>/system/schema/DMF</alias>
 </aliases>
 <sfc:version DomainVersion="3"/>
 </docinfo>
<data>
<xs:schema targetNamespace="http://schemas.microsoft.com/sqlserver/DMF/2007/08"
 elementFormDefault="qualified">
<xs:element name="Policy">
<xs:complexType>
<xs:sequence>
 <xs:any namespace="http://schemas.microsoft.com/sqlserver/DMF/2007/08"
 processContents="skip" minOccurs="0" maxOccurs="unbounded"/>
 </xs:sequence>
 </xs:complexType>
 </xs:element>
<xs:element name="ObjectSet">
<xs:complexType>
<xs:sequence>
 <xs:any namespace="http://schemas.microsoft.com/sqlserver/DMF/2007/08"
 processContents="skip" minOccurs="0" maxOccurs="unbounded"/>
 </xs:sequence>
 </xs:complexType>
 </xs:element>
<xs:element name="Condition">
<xs:complexType>
<xs:sequence>
 <xs:any namespace="http://schemas.microsoft.com/sqlserver/DMF/2007/08"
 processContents="skip" minOccurs="0" maxOccurs="unbounded"/>
 </xs:sequence>
 </xs:complexType>
 </xs:element>
<xs:element name="TargetSet">
<xs:complexType>
<xs:sequence>
 <xs:any namespace="http://schemas.microsoft.com/sqlserver/DMF/2007/08"
 processContents="skip" minOccurs="0" maxOccurs="unbounded"/>
 </xs:sequence>
 </xs:complexType>
 </xs:element>
```

```
<xs:element name="TargetSetLevel">
<xs:complexType>
<xs:sequence>
 <xs:any namespace="http://schemas.microsoft.com/sqlserver/DMF/2007/08"
 processContents="skip" minOccurs="0" maxOccurs="unbounded"/>
 </xs:sequence>
 </xs:complexType>
 </xs:element>
 </xs:schema>
 </data>
 </document>
 </definitions>
<instances>
<document>
<docinfo>
<aliases>
 <alias>/PolicyStore/Policy/Full Database Recovery Model</alias>
 </aliases>
 <sfc:version DomainVersion="3"/>
 </docinfo>
<data>
<DMF:Policy>
<DMF:Parent>
<sfc:Reference sml:ref="true">
 <sml:Uri>/PolicyStore</sml:Uri>
 </sfc:Reference>
 </DMF:Parent>
<DMF:PolicyCondition>
<sfc:Reference sml:ref="true">
 <sml:Uri>/PolicyStore/Condition/Full Recovery Model</sml:Uri>
 </sfc:Reference>
 </DMF:PolicyCondition>
<DMF:PolicyObjectSet>
<sfc:Reference sml:ref="true">
 <sml:Uri>/PolicyStore/ObjectSet/Full Database Recovery Model__ObjectSet</sml:Uri>
 </sfc:Reference>
 </DMF:PolicyObjectSet>
 <DMF:Name type="string">Full Database Recovery Model</DMF:Name>
 <DMF:Description type="string">Policy to make sure a database recovery model
                                                     is set to
Full</DMF:Description>
 <DMF:Condition type="string">Full Recovery Model</DMF:Condition>
 <DMF:ObjectSet type="string">Full Database Recovery Model_ObjectSet</DMF:ObjectSet>
 <DMF:RootCondition type="string"/>
 <DMF:PolicyCategory type="string"/>
 <DMF:Enabled type="boolean">false</DMF:Enabled>
 <DMF:AutomatedPolicyEvaluationMode
type="AutomatedPolicyEvaluationMode">None</DMF:AutomatedPolicyEvaluationMode>
 <DMF:ScheduleUid type="guid">00000000-0000-0000-0000-000000000000
 </DMF:ScheduleUid>
 <DMF:HelpText type="string">Choosing a Recovery Model</DMF:HelpText>
 <DMF:HelpLink type="string">http://msdn.microsoft.com/en-us/library/ms175987.aspx
```

```
</DMF:HelpLink>
 <DMF:ActiveEndDate type="dateTime">0001-01-01T00:00:00</DMF:ActiveEndDate>
 <DMF:ActiveEndTimeOfDay type="long">0</DMF:ActiveEndTimeOfDay>
 <DMF:ActiveStartDate type="dateTime">0001-01-01T00:00:00</DMF:ActiveStartDate>
 <DMF:ActiveStartTimeOfDay type="long">0</DMF:ActiveStartTimeOfDay>
 <DMF:FrequencyInterval type="int">0</DMF:FrequencyInterval>
 <DMF:FrequencyRecurrenceFactor type="int">0</DMF:FrequencyRecurrenceFactor>
 <DMF:FrequencyRelativeIntervals type="FrequencyRelativeIntervals"/>
 <DMF:FrequencySubDayInterval type="int">0</DMF:FrequencySubDayInterval>
 <DMF:FrequencySubDayTypes type="FrequencySubDayTypes">Unknown</DMF:FrequencySubDayTypes>
 <DMF:FrequencyTypes type="FrequencyTypes">Unknown</DMF:FrequencyTypes>
 <DMF:Schedule type="string"/>
 </DMF:Policy>
 </data>
 </document>
<document>
<docinfo>
<aliases>
 <alias>/PolicyStore/ObjectSet/Full Database Recovery Model__ObjectSet</alias>
 </aliases>
 <sfc:version DomainVersion="3"/>
 </docinfo>
<data>
<DMF:ObjectSet>
<DMF:TargetSets>
<sfc:Collection>
<sfc:Reference sml:ref="true">
 <sml:Uri>/PolicyStore/ObjectSet/Full Database Recovery
Model__ObjectSet/TargetSet/Server_/Database</sml:Uri>
 </sfc:Reference>
 </sfc:Collection>
 </DMF:TargetSets>
<DMF:Parent>
<sfc:Reference sml:ref="true">
 <sml:Uri>/PolicyStore</sml:Uri>
 </sfc:Reference>
 </DMF:Parent>
 <DMF:Name type="string">Full Database Recovery Model_ObjectSet</DMF:Name>
 <DMF:Facet type="string">IDatabaseMaintenanceFacet</DMF:Facet>
 </DMF:ObjectSet>
 </data>
 </document>
<document>
<docinfo>
<aliases>
 <alias>/PolicyStore/Condition/Full Recovery Model</alias>
 </aliases>
 <sfc:version DomainVersion="3"/>
 </docinfo>
<data>
<DMF:Condition>
<DMF:Parent>
```

```
<sfc:Reference sml:ref="true">
 <sml:Uri>/PolicyStore</sml:Uri>
 </sfc:Reference>
 </DMF:Parent>
 <DMF:Expression type="string"><Operator><?char 13?> <TypeClass>Bool</TypeClass>
<?char 13?> <OpType>EQ</OpType><?char 13?> <Count>2</Count>
<?char 13?> <Attribute><?char 13?> <TypeClass>Numeric</TypeClass>
<?char 13?> <Name>RecoveryModel</Name><?char 13?> </Attribute>
<?char 13?> <Function><?char 13?> <TypeClass>Numeric</TypeClass>
<?char 13?> <FunctionType>Enum</FunctionType><?char 13?>
 <ReturnType>Numeric</ReturnType><?char 13?> <Count>2</Count>
<?char 13?> <Constant><?char 13?> <TypeClass>String</TypeClass>
<?char 13?> <ObjType>System.String</ObjType><?char 13?>
<Value>Microsoft.SqlServer.Management.Smo.RecoveryModel</Value>
<?char 13?> </Constant><?char 13?> <Constant><?char 13?>
<TypeClass>String</TypeClass><?char 13?> <ObjType>System.String</ObjType>
<?char 13?> <Value>Full</Value><?char 13?> </Constant><?char 13?> </Function>
<?char 13?> </Operator></DMF:Expression>
 <DMF:Name type="string">Full Recovery Model</DMF:Name>
 <DMF:Description type="string">
Condition to check to make sure a database recovery model is set to Full
</DMF:Description>
 <DMF:Facet type="string">IDatabaseMaintenanceFacet</DMF:Facet>
 </DMF:Condition>
 </data>
 </document>
<document>
<docinfo>
<aliases>
 <alias>/PolicyStore/ObjectSet/Full Database Recovery
Model__ObjectSet/TargetSet/Server_/Database</alias>
 </aliases>
 <sfc:version DomainVersion="3"/>
 </docinfo>
<data>
<DMF:TargetSet>
<DMF:Levels>
<sfc:Collection>
<sfc:Reference sml:ref="true">
 <sml:Uri>/PolicyStore/ObjectSet/Full Database Recovery
 Model__ObjectSet/TargetSet/Server_/Database/TargetSetLevel/Server_/Database</sml:Uri>
 </sfc:Reference>
 </sfc:Collection>
 </DMF:Levels>
<DMF:Parent>
<sfc:Reference sml:ref="true">
 <sml:Uri>/PolicyStore/ObjectSet/Full Database Recovery Model__ObjectSet</sml:Uri>
 </sfc:Reference>
 </DMF:Parent>
 <DMF:TargetTypeSkeleton type="string">Server/Database</DMF:TargetTypeSkeleton>
 <DMF:Enabled type="boolean">true</DMF:Enabled>
 </DMF:TargetSet>
```

```
 </data>
 </document>
<document>
<docinfo>
<aliases>
 <alias>/PolicyStore/ObjectSet/Full Database Recovery
Model__ObjectSet/TargetSet/Server_/Database/TargetSetLevel/Server_/Database</alias>
 </aliases>
 <sfc:version DomainVersion="3"/>
 </docinfo>
<data>
<DMF:TargetSetLevel>
<DMF:Parent>
<sfc:Reference sml:ref="true">
 <sml:Uri>/PolicyStore/ObjectSet/Full Database Recovery
Model__ObjectSet/TargetSet/Server_/Database</sml:Uri>
 </sfc:Reference>
 </DMF:Parent>
 <DMF:TargetTypeSkeleton type="string">Server/Database</DMF:TargetTypeSkeleton>
 <DMF:LevelName type="string">Database</DMF:LevelName>
 <DMF:Condition type="string"/>
 </DMF:TargetSetLevel>
 </data>
 </document>
 </instances>
 </model>
```

As you can see by Listing 2-2, a policy is not something you want to create by hand. But for all of you curious types, interrogating an XML file for a policy is a great way to see what is going on behind the scenes. You may also notice many tags begin with **DMF**, which stands for Declarative Management Framework. DMF was the original name of Policy-Based Management, but Microsoft changed the name prior to the final release of SQL Server 2008.

Exporting Current State As Policy

Many policies can be exported based on the current state of a facet. Once you have configured the properties of the facet for a given object, you can export the current state of the facet as a policy.

If you are familiar with SQL Server 2005, you may have noticed that the Surface Area Configuration tool is not available when you install SQL Server 2008. The configuration of the Database Engine features is now managed using the Surface Area Configuration facet in Policy-Based Management. This section will walk you through exporting a Surface Area Configuration policy using the current state.

In SQL Server Management Studio, right-click the server instance you would like to configure and select Facets from the context menu.

You can now select and manage any of the server-level facets, including the following:

- Server

- Server Audit

- Server Configuration

- Server Installation Settings

- Server Performance

- Server Security

- Server Settings

- Surface Area Configuration

For this example, change the Facet option to Surface Area Configuration, as shown in Figure 2-15.

■ **Note**: You can right-click other objects, such as databases and tables, to manage facets directly related to those objects. For example, if you right-click a database and select Facets from the context menu, you will be able to manage the following facets from the View Facets dialog box: Database, Database Maintenance, Database Options, Database Performance, and Database Security.

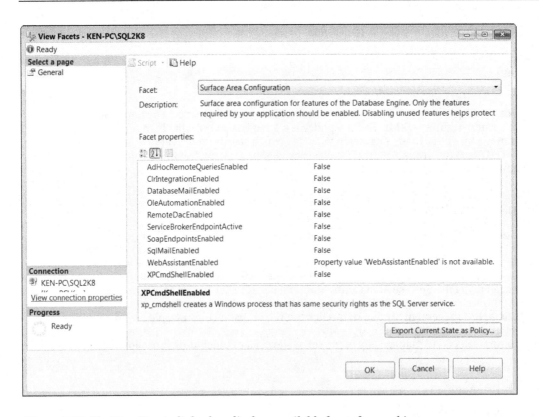

Figure 2-15. The View Facets dialog box displays available facets for an object.

From the View Facets dialog box, you can configure the values for the facet. If you had previously configured the options using **sp_configure**, they would show up as the current state.

You can also export the current configurations as a policy to the local server or to a file that you can import and apply to multiple servers across the organization. Click the Export Current State as Policy button to bring up the Export as Policy dialog box, as shown in Figure 2-16.

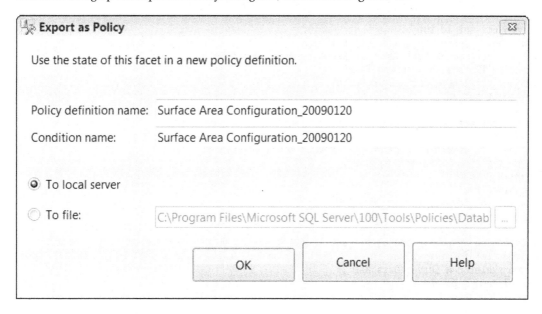

Figure 2-16. Export as Policy dialog box

The Export as Policy dialog box allows you to name the policy and condition that will be created. By default, the policy and condition name will be *FacetName_YYYYMMDD*. For this demonstration, save the policy to the local server and click OK. Click OK again to close the View Facets dialog box.

You should now be able to see your new policy and condition in the Policy Management node in SQL Server Management Studio. You can manage the policy using the same methods as if you created it manually.

Creating Policies with T-SQL

Another way to create policies is by using use T-SQL. This makes policies extremely portable. You can script custom policies and share them with other DBAs or even create a postinstallation script that will apply all the standard policies for your organization within seconds.

One of the advantages of using T-SQL to create policies over using XML files is the ability to place all the policies in a single script file. This way, there are fewer steps needed to deploy the policies throughout your environment. You can also take advantage of a Central Management Server (you will learn more about Central Management Servers in Chapter 3) to deploy all of your policies to a group of servers with a single click.

To generate the T-SQL for the Full Database Recovery Model policy we created earlier in this chapter, right-click the policy and select Script Policy as → Create to → New Query Editor Window. Listing 2-3 shows the T-SQL script that is generated.

Listing 2-3. T-SQL script to create the Full Database Recovery Model policy

```
Declare @object_set_id int
EXEC msdb.dbo.sp_syspolicy_add_object_set
    @object_set_name=N'Full Database Recovery Model_ObjectSet',
    @facet=N'IDatabaseMaintenanceFacet',
    @object_set_id=@object_set_id OUTPUT
Select @object_set_id

Declare @target_set_id int
EXEC msdb.dbo.sp_syspolicy_add_target_set
    @object_set_name=N'Full Database Recovery Model_ObjectSet',
    @type_skeleton=N'Server/Database',
    @type=N'DATABASE',
    @enabled=True,
    @target_set_id=@target_set_id OUTPUT
Select @target_set_id

EXEC msdb.dbo.sp_syspolicy_add_target_set_level
    @target_set_id=@target_set_id,
    @type_skeleton=N'Server/Database',
    @level_name=N'Database',
    @condition_name=N'',
    @target_set_level_id=0

GO

Declare @policy_id int
EXEC msdb.dbo.sp_syspolicy_add_policy
    @name=N'Full Database Recovery Model',
    @condition_name=N'Full Recovery Model',
    @policy_category=N'',
    @description=N'Policy to make sure a database recovery model is set to Full',
    @help_text=N'Choosing a Recovery Model',
    @help_link=N'http://msdn.microsoft.com/en-us/library/ms175987.aspx',
    @schedule_uid=N'00000000-0000-0000-0000-000000000000',
    @execution_mode=0,
    @is_enabled=False,
    @policy_id=@policy_id OUTPUT,
    @root_condition_name=N'',
    @object_set=N'Full Database Recovery Model_ObjectSet'
Select @policy_id

GO
```

The script in Listing 2-3 executes a few stored procedures in the **msdb** database, which ultimately insert the policy definition into the internal policy tables also located in the **msdb** database. These stored procedures are not documented, so it would not be a good idea to try to use them to create a policy from scratch. We will discuss the internals of Policy-Based Management in detail in Chapter 6, including internal tables and procedures.

Managing Policy Categories

Policy categories help you group like policies in order to ease policy administration. For example, you can sort by category in order to help you quickly identify a set of policies you would like to evaluate. You can also create custom categories that mandate target subscriptions to the policies within the category or just allow targets to subscribe to each category on an as-needed basis.

Creating Policy Categories

To create policy categories, right-click Policy Management in SQL Server Management Studio Object Explorer and select Manage Categories from the context menu. This will display the Manage Policy Categories dialog box, shown in Figure 2-17.

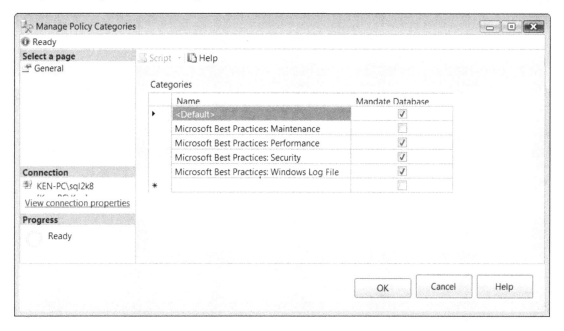

Figure 2-17. Manage Policy Categories dialog box

To add a new category, just type the name of a new category on the empty line, choose whether to mandate subscriptions, and click OK. If a category is mandated, it will be evaluated against all targets. If you do not choose to mandate subscriptions, you will need to specifically designate the targets that will be evaluated. This allows individual database owner to determine if the policy is relevant to their database and subscribe as necessary.

All policies must be assigned to a category, and if no category is specifically chosen, the policy will be assigned to the Default category. Note that for the Default category, you cannot remove the Mandate Database check box. All policies that remain in the Default category will be mandated against all targets.

You can also add a new category from the Description page of the Open Policy dialog box by selecting the New button next to the Category drop-down list, as shown in Figure 2-18.

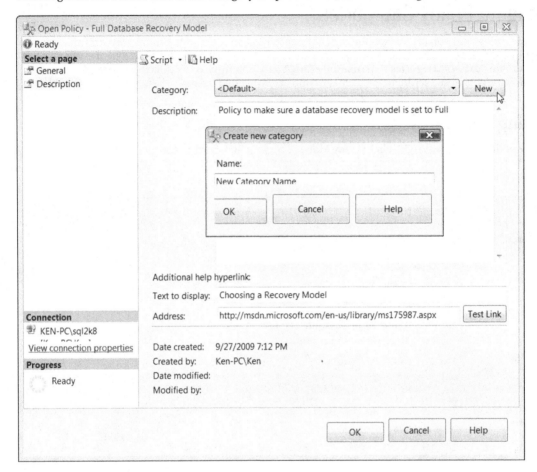

Figure 2-18. *Choosing New next to the the Category drop-down list in the Open Policy dialog box displays the Create New Category dialog box.*

Notice that in the Create New Category dialog box, you can specify only the category name; you cannot select to mandate database subscriptions. In this case, a new category will be created with the default option to mandate subscriptions. This is somewhat of a shortcut if you want to mandate subscriptions to the policies in the new category. If you do not want to mandate subscriptions, you will need to go to the Manage Policy Category dialog box to change the setting, so you may as well create the new category from there, rather than taking the Open Policy dialog box route.

Once you have created your categories, you can start assigning policies to them by selecting the Category drop-down list on the Description page of the Open Policy dialog box (see Figure 2-18). You can tell which policies are assigned to each category by running the query in Listing 2-4.

Listing 2-4. Query used to view policies by category

```
SELECT  B.name AS 'CategoryName',
        A.name AS 'PolicyName',
        B.mandate_database_subscriptions,
        A.is_enabled
FROM  msdb.dbo.syspolicy_policies_internal A INNER JOIN
                msdb.dbo.syspolicy_policy_categories_internal B ON
                    A.policy_category_id = B.policy_category_id
ORDER BY B.name,
        A.name
```

Figure 2-19 shows a sample result set returned by running the query in Listing 2-4. As you can see, this query will come in handy as you start incorporating more policies into your environment.

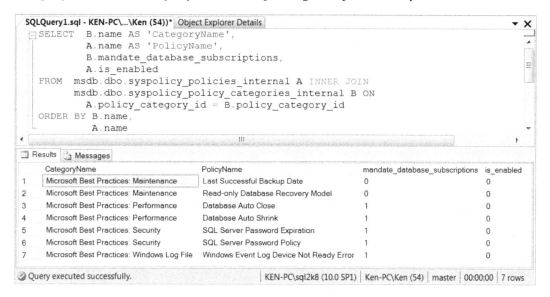

Figure 2-19. Results returned from running the query in Listing 2-4

Subscribing to Categories

We mentioned earlier that a target could choose to subscribe to a category if the category is not mandated. You can subscribe a database to a category, and all the policies within that category that apply to the database, or any object within the database, will be checked when you evaluate a policy within the category. However, you must be the database owner (dbo) or system administrator (sa) in order to subscribe a database to a category. If you allow each database to subscribe to a category, the policy administrators do not necessarily need to know which policies are relevant for each database.

To subscribe to a category, right-click a database and select Policies → Categories from the context menu to display the Categories dialog box, as shown in Figure 2-20. Select the Subscribed check box beside each category name that you wish to enforce, and then click OK.

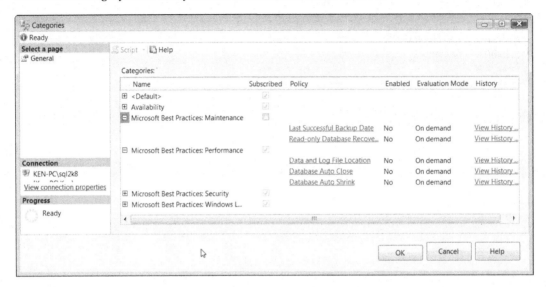

Figure 2-20. *Categories dialog box*

In the example in Figure 2-20, notice that the only category you can control is Microsoft Best Practices: Maintenance; all of the check boxes for the other categories are disabled. If you look at Figure 2-17, you will see that the Microsoft Best Practices: Maintenance category is the only one that does not have the Mandate Database option selected. It is important to remember that you cannot remove the Mandate Database option from the Default category, and all policies are placed in the Default category if you do not explicitly specify a different one. Therefore, if you want to allow database owners to manage their own categories, you need to make sure to put a little extra thought into creating categories and adding policies.

Creating Advanced Conditions

Thus far, we have showed you how to create policies and conditions based on predefined attributes of a given facet. However, you can create advanced conditions that extend the realm of Policy-Based Management far beyond the predefined attributes. The following is a list of available functions you can use to create advanced conditions:

```
Add()            Enum()           Multiply()
Array()          ExecuteSql()     Power()
Avg()            ExecuteWql()     Round()
BitwiseAnd()     False()          String()
```

```
BitwiseOr()        GetDate()        Subtract()
Count()            Guid()           Sum()
DateAdd()          IsNull()         True()
DatePart()         Len()            Upper()
DateTime()         Lower()
Divide()           Mod()
```

Not only can you use these functions in your conditions, but you can also access the properties that apply to the facet you are using to create the condition.

Two very powerful functions in the preceding list are `ExecuteSql()` and `ExecuteWql()`. Windows Management Instrumentation (WMI) allows you access information about the operating system, such as disk and processor information. By taking advantage of WMI Query Language (WQL), you can use the `ExecuteWql()` function to create policies using logic based on the state of the operating system. You can use the `ExecuteSql()` function to run any valid SQL statement that you can think of to help you enforce rules in your environment. You can use a property, function, or constant on either side of the operator.

The basic syntax for an advanced condition is as follows:

```
{property | function | constant}
 {operator}
{property | function | constant}
```

The biggest limiting factor for using advanced conditions is figuring out when and how you can use them, because it is up to you to think of usage scenarios for your environment.

Let's look at a situation where you can use an advanced operator. Let's say you have servers in your development environment and you want to create a policy to know if developers are creating an excessive number of databases. You can create a policy using an advanced condition that compares the number of databases on the server to a given value. If the number of databases exceeds that value, the policy will fail when evaluated against that server. Follow these steps to create the policy:

1. Right-click the Policies folder in SQL Server Management Studio and select New Policy from the context menu. Give the policy a descriptive name, such as **Check Number of Databases**.

2. Click the Conditions drop-down list and select New Condition to display the Create New Condition dialog box. Give the condition a descriptive name, such as **Check Number of Databases**.

3. Click the Facet drop-down list and select the Server facet, since we will be checking this policy at the server level.

4. Click the ellipsis button next to the Field column in the Expression grid to display the Advanced Edit dialog box.

5. When you highlight a function in the Advanced Dialog box, you get a lot of useful information in the Details section on the right side of the dialog box, including an example of how to execute each function. We want to get a count of all the databases on the server. Enter the following command in the Cell Value text box, as shown in Figure 2-21:

ExecuteSql('Numeric', 'SELECT COUNT(*) FROM sys.databases')

■ **Note** If you have any single quotes in your SQL statement, they need to be escaped by another single quote, just as in dynamic SQL. For example, notice there are two single quotes around `master` in the following statement instead of just one: `ExecuteSql('Numeric', 'SELECT COUNT(*) FROM sys.databases WHERE name <> ''master''')`.

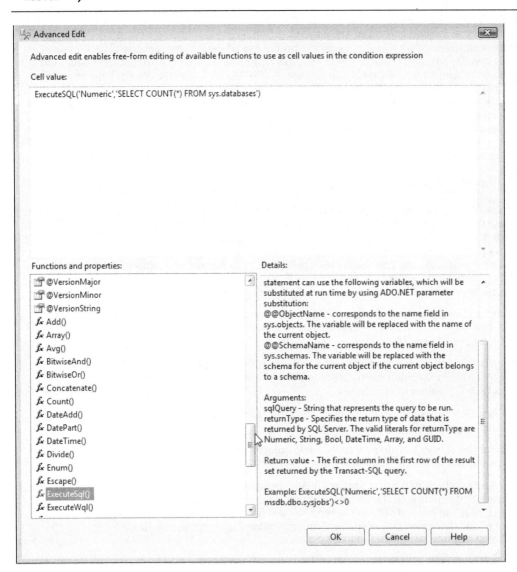

Figure 2-21. Advanced Edit dialog box

6. Click OK in the Advanced Edit dialog box to return to the Create New Condition dialog box.

7. For this example, we want the policy to fail if there are more than ten databases. Change the Operator to <= and type **10** in the Value field. Figure 2-22 shows the completed condition.

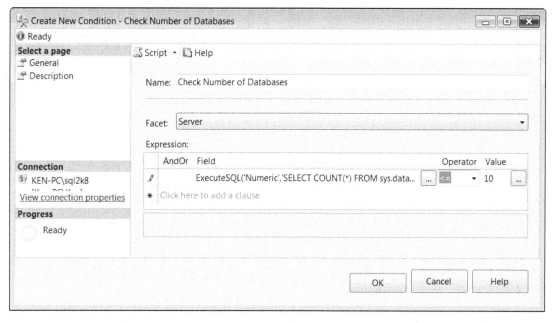

Figure 2-22. The condition for the Check Number of Databases policy in the Create New Condition dialog box

8. Click OK to return to the Create Policy dialog box.

9. Enter any remaining information you would like for the policy, such as a brief description and category.

10. Click OK to create the new policy.

Figure 2-23 shows a sample result of the policy once it has been evaluated. We will explain how to evaluate policies in Chapter 3.

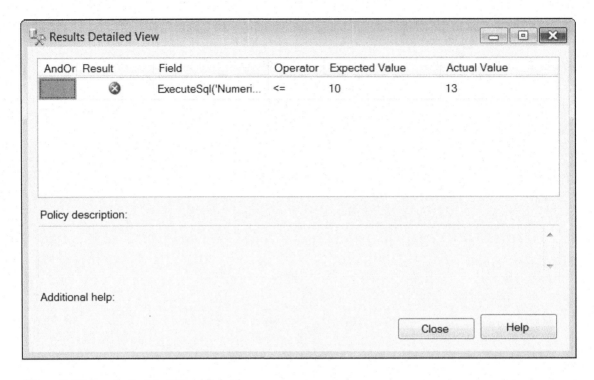

Figure 2-23. Results Detailed View dialog box

As you can see in Figure 2-23, the expected value was <= 10 (which we hard-coded in our condition), and the actual value is 13 (which was derived by executing the query we defined using the Advanced Edit dialog box). Obviously, since 13 is greater than 10, the policy results in a failure. You should also be aware that `ExecuteSql()` evaluates only the first column from the first row of a result set.

As you can see, by creating advanced conditions, you can greatly expand the capabilities of Policy-Based Management based on the needs of your environment.

Defining Conditions for System Databases

When you create a new policy, you will notice that the target is set to Every Database, which is misleading, because it applies the policy against every *user* database. This means if you want to ensure `AUTOSHRINK` is not enabled on your system databases (`master`, `msdb`, `model`, and `tempdb`), for example, applying a policy with this default target setting will not work.

So, how can you create a new condition that allows you to run a policy against both user and system databases? You can create a new custom condition by using the following procedure, which allows you to look at both system and user database targets.

1. Right-click the Conditions folder under the Policy Management node in SQL Server Management Studio and select New Condition from the context menu.

2. Give the condition a meaningful name, such as **Every Database – User and System**.

3. Choose the appropriate facet. For this particular condition, you want to use the Database facet.

4. Click the Field column and select the **@IsSystemObject** property from the drop-down list.

5. Make sure the Operator column is set to =.

6. Click the Value column and select True from the drop-down list.

7. Select the next line in the Expression grid that reads "Click here to add a clause," and change the AndOr operator to OR.

8. Click the Field column and select the **@IsSystemObject** property from the drop-down list.

9. Make sure the Operator column is set to =.

10. Click the Value column and select False from the drop-down list.

11. Select the Description page and enter a meaningful description, such as **Condition that allows you to evaluate both user and system databases**.

12. Click OK to create the new condition.

After following the preceding steps, your new condition should look like the condition shown in Figure 2-24.

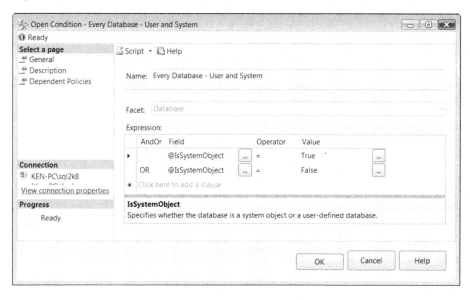

Figure 2-24. *Condition to evaluate both user and system databases*

Alternatively, you can execute the T-SQL script in Listing 2-5 to easily create the condition on your servers.

Listing 2-5. Script to create a condition to evaluate both user and system databases

```
DECLARE @condition_id int

EXEC msdb.dbo.sp_syspolicy_add_condition
    @name=N'Every database - User and System',
    @description=N'Condition that allows you to evaluate both user and system databases.',
    @facet=N'Database',
    @expression=N'<Operator>
  <TypeClass>Bool</TypeClass>
  <OpType>OR</OpType>
  <Count>2</Count>
  <Operator>
    <TypeClass>Bool</TypeClass>
    <OpType>EQ</OpType>
    <Count>2</Count>
    <Attribute>
      <TypeClass>Bool</TypeClass>
      <Name>IsSystemObject</Name>
    </Attribute>
    <Function>
      <TypeClass>Bool</TypeClass>
      <FunctionType>True</FunctionType>
      <ReturnType>Bool</ReturnType>
      <Count>0</Count>
    </Function>
  </Operator>
  <Operator>
    <TypeClass>Bool</TypeClass>
    <OpType>EQ</OpType>
    <Count>2</Count>
    <Attribute>
      <TypeClass>Bool</TypeClass>
      <Name>IsSystemObject</Name>
    </Attribute>
    <Function>
      <TypeClass>Bool</TypeClass>
      <FunctionType>False</FunctionType>
      <ReturnType>Bool</ReturnType>
      <Count>0</Count>
    </Function>
  </Operator>
</Operator>', @is_name_condition=0, @obj_name=N'', @condition_id=@condition_id OUTPUT

SELECT @condition_id

GO
```

Once you have created the new condition, you can use it when creating your policies by selecting it from the drop-down list in the Against Targets section.

■ **Caution**: Be cautious when applying policies to your system databases. Some policies may make sense to apply to system databases; others may not. For example, you may not care if the data and log files of the `model` database reside on the same drive. On the other hand, you wouldn't want `AUTOSHRINK` enabled for your `msdb` database.

With the appropriate policies in place, you can make sure to manage your entire environment, not just your user databases.

Summary

In this chapter, we discussed many aspects of creating and managing policies. Working with the SQL Server Management Studio GUI, you can create a condition, create a policy, and even view the policies that are dependent on each condition.

We covered the various ways of importing and exporting policies, including exporting existing policies and exporting the current state of a facet to create a policy. We also showed you how to manage policies using T-SQL, along with some advantages of doing so. We talked about the importance of managing categories, including how to create new categories and how to subscribe to categories that are not mandated. We demonstrated how powerful Policy-Based Management can be by using advanced conditions. Finally, you saw how to create conditions that will include your system databases as well as your user databases.

In the next chapter, you will see the many ways you can evaluate and enforce these policies to maintain consistency and control in your environment.

CHAPTER 3

■ ■ ■

Evaluating Policies

Evaluating a policy is the process of executing a policy and reviewing the results against the desired configuration on the target instance. Policy-Based Management provides several options and configurations for evaluating policies:

- You can evaluate policies against a single registered SQL Server instance or a group of instances.

- You can configure policy evaluation to check on change, on schedule, or on demand.

- You can configure Policy-Based Management to allow and log the noncompliant changes, or to prevent and roll back changes.

- You can schedule evaluation of single or multiple policies against a given SQL Server instance.

All of these techniques will be covered in this chapter.

Evaluation Modes

As discussed in the previous chapters, you have up to four choices on how you would like the policy to be evaluated. Note that not all evaluation modes will be available for all the policies, due to the characteristics of the facets used by the policy. Table 3-1 summarizes how the modes work and their availability. We'll look at using each of these modes in the following sections.

Table 3-1. Summary of Evaluation Modes

Evaluation Mode	Description	Availability
On Demand	Evaluate the policy only when the user has requested.	Always available
On Schedule	Evaluate the policy on a schedule for a job using the SQL Server Agent. This is an automated evaluation mode.	Always available
On Change: Log Only	Allow a change to be made that does not conform to the policy defined, and then log the change to the event log. This is an automated evaluation mode.	Available only if the change of the state of the facet can be captured by an event

Table 3-1. Continued

On Change: Prevent	Disallow a change if it does not conform to the policy defined. This is an automated evaluation mode. It uses DDL triggers.	Available only if there is transactional support for the DDL statements that change the state of the facet

Evaluation on Demand

When evaluating a policy on demand, you can either evaluate a single policy or evaluate multiple policies at once. Let's start with the evaluation of a single policy on demand.

Evaluating a Single Policy on Demand

Evaluating a single policy on demand is a quick way to give the target instance a once-over if you think something may be awry. As an example, we'll walk through the procedure for making sure that autoshrink is disabled for all of your databases.

Begin by expanding the Policies folder. Right-click the policy that you want to evaluate and select Evaluate from the context menu, as shown in Figure 3-1. In our scenario, we are choosing the Database Auto Shrink policy. If you do not have the Database Auto Shrink policy, you can import it from the predefined policies location that is part of the SQL Server installation, as described in Chapter 2. (Actually, any policy you choose will be fine.)

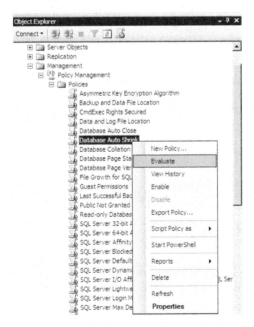

Figure 3-1. *Choosing to evaluate a single policy*

Since you selected only one policy, that policy is immediately executed, and you are taken to the Evaluation Results page of the Evaluate Policies dialog box, as shown in Figure 3-2. The Evaluation Results page has two sections: Results and Target Details.

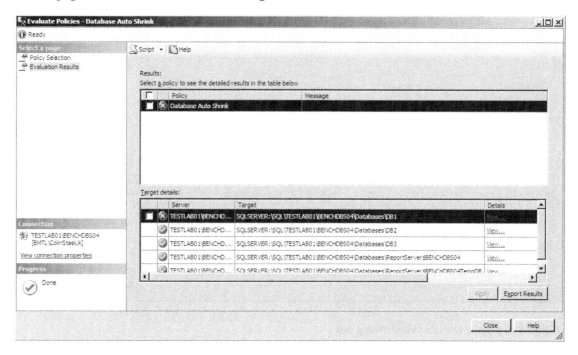

Figure 3-2. The Evaluation Results page of the Evaluate Policies dialog box

In the Target Details section in Figure 3-2, you can see that the policy ran against all of the user databases (as defined by the Database Auto Shrink policy), and the database named **DB1** failed to evaluate successfully against the policy.

To determine the problem, click the View link in the Details column. In the Results Detailed View dialog box, you will see the expected value that the policy is checking for and the actual value at the time of evaluation, as shown in Figure 3-3. If the policy creator added a policy description and a help link, you will find that information here as well.

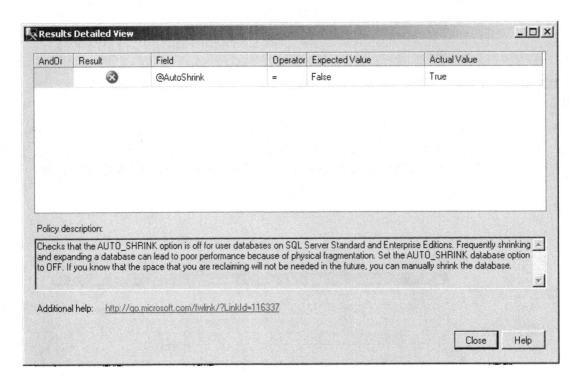

Figure 3-3. *Results Detailed View dialog box*

Close the Results Detailed View dialog box and return to the Evaluate Policies dialog box. Select the check box to the left of the failed evaluation of the policy. Now the Apply button that was previously disabled is enabled, as shown in Figure 3-4. Clicking the Apply button will change the facet's current configuration value to the expected value of the policy.

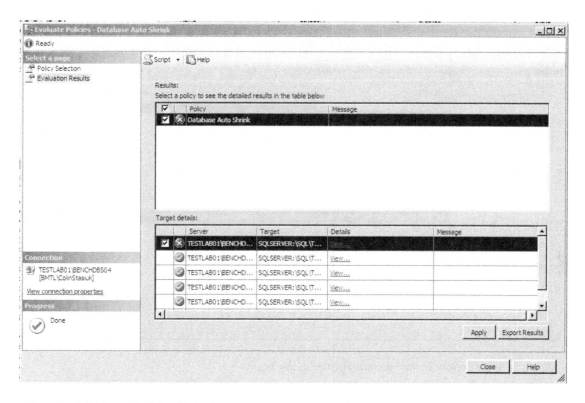

Figure 3-4. *Evaluate Policies dialog box*

If multiple targets had failed the policy evaluation, a check box would appear beside each of the failed targets. Alternatively, you can select the check box beside the policy name in the Results section to select all of the failed targets at once. Note that not all failed policies can be resolved in this manner, as some policies require more steps than a single configuration change for their condition to return true.

You could also script out the changes that would be made if you clicked the Apply button by selecting the targets that you want to fix and choosing an option from the Script drop-down list, as shown in Figure 3-5.

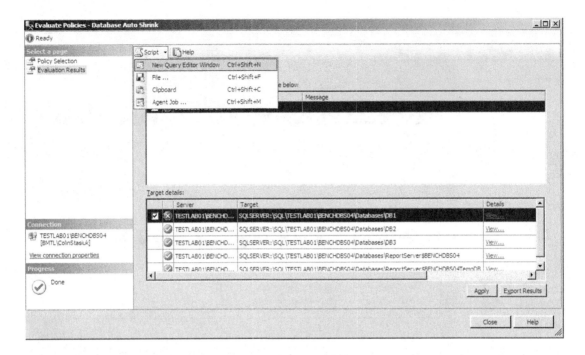

Figure 3-5. *Script options in the Evaluate Policies dialog box*

After selecting the failed targets that you want to fix, click the Apply button. A message box will appear, as shown in Figure 3-6. This asks you to confirm that you want to change the actual value of the targets selected to the expected values as defined in the policy.

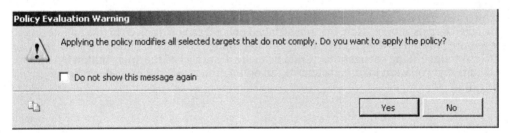

Figure 3-6. *Policy Evaluation Warning message box*

After you click Yes to acknowledge the warning, the changes will be applied immediately, and the policy will be reevaluated. The results will be updated in the Evaluate Policies dialog box, as shown in Figure 3-7.

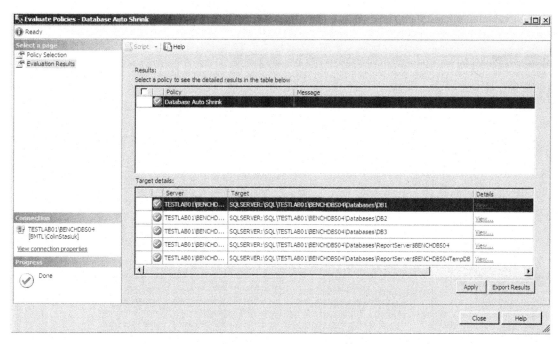

Figure 3-7. Evaluate Policies dialog box after fixing the failed target

Evaluating Multiple Policies on Demand

Evaluating multiple policies on demand is a good example of where correctly managing your policy categories comes in handy. If you have created meaningful category names, you can quickly select and evaluate all the policies for a given category.

　　To evaluate multiple policies at once, right-click the Policies folder and select Evaluate, as shown in Figure 3-8.

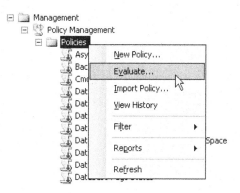

Figure 3-8. Choosing to evaluate multiple policies

The Evaluate Policies dialog box will list all of the policies that are defined on the server, as shown in Figure 3-9. A check box is beside each available policy so that you can choose multiple policies.

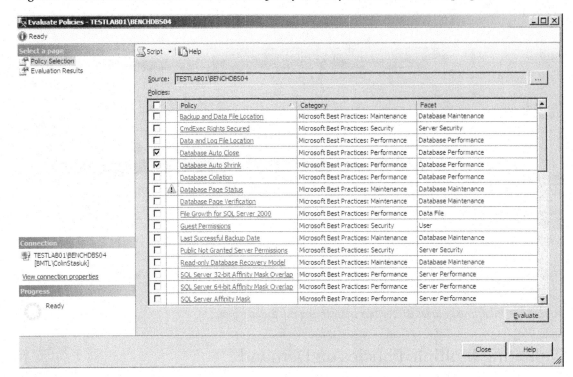

Figure 3-9. Evaluate Policies dialog box showing all the policies available on the server

---

◼ **Tip**: The Database Page Status policy has a warning flag beside it because the policy contains scripts. You should run policies like this only from a trustworthy source.

The Evaluation Results page of the Evaluate Policies dialog box will show a list of the policies you selected to evaluate. You can select single or multiple targets to change so that the actual value will match the expected value of the policy. Once you've selected the targets you want to fix, the Apply button will be enabled, as shown in Figure 3-10.

▪ **Tip**: If you highlight multiple policies using the Object Explorer Details window, they will be preselected in the Evaluate Policies dialog box. You can display the Object Explorer Details window by pressing F7 in SQL Server Management Studio.

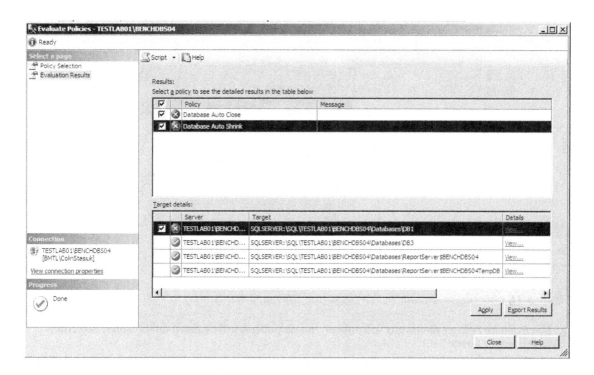

Figure 3-10. Evaluate Policies dialog box ready to apply changes

After you click the Apply button, the changes are applied immediately, and the policies are reevaluated. The results are updated and shown on the Evaluation Results page of the Evaluate Policies dialog box.

Evaluating Policies Against a Different Instance

Using SQL Server Management Studio, you can evaluate policies against an instance different from the one where the policies are stored. This is particularly useful if you have pre-SQL Server 2008 instances. Although you cannot create or store policies on versions of SQL Server earlier than 2008, you can still evaluate certain policies against them. (Policies that pertain to specific features can be evaluated only against versions of SQL Server that include that particular feature.)

To evaluate against a different instance, right-click an instance of SQL Server that is not your Policy-Based Management policy store and select Evaluate Policies, as shown in Figure 3-11.

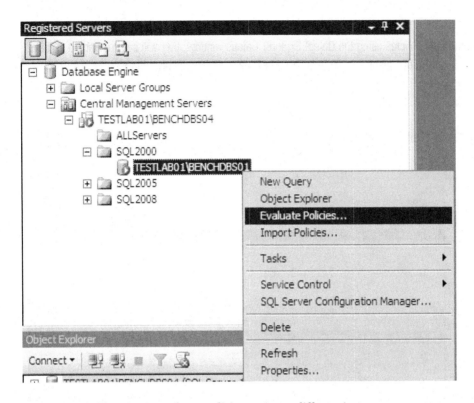

Figure 3-11. Choosing to evaluate policies against a different instance

The Evaluate Policies dialog box will appear, but no policies will be listed on the Policy Selection page, as shown in Figure 3-12.

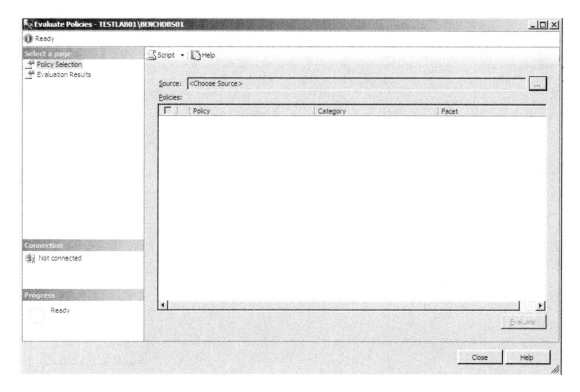

Figure 3-12. Evaluate Policies dialog box after choosing to evaluate against a policy on a different instance

Click the ellipsis button next to the Source box at the top of the dialog box to open the Select Source dialog box, as shown in Figure 3-13. The source can be either a path to a directory of policies or a SQL Server instance. For this example, we will choose the SQL Server instance we have been using in previous examples

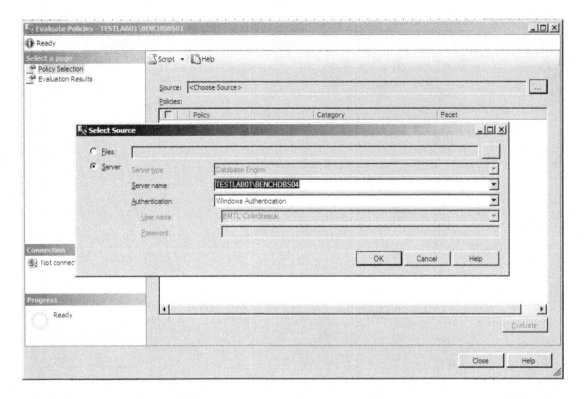

Figure 3-13. *Select Source dialog box*

Once you select your policy store server and click OK, the Evaluate Policies dialog box will populate with all the policies that are stored on that SQL Server instance (see Figure 3-9). You can now select one or many policies to evaluate against this SQL Server instance.

■ **Note**: When evaluating policies that are not on the same server as the policy store, you cannot apply the changes using the Apply button.

Evaluation on Schedule

Scheduling a policy allows you to perform routine checks to ensure your servers comply with the policies you have enabled. When scheduling a policy, you can either create a new schedule or choose from a schedule that already exists. Let's look at creating a schedule first.

Creating a Schedule

Scheduling a policy is a straightforward process. Just like many things in SQL Server, it's a simple point-and-click operation.

To create a schedule, right-click the policy of interest and select Properties from the context menu, as shown in Figure 3-14. Alternatively, you can double-click the policy to open the Properties dialog box.

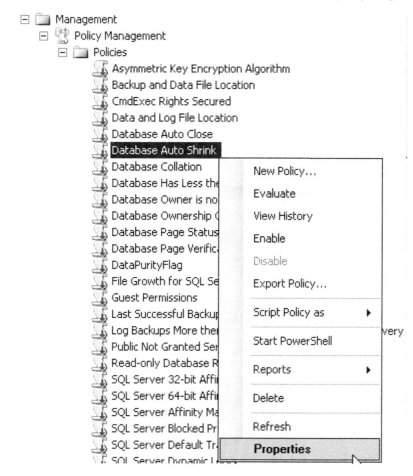

Figure 3-14. Choosing to view the properties of a policy

In the Open Policy dialog box, click the Evaluation Mode drop-down list and select On Schedule, as shown in Figure 3-15.

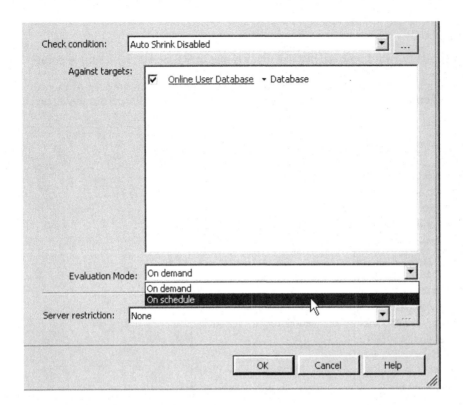

Figure 3-15. *Choosing the On Schedule evaluation mode*

After you have selected On Schedule, a Schedule area will become available. Here, you can choose to pick a current job schedule to append the policy to (as described in the next section) or select a new job schedule, as shown in Figure 3-16.

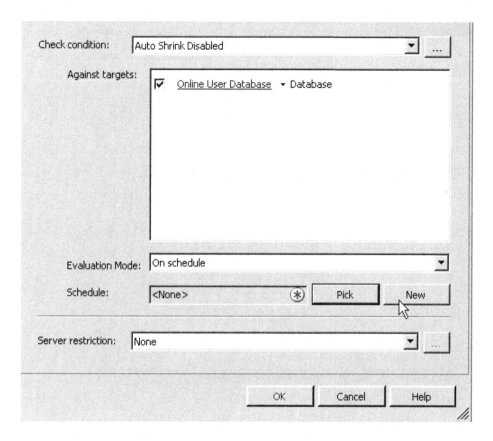

Figure 3-16. Open Policy dialog box after choosing On Schedule

Click the New button to open the New Job Schedule dialog box, as shown in Figure 3-17. Here, you specify the schedule type, frequency, and duration. When you click OK, a new SQL Server Agent job will be created (if one doesn't already exist) to evaluate your policy on the defined schedule.

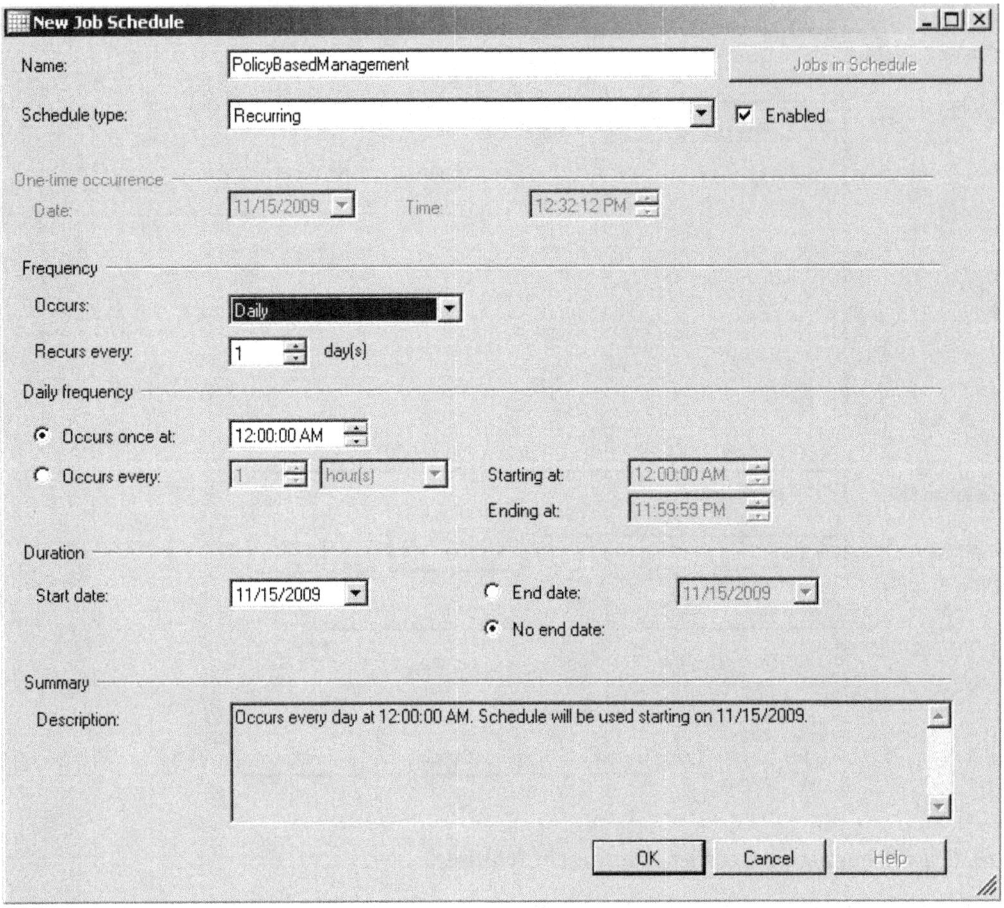

Figure 3-17. New Job Schedule dialog box

In order for the policy to actually be evaluated according to the defined schedule, you need to enable the policy by selecting the Enabled check box in the Open Policy dialog box, as shown in Figure 3-18. If the policy is not enabled, SQL Server will simply ignore the scheduled job, and you will be none the wiser.

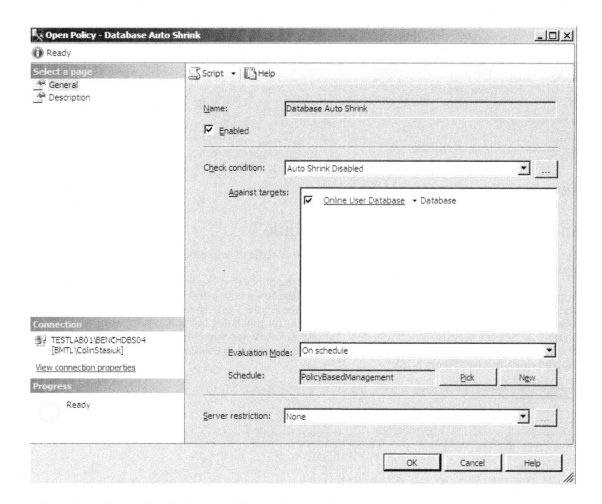

Figure 3-18. Open Policy dialog box with the policy enabled

After the scheduled job has executed, if an evaluated policy failed, two rows will be entered into the SQL Server log, as shown in Figure 3-19. The list in the log is arranged with the earliest entry at the bottom. The earliest entry contains the error number that was raised by the failure, and the next entry (going upward) contains the name of the policy that was violated. The usefulness of the SQL Server log entries is limited, as they do not provide any additional information about which database actually failed the policy. You will see how you can use the error number raised by the policy violation to receive automatic notifications in Chapter 5.

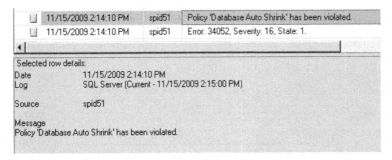

| | 11/15/2009 2:14:10 PM | spid51 | Policy 'Database Auto Shrink' has been violated. |
| | 11/15/2009 2:14:10 PM | spid51 | Error: 34052, Severity: 16, State: 1. |

Selected row details:
Date   11/15/2009 2:14:10 PM
Log   SQL Server (Current - 11/15/2009 2:15:00 PM)

Source   spid51

Message
Policy 'Database Auto Shrink' has been violated.

Figure 3-19. SQL Server log showing failed policies

Adding Policies to an Existing Schedule

If you want to schedule a policy to run at the same time as some of your other policies, you can pick an existing schedule instead of creating a new one.

To add a policy to an existing schedule, right-click the policy that you want to schedule and select Properties from the context menu (see Figure 3-14). In the Open Policy dialog box, drop-down the Evaluation Mode combo box and select On Schedule (see Figure 3-15). After you select On Schedule, click the Pick button (see Figure 3-16). The Pick Schedule for Job dialog box will appear, as shown in Figure 3-20. Select a preexisting job schedule and click OK. As when you create a new schedule, in order for the policy to be evaluated as part of the job schedule, you need to enable the policy by checking the Enabled check box (see Figure 3-18).

Pick Schedule for Job -   _ □ x

Available schedules:

ID	Name	Enabled	Description	Jobs in ...
3	CollectorSchedule_Every...	☑	Occurs every day every 10 minute(s)...	0
4	CollectorSchedule_Every...	☑	Occurs every day every 15 minute(s)...	0
5	CollectorSchedule_Every...	☑	Occurs every day every 30 minute(s)...	0
2	CollectorSchedule_Every...	☑	Occurs every day every 5 minute(s) ...	0
6	CollectorSchedule_Every...	☑	Occurs every day every 60 minute(s)...	0
7	CollectorSchedule_Every...	☑	Occurs every day every 6 hour(s) be...	0
9	PolicyBasedManagement	☑	Occurs every week on Sunday at 12...	1
1	RunAsSQLAgentService...	☑	Start automatically when SQL Server...	0
8	syspolicy_purge_history_s...	☑	Occurs every day at 2:00:00 AM. Sc...	1

Properties

Help   OK   Cancel

Figure 3-20. Pick Schedule for Job dialog box

You can have separate schedules for different grouping of policies. If you want to check to see which policies are part of which job schedule, you can run the query shown in Listing 3-1.

Listing 3-1. Query to return policy schedules

```
SELECT  c.name as 'JobName', a.policy_id, a.name as 'PolicyName', a.is_enabled
FROM    msdb.dbo.syspolicy_policies a INNER JOIN
                msdb.dbo.sysjobschedules b ON a.job_id = B.job_id INNER JOIN
                msdb.dbo.sysjobs c ON b.job_id = c.job_id
WHERE   a.execution_mode = 4
```

Evaluation on Change: Log Only

The On Change: Log Only mode uses event notifications to evaluate a policy when a change has been made. If a change goes against the policy, the change will be allowed, and entries will be made in the SQL Server event log for tracking purposes.

As shown earlier in Table 3-1, not all policies can be evaluated in this mode. To determine which policies can be evaluated in this mode, you can use the query shown in Listing 3-2.

Listing 3-2. Query to determine which policies you can evaluate using On Change: Log Only

```
SELECT  a.name as 'PolicyName'
FROM    msdb.dbo.syspolicy_policies a INNER JOIN
                msdb.dbo.syspolicy_conditions b ON a.condition_id = b.condition_id INNER JOIN
                msdb.dbo.syspolicy_management_facets c ON b.facet = c.name
WHERE   c.execution_mode & 2 = 2
```

The **execution_mode** column in the **syspolicy_management_facets** table is a bitwise operator with the following values:

- **4 (100)**: On Demand, On Schedule
- **2 (10)**: On Change: Log Only
- **1(1)**: On Change: Prevent

To configure a policy for On Change: Log Only evaluation, right-click the policy that you want to configure and select Properties from the context menu (or double-click the policy). We will be using the SQL Server Password Expiration policy in this example, as shown in Figure 3-21. If you don't have the Server Password Expiration policy, you can import it from the predefined policies location that is part of the SQL Server installation, as described in Chapter 2.

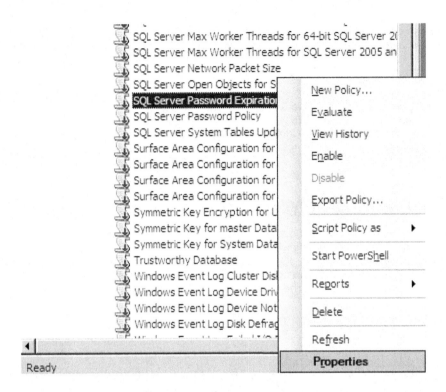

Figure 3-21. Choosing to view the properties of the SQL Server Password Expiration policy

In the Open Policy dialog box, select the On Change: Log Only option from the Evaluation Mode combo box. Then enable the policy by selecting the Enabled check box, as shown in Figure 3-22.

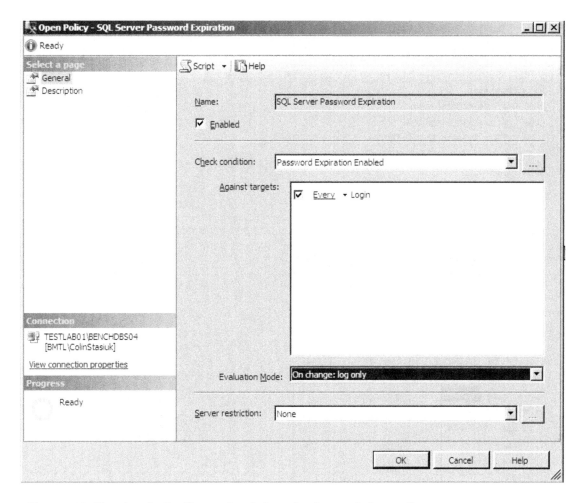

Figure 3-22. Choosing the On Change: Log Only evaluation mode for a policy

Now that this policy is set to log the change when the evaluation fails, let's test it and review the results. In Object Explorer, expand Security and then Logins, right-click a SQL login, and select Properties, as shown in Figure 3-23. (Alternatively, you can double-click the SQL login to display the Login Properties dialog box.)

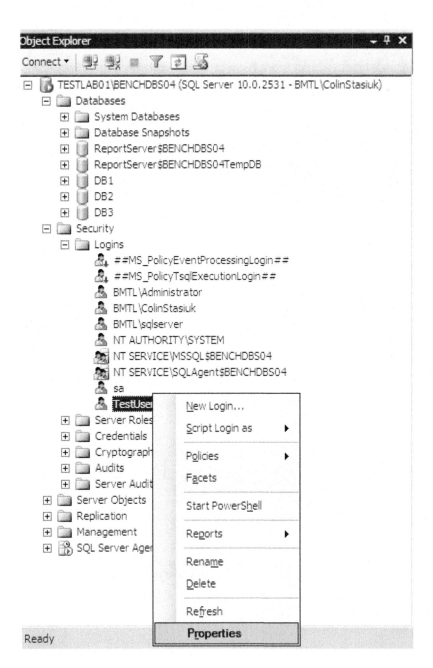

Figure 3-23. Choosing to view login properties

In the Login Properties dialog box, uncheck the Enforce Password Expiration check box and the Enforce Password Policy check box, as shown in Figure 3-24, and then click OK.

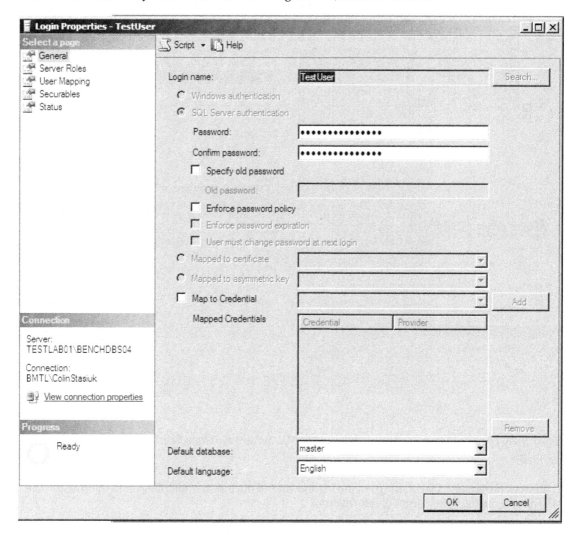

Figure 3-24. Turning off password policy and expiration in the Login Properties dialog box

Now open the SQL Server event log. You will see multiple new entries tracking the change, as shown in Figure 3-25.

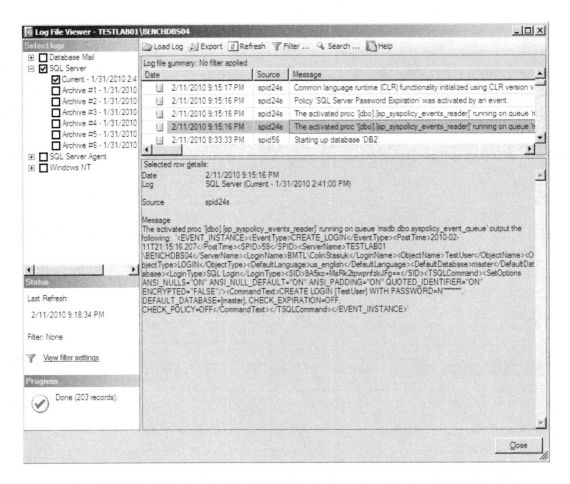

Figure 3-25. *Log File Viewer dialog box showing the SQL Server event log after the policy has been executed*

Review the detailed XML message in the log showing all the information relevant to the change. The XML will give the following pieces of information:

- **EventType**: Type of the event

- **PostTime**: Date/time when the change took place

- **SPID**: SQL Server internal process ID

- **ServerName**: Name of the server where the change took place

- **LoginName**: Login name used to make the change

- **ObjectName**: Name of the object that the change affected

- **ObjectType**: Type of the object that the change affected

- **DefaultLanguage**: Default language of the login

- **DefaultDatabase**: Default database of the login

- **LoginType**: Windows or SQL Server login

- **SID**: Security ID of the login that the change affected

- **TSQLCommand**: Actual command issued against the database to make the change

Also notice the quick summary message in the SQL Server event log, as shown in Figure 3-26.

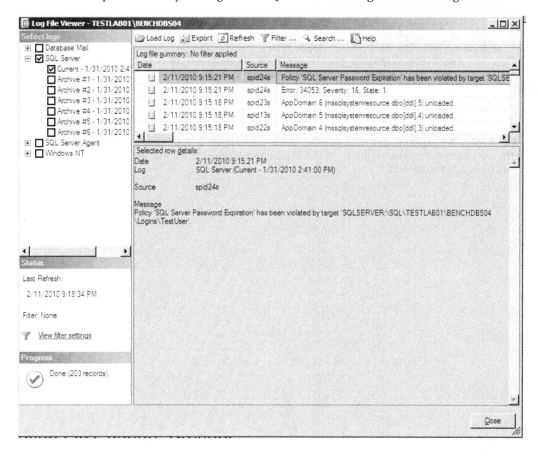

Figure 3-26. Summary message in the SQL Server event log

73

Evaluation on Change: Prevent

Configuring a policy to use the On Change: Prevent evaluation mode is a great way to prevent something from happening in your environment. For example, you will often see On Change: Prevent policies enforcing things such as naming conventions for tables and procedures.

As shown earlier in Table 3-1, not all policies can be evaluated in the On Change: Prevent mode. For a policy to be able to be evaluated using this mode, all the properties of the included facets must be able to raise a DDL event. To determine which policies you can evaluate using the On Change: Prevent mode, you can run the query shown in Listing 3-3.

Listing 3-3. Query to determine which policies you can evaluate using On Change: Prevent

```
SELECT  a.name as 'PolicyName'
FROM    msdb.dbo.syspolicy_policies a INNER JOIN
                msdb.dbo.syspolicy_conditions b ON a.condition_id = b.condition_id INNER JOIN
                msdb.dbo.syspolicy_management_facets c ON b.facet = c.name
WHERE   c.execution_mode & 1 = 1
```

To configure a policy to use the On Change: Prevent evaluation mode, right-click the policy and select Properties from the context menu. As in the previous example, we will be using the SQL Server Password Expiration policy to demonstrate this mode (see Figure 3-21). In the Open Policy dialog box, select the On Change: Prevent option from the Evaluation Mode drop-down list, and then enable the policy, as shown in Figure 3-27.

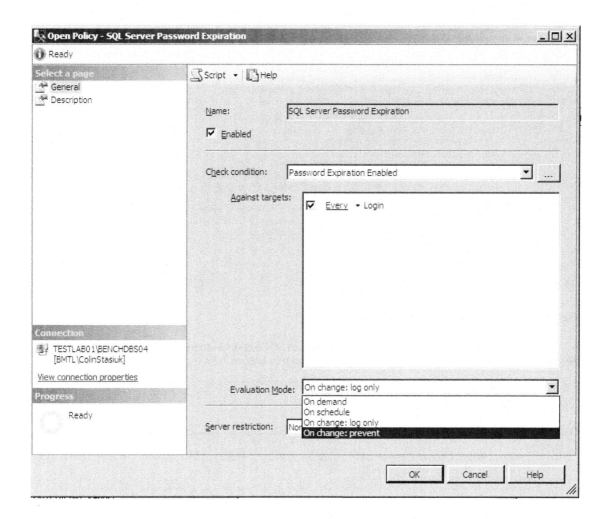

Figure 3-27. Choosing the On Change: Prevent evaluation mode for a policy

Now let's test this policy. In Object Explorer, expand Security and then Logins, right-click a SQL login, and select Properties (see Figure 3-23). In the Login Properties dialog box, uncheck the Enforce Password Expiration and Enforce Password Policy check boxes (see Figure 3-24), and then click OK.

An error message box will appear with information about the policy that you violated, as shown in Figure 3-28.

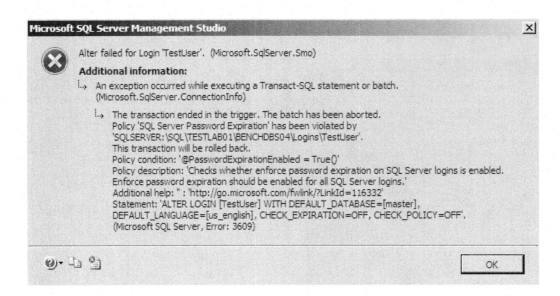

Figure 3-28. Error message box for failed policy

If you were to try to make the change using T-SQL in SQL Server Management Studio, you would see the same error information in the Messages tab, as shown in Figure 3-29.

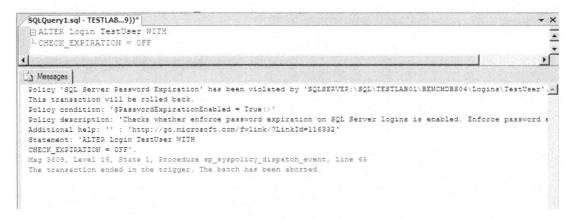

Figure 3-29. Error message for failed policy on the Messages tab

Using a Central Management Server

Central Management Servers are new in SQL Server 2008. They provide you with a central location to execute multiserver queries and evaluate policies against defined server groups. Central Management Servers are managed using the Registered Servers window in SQL Server Management Studio. A Central

Management Server is a designated database instance that maintains a collection or grouping of SQL Servers, much like registered server groups.

Creating a Central Management Server

In order to make use of a Central Management Server, you must have at least one SQL Server 2008 instance in your environment. You can register and manage previous versions of SQL Server with the Central Management Server, but the Central Management Server itself needs to be configured on a SQL Server 2008 instance.

Windows authentication is the only method of connecting to each registered server, which means that no usernames or passwords are stored on the Central Management Server. Using Windows authentication also means that you may have different levels of security access on each server, depending on how your account is configured on that individual server.

To create a Central Management Server, right-click the Central Management Servers folder located in the Registered Servers window in SQL Server Management Studio and select Register Central Management Server from the context menu, as shown in Figure 3-30.

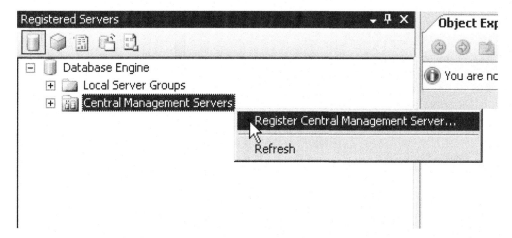

Figure 3-30. *Choosing to register a Central Management Server*

You will see the New Server Registration dialog box, as shown in Figure 3-31. Enter the name of the SQL Server instance that will be designated as the Central Management Server, along with the appropriate connection information. Notice that you can use SQL Server authentication to create the Central Management Server; the Windows authentication rule applies to only the registered servers being managed by the Central Management Server.

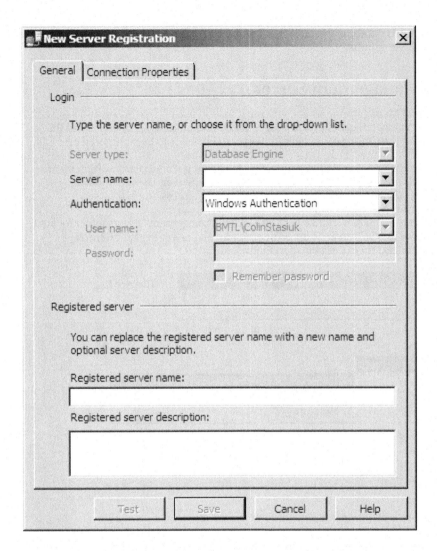

Figure 3-31. *New Server Registration dialog box, used to create a Central Management Server*

Click Test to test the connection. If the connection is successful, click Save to create the Central Management Server.

Creating a Central Management Server Group

You could just stop at creating a Central Management Server and start registering the SQL Server instances in your environment. However, we have found that in order to maximize the value of the Central Management Server, it is best to group your servers. That way, you can run certain policies against certain groups depending on their requirements. How you group your servers is a personal decision based on your environment and how you plan to utilize Policy-Based Management.

A very popular grouping organization is by environment, such as development, user acceptance testing, and production. As an example, we will create groups for those three environments.

To create a Central Management Server group, right-click the Central Management Server you just created and select New Server Group from the context menu, as shown in Figure 3-32.

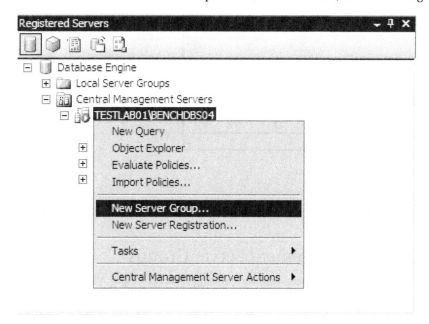

Figure 3-32. Choosing to create a new server group

You will see the New Server Group dialog box, as shown in Figure 3-33. Enter **PROD** as the group name and enter a group description, such as **Production SQL Server Group**. Click OK to close the dialog box and create the group.

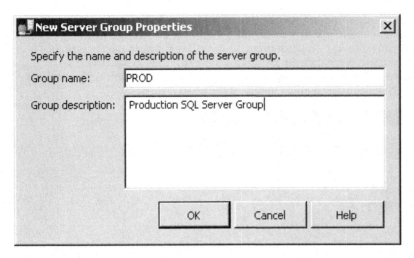

Figure 3-33. *New Server Group Properties dialog box*

Repeat this procedure to create two more Central Management Server groups, named DEV (for development) and UAT (for user acceptance testing).

Adding Servers to Central Management Server Groups

Now that you have created server groups, the next step is to start adding servers to them. You can add servers individually, or, if you have already registered services and groups, you can import them.

■ **Note**: You cannot register a Central Management Server to be a part of its own group.

Registering a Server to a Group

Right-click the Production group you just created and select New Server Registration from the context menu. The New Server Registration dialog box that appears is similar to the dialog box used to register the Central Management Server, with one small exception: The Authentication selection is preset to Windows Authentication and cannot be changed, as shown in Figure 3-34.

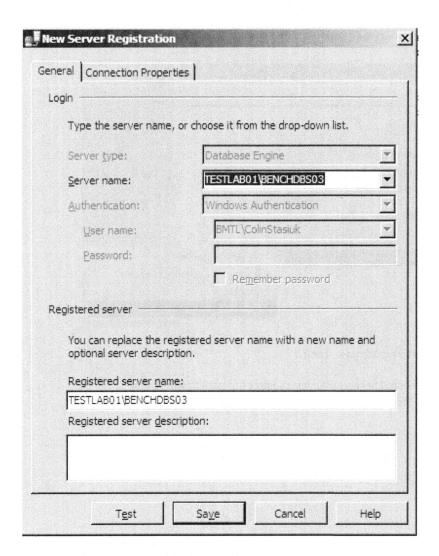

Figure 3-34. Dialog box used to register a server to be managed by a Central Management Server

Click Test to test the connection. If the connection is successful, click Save to complete the registration.

Repeat the process a couple of times to add a few other servers to the Production group.

Importing Registered Servers and Groups

If you have groups and servers registered already, you can export your list of registered servers and groups and then import them to your Central Management Server, as follows:

1. Right-click the Local Server Group folder and select Tasks → Export, as shown in Figure 3-35.

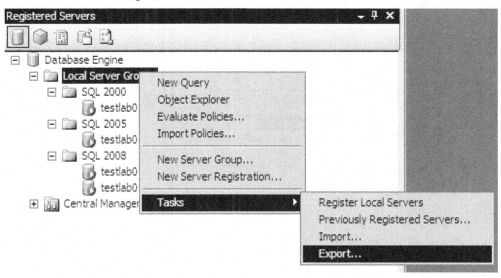

Figure 3-35. Choosing to export a registered server list

2. In the Export Registered Servers dialog box, enter the path to where you would like the export file saved, as shown in Figure 3-36, and then click OK.

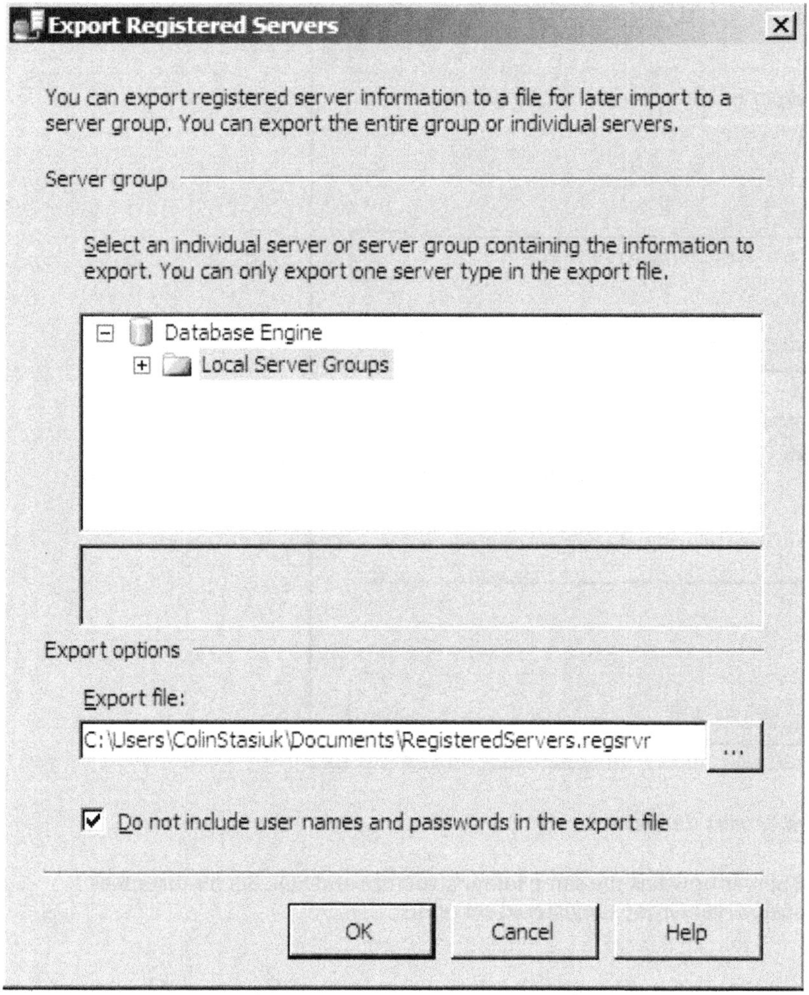

Figure 3-36. Export Registered Servers dialog box

3. Right-click the Central Management Server folder and select Tasks →
   Import.

4. In the Import Registered Servers dialog box, browse to the file you saved, as
   shown in Figure 3-37, and then click OK.

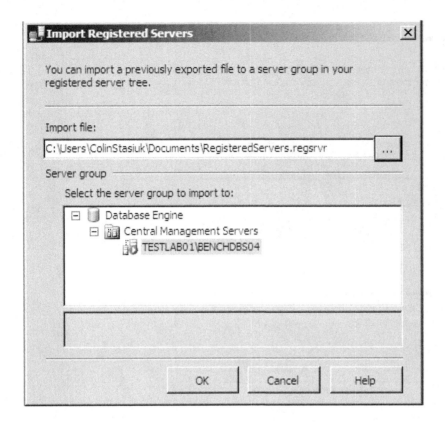

Figure 3-37. Import Registered Servers dialog box

The Central Management Server now has the same folder structure and SQL Server instances registered as defined in the Local Server Groups registered server list.

Evaluating Policies against a Central Management Server Group

Right-clicking a server group provides you with a few options that you can execute against all the servers in the group, as shown in Figure 3-38. In this section, we'll look at the Evaluate Policies option for a Central Management Server group.

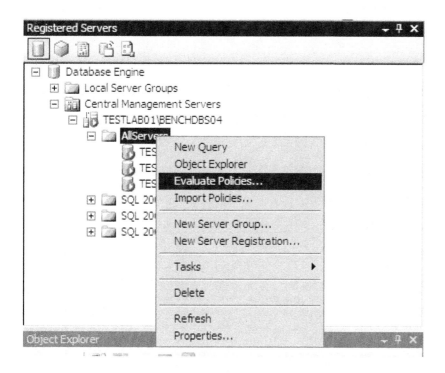

Figure 3-38. Central Management Server group options

Now that you have servers in you Central Management Server groups, you can see the real power of using Policy-Based Management with Central Management Servers.

Execute one or more policies against all of the servers in a server group by following these steps:

1. Right-click a Central Management Server group and select Evaluate Policies (see Figure 3-38),

2. In the Evaluate Policies dialog box, you'll need to select the source for your policy store. Click the ellipsis button next to the Source field (see Figure 3-12).

3. In the Select Source dialog box, select whether your policies are on the file system or stored on a SQL Server instance. For this walk-through, we're going to use the ones stored on our SQL Server 2008 instance (see Figure 3-9).

4. The Evaluate Policies dialog box will now be populated with the policies that are stored on the server (see Figure 3-13).

5. Select a single or multiple policies to evaluate, as shown in Figure 3-39, and then click the Evaluate button.

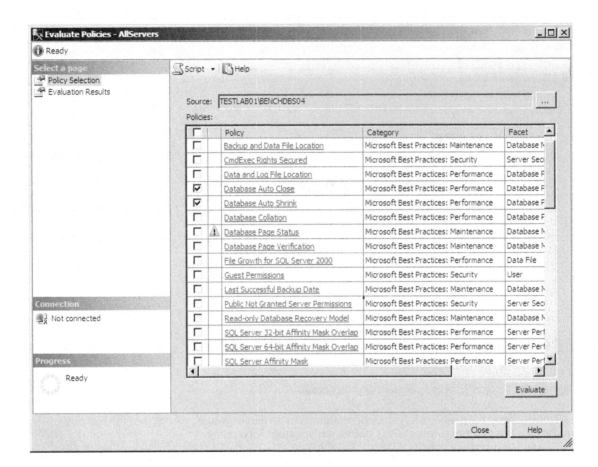

Figure 3-39. *Selecting policies to evaluate against a Central Management Server group*

You've now evaluated the selected policies against all the servers in the group at the same time. The Evaluate Policies dialog box will show the evaluation status of each object (in this example, databases) in the Targets Details section, as shown in Figure 3-40.

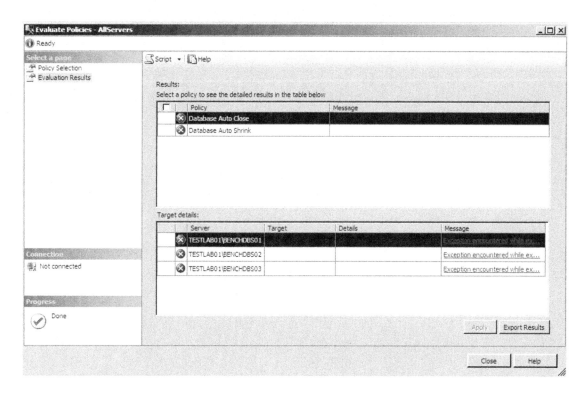

Figure 3-40. Evaluate Policies dialog box showing results of evaluating against a Central Server Management group

Summary

In this chapter, we introduced you to the different execution modes you can use to evaluate policies. We have shown the out-of-the-box ways to evaluate a single policy, as well as to evaluate multiple policies at once. We also demonstrated how you can configure a Central Management Server that will allow you to evaluate your policies against multiple SQL Server instances.

## CHAPTER 4

Policy-Based Management Using PowerShell

PowerShell is a very useful scripting tool that enables system administrators to automate server administration, gather information, and deploy applications. Microsoft introduced support for Windows PowerShell version 1 with SQL Server 2008, and support for Windows PowerShell version 2 will be released with SQL Server 2008 Release 2.

In this chapter, we will create some basic PowerShell scripts to demonstrate how to use this tool with Policy-Based Management. We will use PowerShell to run a single policy against a single instance of SQL Server, and then to run a group of policies against a single instance of SQL Server. We will then store and query the policy results. Finally, we will tie in the use of a Central Management Server to execute and store the results of a category of policies against all the instances in a server group.

Creating a Basic PowerShell Script

When you create a PowerShell script, there are two ways of connecting to and querying a SQL Server instance: using T-SQL and using SQL Server Management Objects (SMO). We'll look at both the T-SQL and SMO methods, and then demonstrate how to interrogate the class to find out the properties and methods available to you.

Using T-SQL

You can connect to a database from PowerShell, run a T-SQL query against the database, and return a result set back to PowerShell. The procedure is as follows:

1. Create a connection to SQL Server using the .NET data provider.

2. Build your connection string.

3. Create a T-SQL command to run against a SQL Server database.

4. Populate a container (**DataSet**) with the results of the T-SQL query.

5. Return the results stored in the container to the shell window.

6. Close the connection to SQL Server.

Listing 4-1 shows an example of connecting to and querying a database using T-SQL in PowerShell.

Listing 4-1. Connecting to and querying a SQL Server instance using T-SQL in PowerShell

```
$SQLCon = New-Object System.Data.SqlClient.SqlConnection

$SQLCon.ConnectionString
    = "Server = TESTLAB01\BENCHDBS04TESTLAB01\BENCHDEV04; Database = msdb;
Integrated Security = True"

$SQLCmd = New-Object System.Data.SqlClient.SqlCommand
$SQLCmd.CommandText = "SELECT [name] FROM dbo.syspolicy_policies"
$SQLCmd.Connection = $SQLCon

$SQLDataAdapter = New-Object System.Data.SqlClient.SqlDataAdapter
$SQLDataAdapter.SelectCommand = $SQLCmd

$DataSet = New-Object System.Data.DataSet
$SQLDataAdapter.Fill($DataSet)
$DataSet.Tables[0]

$SQLCon.Close()
```

Edit the code in Listing 4-1 so that the server is your SQL Server 2008 Policy-Based Management instance. Then save it as Example4-1.ps1.

Execute Example4-1.ps1 by opening a command prompt and running the **sqlps** utility, as shown in Figure 4-1. The results should list the policies that you currently have stored, as shown in the example in Figure 4-2.

Figure 4-1. Running Example4-1.ps1

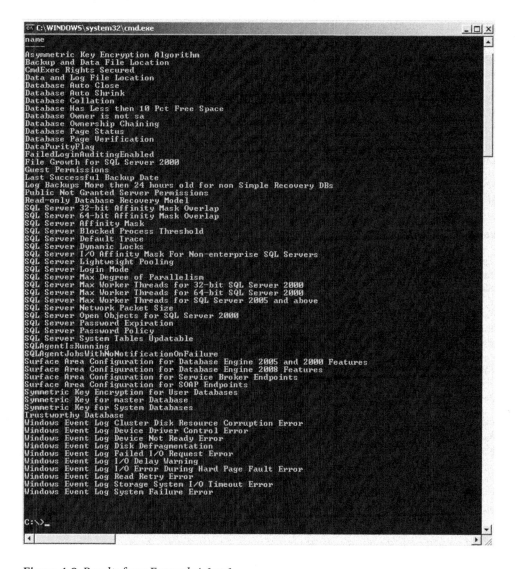

Figure 4-2. Results from Example4-1.ps1

Using SQL Server Management Objects

Another way to connect to and query an instance is to use SMO classes. In this section we're going to look at the following namespaces and objects:

> `Microsoft.SQLServer.Management.sdk.sfc`: A namespace that contains a set of classes, interfaces, structures, delegates, and enumerations that support SQL SMO.

> **Microsoft.SQLServer.Management.DFM**: A namespace that contains classes that represent the SQL Server Policy-Based Management objects.
>
> **SQLStoreConnection**: A class in the **Microsoft.SQLServer.Management.sdk.sfc** namespace that represents a connection to a SQL Server instance.
>
> **PolicyStore**: An object in the **Microsoft.SQLServer.Management.DFM** namespace that represents a Policy-Based Management policy store that holds information about policies, conditions, object sets, and subscriptions

Furthermore, our SMO example makes use of an important SMO class known as **$Policy.Name**. It's a useful class that implements many properties and methods to help you work with Policy-Based Management from PowerShell.

Listing 4-2 shows how to connect and query for the same information as in Listing 4-1. The difference is that this time we are using SMO rather than T-SQL.

Listing 4-2. Connecting to and querying a SQL Server instance using SMO in PowerShell

```
$SQLPBMConnection = new-object
Microsoft.SQLServer.Management.Sdk.Sfc.SqlStoreConnection("server=
TESTLAB01\BENCHDBS04TESTLAB01\BENCHDEV04;
        Trusted_Connection=true");

$SQLPolicyStore = new-object
Microsoft.SqlServer.Management.DMF.PolicyStore($SQLPBMConnection);

foreach ($Policy in $SQLPolicyStore.Policies)
{
        $Policy.Name
}
```

Edit the code in Listing 4-2 so that the server is your SQL Server 2008 Policy-Based Management instance. Then save it as Example4-2.ps1. Execute Example4-2.ps1. The results should look similar to Figure 4-3 and identical to the results from Listing 4-1.

```
C:\WINDOWS\system32\cmd.exe                                                    _ |□| x|
C:\>sqlps C:\PowerShell\Example4-2.ps1
Asymmetric Key Encryption Algorithm
Backup and Data File Location
CmdExec Rights Secured
Data and Log File Location
Database Auto Close
Database Auto Shrink
Database Collation
Database Has Less then 10 Pct Free Space
Database Owner is not sa
Database Ownership Chaining
Database Page Status
Database Page Verification
DataPurityFlag
FailedLoginAuditingEnabled
File Growth for SQL Server 2000
Guest Permissions
Last Successful Backup Date
Log Backups More then 24 hours old for non Simple Recovery DBs
Public Not Granted Server Permissions
Read-only Database Recovery Model
SQL Server 32-bit Affinity Mask Overlap
SQL Server 64-bit Affinity Mask Overlap
SQL Server Affinity Mask
SQL Server Blocked Process Threshold
SQL Server Default Trace
SQL Server Dynamic Locks
SQL Server I/O Affinity Mask For Non-enterprise SQL Servers
SQL Server Lightweight Pooling
SQL Server Login Mode
SQL Server Max Degree of Parallelism
SQL Server Max Worker Threads for 32-bit SQL Server 2000
SQL Server Max Worker Threads for 64-bit SQL Server 2000
SQL Server Max Worker Threads for SQL Server 2005 and above
SQL Server Network Packet Size
SQL Server Open Objects for SQL Server 2000
SQL Server Password Expiration
SQL Server Password Policy
SQL Server System Tables Updatable
SQLAgentIsRunning
SQLAgentJobsWithNoNotificationOnFailure
Surface Area Configuration for Database Engine 2005 and 2000 Features
Surface Area Configuration for Database Engine 2008 Features
Surface Area Configuration for Service Broker Endpoints
Surface Area Configuration for SOAP Endpoints
Symmetric Key Encryption for User Databases
Symmetric Key for master Database
Symmetric Key for System Databases
Trustworthy Database
Windows Event Log Cluster Disk Resource Corruption Error
Windows Event Log Device Driver Control Error
Windows Event Log Device Not Ready Error
Windows Event Log Disk Defragmentation
Windows Event Log Failed I/O Request Error
Windows Event Log I/O Delay Warning
Windows Event Log I/O Error During Hard Page Fault Error
Windows Event Log Read Retry Error
Windows Event Log Storage System I/O Timeout Error
Windows Event Log System Failure Error

C:\>_
```

Figure 4-3. Results from Example4-2.ps1

Interrogating for Members and Properties

SMO enables you to interrogate a class for the members and properties that it implements. We've been working with the **$Policy.Name** class. Listing 4-3 shows how you can invoke the **Get-Member** cmdlet to interrogate that class for the properties and methods it implements.

Listing 4-3. Using the Get-Member cmdlet to retrieve a listing of available properties and methods

```
$SQLPBMConnection = new-object
Microsoft.SQLServer.Management.Sdk.Sfc.SqlStoreConnection("server=TESTLAB01\BENCHDBS04;
Trusted_Connection=true");
$SQLPolicyStore = new-object
Microsoft.SqlServer.Management.DMF.PolicyStore($SQLPBMConnection);
$SQLPolicyStore | get-member
```

Again, edit this code so that the server is your SQL Server 2008 Policy-Based Management instance, save it as Example4-3.ps1, and then execute Example4-3.ps1. The results should look similar to Figure 4-4.

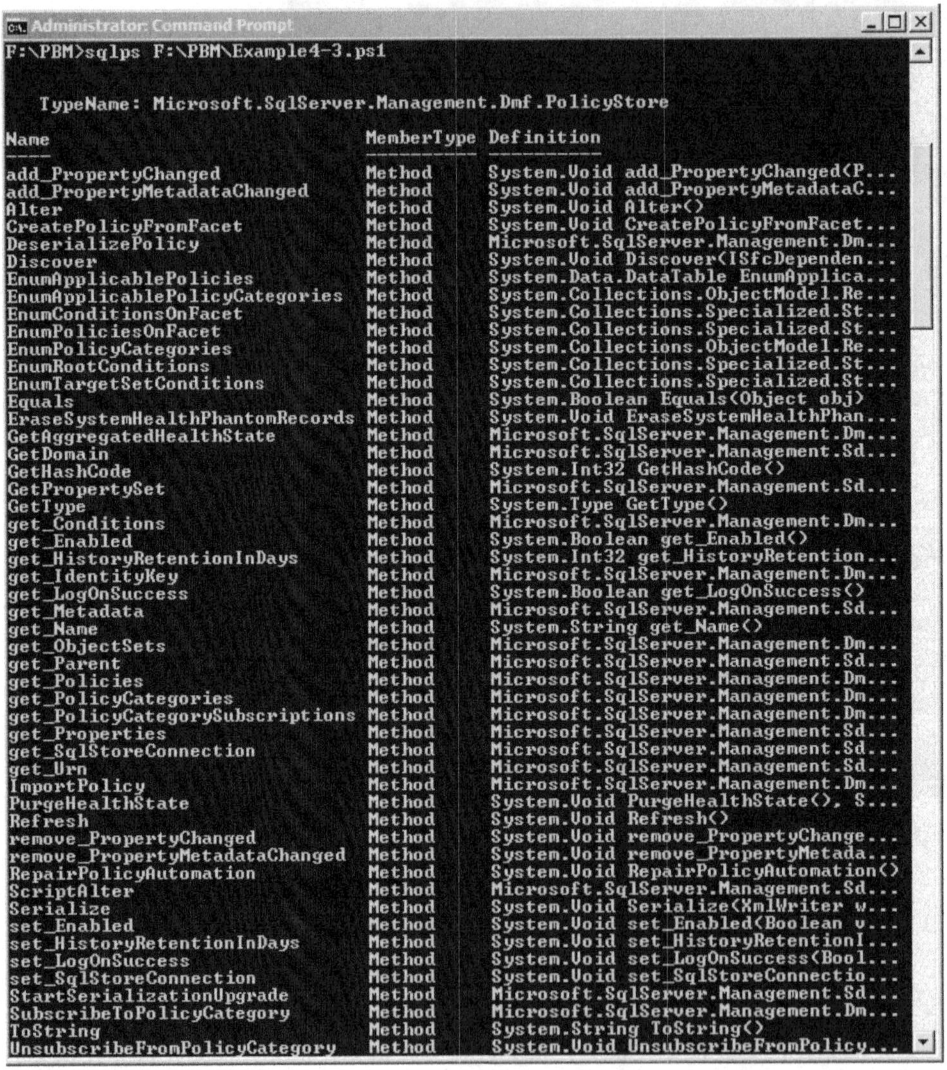

```
Administrator: Command Prompt
F:\PBM>sqlps F:\PBM\Example4-3.ps1

   TypeName: Microsoft.SqlServer.Management.Dmf.PolicyStore

Name                                MemberType Definition
----                                ---------- ----------
add_PropertyChanged                 Method     System.Void add_PropertyChanged(P...
add_PropertyMetadataChanged         Method     System.Void add_PropertyMetadataC...
Alter                               Method     System.Void Alter()
CreatePolicyFromFacet               Method     System.Void CreatePolicyFromFacet...
DeserializePolicy                   Method     Microsoft.SqlServer.Management.Dm...
Discover                            Method     System.Void Discover(ISfcDependen...
EnumApplicablePolicies              Method     System.Data.DataTable EnumApplica...
EnumApplicablePolicyCategories      Method     System.Collections.ObjectModel.Re...
EnumConditionsOnFacet               Method     System.Collections.Specialized.St...
EnumPoliciesOnFacet                 Method     System.Collections.Specialized.St...
EnumPolicyCategories                Method     System.Collections.ObjectModel.Re...
EnumRootConditions                  Method     System.Collections.Specialized.St...
EnumTargetSetConditions             Method     System.Collections.Specialized.St...
Equals                              Method     System.Boolean Equals(Object obj)
EraseSystemHealthPhantomRecords     Method     System.Void EraseSystemHealthPhan...
GetAggregatedHealthState            Method     Microsoft.SqlServer.Management.Dm...
GetDomain                           Method     Microsoft.SqlServer.Management.Sd...
GetHashCode                         Method     System.Int32 GetHashCode()
GetPropertySet                      Method     Microsoft.SqlServer.Management.Sd...
GetType                             Method     System.Type GetType()
get_Conditions                      Method     Microsoft.SqlServer.Management.Dm...
get_Enabled                         Method     System.Boolean get_Enabled()
get_HistoryRetentionInDays          Method     System.Int32 get_HistoryRetention...
get_IdentityKey                     Method     Microsoft.SqlServer.Management.Dm...
get_LogOnSuccess                    Method     System.Boolean get_LogOnSuccess()
get_Metadata                        Method     Microsoft.SqlServer.Management.Sd...
get_Name                            Method     System.String get_Name()
get_ObjectSets                      Method     Microsoft.SqlServer.Management.Dm...
get_Parent                          Method     Microsoft.SqlServer.Management.Sd...
get_Policies                        Method     Microsoft.SqlServer.Management.Dm...
get_PolicyCategories                Method     Microsoft.SqlServer.Management.Dm...
get_PolicyCategorySubscriptions     Method     Microsoft.SqlServer.Management.Dm...
get_Properties                      Method     Microsoft.SqlServer.Management.Sd...
get_SqlStoreConnection              Method     Microsoft.SqlServer.Management.Sd...
get_Urn                             Method     Microsoft.SqlServer.Management.Sd...
ImportPolicy                        Method     Microsoft.SqlServer.Management.Dm...
PurgeHealthState                    Method     System.Void PurgeHealthState(), S...
Refresh                             Method     System.Void Refresh()
remove_PropertyChanged              Method     System.Void remove_PropertyChange...
remove_PropertyMetadataChanged      Method     System.Void remove_PropertyMetada...
RepairPolicyAutomation              Method     System.Void RepairPolicyAutomation()
ScriptAlter                         Method     Microsoft.SqlServer.Management.Sd...
Serialize                           Method     System.Void Serialize(XmlWriter w...
set_Enabled                         Method     System.Void set_Enabled(Boolean v...
set_HistoryRetentionInDays          Method     System.Void set_HistoryRetentionI...
set_LogOnSuccess                    Method     System.Void set_LogOnSuccess(Bool...
set_SqlStoreConnection              Method     System.Void set_SqlStoreConnectio...
StartSerializationUpgrade           Method     Microsoft.SqlServer.Management.Sd...
SubscribeToPolicyCategory           Method     Microsoft.SqlServer.Management.Dm...
ToString                            Method     System.String ToString()
UnsubscribeFromPolicyCategory       Method     System.Void UnsubscribeFromPolicy...
```

Figure 4-4. Results from Example4-3.ps1

Now that you have seen how to connect to a SQL Server instance using PowerShell, we will look at using PowerShell to run a single policy against a SQL Server instance.

Running a Policy Against a SQL Server Instance

PowerShell can be used to run a policy against an instance of SQL Server to determine if the instance is compliant with the condition of the policy. In this section, we're going to show you how to do the following:

- Use the **Invoke-PolicyEvaluation** cmdlet to run a policy stored on the file system.

- Get detailed results in XML form by using the **–OutputXML** parameter to specify an output location.

- Use the **Invoke-PolicyEvaluation** cmdlet to run a policy stored on a server.

Invoking a Policy from a File

The **Invoke-PolicyEvaluation** cmdlet reports whether or not a target set of SQL Server objects complies with the conditions specified in one or more Policy-Based Management policies. Listing 4-4 shows how to invoke a policy defined in a file stored on your file system. This policy checks that all databases for the evaluated instance have autoshrink disabled.

Listing 4-4. Using the Invoke-PolicyEvaluation cmdlet to run a policy stored on the file system

```
Set-Location "C:\Program Files\Microsoft SQL Server\100\Tools\Policies\DatabaseEngine\1033"
Invoke-PolicyEvaluation -Policy "Database Auto Shrink.xml" -TargetServer
"TESTLAB01\BENCHDBS04"
```

The path for **Set-Location** is the local path that is storing policies on the file system. Edit the code in Listing 4-4 so that the **TargetServer** is the SQL Server instance that you would like to run this policy against. Save the code as Example4-4.ps1, and then execute it. Figure 4-5 shows an example of the results.

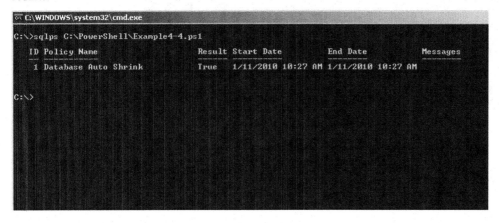

Figure 4-5. Results from Example4-4.ps1

In this example, the SQL Server instance did not have any databases with autoshrink enabled. If any databases had autoshrink enabled, the result column for the execution would read **False**. The information provided here is very limited, as it does not give you any details on which databases passed or failed the policy check. In the next section, we'll show you how to output detailed results to an XML file and review the information in that file.

Getting Detailed Results

Listing 4-5 shows how to invoke a policy evaluation and write detailed results to an output file. The output will be in XML form, and you specify the file using the **–OutputXML** parameter.

Listing 4-5. Using the Invoke-PolicyEvaluation cmdlet to run a policy stored on the file system and saving the results to an XML file

```
Set-Location "C:\Program Files\Microsoft SQL Server\100\Tools\Policies\DatabaseEngine\1033"
Invoke-PolicyEvaluation -Policy "Database Auto Shrink.xml" -TargetServer "TESTLAB\BENCHDBS01"
-OutputXML > C:\AutoShrink.xml
```

■ **Note**: The –OutputXML path can be either a local path or a UNC path.

Edit the code so that the **TargetServer** is the SQL Server instance that you would like to run this policy against, and change the **OutputXML** path to where you would like the XML results file to be generated. Save the code as Example4-5.ps1, and then execute it, as shown in Figure 4-6.

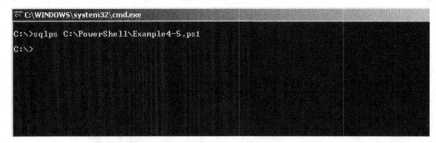

Figure 4-6. Results from Example4-5.ps1

The results of the policy execution are not reflected in the command prompt window, because we wrote the results to an XML file. To review those results, you will need to open that XML file. You can do that using any text editor or an XML editor. When you open the file, you will see XML in the form shown in Listing 4-6, which shows a small subset of the entire XML file.

Listing 4-6. Portion of an XML file with results from Example4-5.ps1

```
<DMF:ResultDetail type="string"><Operator><?char 13?> <TypeClass>Bool</TypeClass><?char 13?>
<OpType>EQ</OpType><?char 13?> <ResultObjType>System.Boolean</ResultObjType><?char 13?>
<ResultValue>True</ResultValue><?char 13?> <Count>2</Count><?char 13?> <Attribute><?char 13?>
<TypeClass>Unsupported</TypeClass><?char 13?> <Name>AutoShrink</Name><?char 13?>
<ResultObjType>System.Boolean</ResultObjType><?char 13?>
<ResultValue>False</ResultValue><?char 13?> </Attribute><?char 13?> <Function><?char 13?>
<TypeClass>Bool</TypeClass><?char 13?> <FunctionType>False</FunctionType><?char 13?>
<ReturnType>Bool</ReturnType><?char 13?> <ResultObjType>System.Boolean</ResultObjType><?char
13?> <ResultValue>False</ResultValue><?char 13?> <Count>0</Count><?char 13?> </Function><?char
13?> </Operator></DMF:ResultDetail>
  <DMF:TargetQueryExpression
type="string">SQLSERVER:\SQL\TESTLAB01\BENCHDBS01\Databases\Northwind</DMF:TargetQueryExpressi
on>
  <DMF:ID type="long">1</DMF:ID>
  <DMF:Result type="boolean">true</DMF:Result>
```

The **<DMF: TargetQueryExpression>** tag shows the database that this policy was evaluated against, and the **<DMF: Result>** tag shows the results. In this example, for the Northwind database, the Auto Shrink Enabled policy evaluated to **true**.

Invoking a Policy Defined on the Server

Listing 4-4 showed how to invoke a policy when the definition is stored in a file on the file system. You can also store policy definitions in a SQL Server instance. Listing 4-7 shows how to invoke such policies.

Listing 4-7. Using the Invoke-PolicyEvaluation cmdlet to run a policy stored in a SQL Server instance

```
Set-Location SQLSERVER:\SQLPolicy\TESTLAB01\BENCHDBS04\Policies
Get-ChildItem | Where-Object {$_.Name -eq "Database Auto Shrink"} |
Invoke-PolicyEvaluation -TargetServer "TESTLAB01\BENCHDBS04"
```

■ **Note**: The example instance is TESTLAB01\BENCHDBS04\. If you are not using a named instance, then it would be TESTLAB01\DEFAULT\.

Again, be sure to change the **Set-Location** value to the SQL Policy store the SQL Server instance that is storing the policies and the **TargetServer** value to the instance that you want to evaluate the policy against. Save the code as Example4-6.ps1 and execute it. Figure 4-7 shows an example of the results.

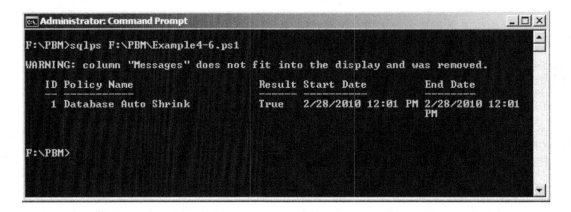

Figure 4-7. Results from Example4-6.ps1

Running Multiple Policies Against a SQL Server Instance

In this section, we will show you how to run multiple policies against an instance in one go. There are different approaches you can take to that problem. We'll look at the following three possible solutions:

- Add file system policies to the **Invoke-PolicyEvaluation** cmdlet.

- Search for a policy category on the file system.

- Search for a policy category in a SQL Server instance.

Invoking Multiple Policies from the Cmdlet

Listing 4-4 demonstrated how to use the **Invoke-PolicyEvaluation** cmdlet to run a single policy from PowerShell. Running multiple policies is a simple extension of what you saw earlier. Simply list more than one policy name, as shown in Listing 4-8. Notice the list of file names following the **–Policy** parameter.

Listing 4-8. Running multiple policies by adding file system policies

```
Set-Location "C:\Program Files\Microsoft SQL Server\100\Tools\Policies\DatabaseEngine\1033"
Invoke-PolicyEvaluation -Policy "Database Auto Shrink.xml", "Database Auto Close.xml" -
TargetServer "TESTLAB01\BENCHDBS04"
```

Edit the code in Listing 4-8 so that the **TargetServer** is the SQL Server instance that you would like to run this policy against. Save the code as Example4-7.ps1 and execute it. Figure 4-8 shows an example of the results. The Database Auto Shrink policy and the Database Auto Close policy were evaluated, and the results were returned to the command prompt window.

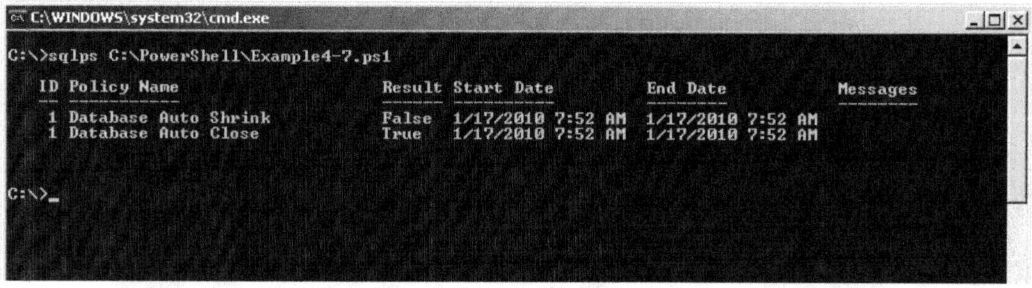

Figure 4-8. Results from Example4-7.ps1

Invoking a Category of Policies from the File System

When you define policies, you can group them into categories. You can take advantage of that grouping to invoke an entire collection of policies to evaluate at once. Listing 4-9 shows how to invoke all of the policies in the Microsoft Best Practices: Maintenance category.

Listing 4-9. Running multiple policies by searching for a policy category on the file system

```
Set-Location "C:\Program Files\Microsoft SQL Server\100\Tools\Policies\DatabaseEngine\1033"
$AllPolicies = get-childitem -Name
foreach ( $Policy in $AllPolicies)
{
        $PolicyInCategory = select-string "Microsoft Best Practices: Maintenance" $Policy
        If ($PolicyInCategory -ine $null)
        {
                Invoke-PolicyEvaluation -Policy $policy -TargetServer "TESTLAB01\BENCHDBS04"
        }
}
```

Edit the code so that the **TargetServer** is the SQL Server instance that you would like to run this policy against. Save the code as Example4-8.ps1 and execute it. As shown in the example in Figure 4-9, multiple policies are evaluated at the same time, and the results are returned to the command prompt window.

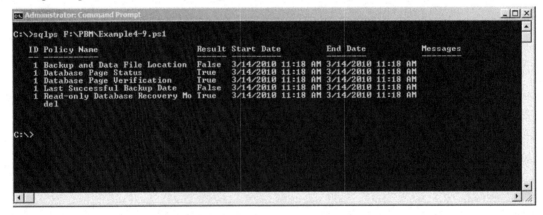

Figure 4-9. Results from Example4-8.ps1

Invoking a Category of Policies from an Instance

If you store your policy definitions in a SQL Server instance, you can still invoke them by category. Listing 4-10 shows how to do that.

Listing 4-10. Using the Invoke-PolicyEvaluation cmdlet to run a category of policies stored on a server

```
Set-Location SQLSERVER:\SQLPolicy\TESTLAB01\BENCHDBS04\Policies
Get-ChildItem | Where-Object {$_.PolicyCategory -eq "Microsoft Best Practices: Maintenance"}
| Invoke-PolicyEvaluation -TargetServer "TESTLAB01\BENCHDBS04"
```

Edit the code so that the server is the SQL Server instance that contains the policies and **TargetServer** is the SQL Server Instance that you would like to run this policy against. Save the code as Example4-9.ps1, and then execute it. Figure 4-10 shows an example of the results.

Figure 4-10. Results from Example4-9.ps1

One advantage to having policies defined and stored in an instance is that you can more easily confirm that they have run as you expected. For example, if you want to validate that the code from Listing 4-10 worked properly, and that only the policies that are categorized as Microsoft Best Practices: Maintenance were evaluated, you can do that. To do so, open SQL Server Management Studio and connect to the instance that contains the policies. Then expand Management, expand Policy Management, and select the folder called Policies. You should see a list of the policies that are categorized as Microsoft Best Practices: Maintenance. If the instance that stores the policies is the same instance that you used as your **TargetServer** value, the state is equivalent to the evaluation result. In the Object Explorer Details window, the information should look similar to that shown in Figure 4-11, depending on the target server you chose and the evaluation results.

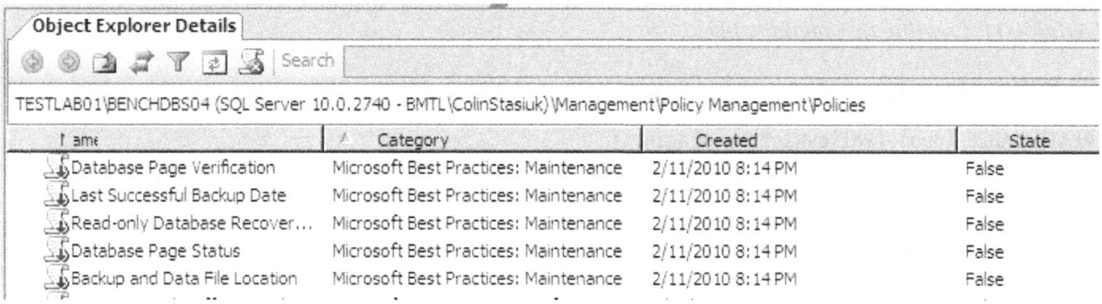

Object Explorer Details				
⊕ ⊕ ⓓ ⥂ ▽ ⊡ ⓔ	Search			
TESTLAB01\BENCHDBS04 (SQL Server 10.0.2740 - BMTL\ColinStasiuk)\Management\Policy Management\Policies				
Name	Category	Created	State	
Database Page Verification	Microsoft Best Practices: Maintenance	2/11/2010 8:14 PM	False	
Last Successful Backup Date	Microsoft Best Practices: Maintenance	2/11/2010 8:14 PM	False	
Read-only Database Recover...	Microsoft Best Practices: Maintenance	2/11/2010 8:14 PM	False	
Database Page Status	Microsoft Best Practices: Maintenance	2/11/2010 8:14 PM	False	
Backup and Data File Location	Microsoft Best Practices: Maintenance	2/11/2010 8:14 PM	False	

Figure 4-11. Object Explorer Details window showing policies

Querying and Storing Policy Execution Results

Earlier in this chapter, you saw how to save the policy evaluation results from PowerShell to an XML file. Saving the results to a file is fine when only one policy is involved. However, when you are evaluating multiple policies at the same time, things get more complicated. Writing all the output to a single file makes it difficult to work with the results. You can make your job easier by moving that XML into a database table.

▪ **Note**: The scripts presented in the remainder of this chapter are based on the great work of Lara Rebbulke, Technology Solution Professional; Dmitri Tchikatilov, Technology Solution Professional; and Tom Davidson, Solution Specialist—all with Microsoft. They developed the Enterprise Policy Management Framework, introduced in Chapter 1, which should be the cornerstone of any Policy-Based Management implementation. We use their scripts here by permission.

In this section, you're going to learn how to do the following:

- Create a staging table.

- Load policy evaluation history into that table.

- Query policy evaluation history results using T-SQL.

Creating a Staging Table

To create a staging table, execute the statements shown in Listing 4-11. The result from Listing 4-11 will be a table named **PolicyHistory_staging**, with columns that give easy access to results from policy evaluations. You may want to create your table in a reporting schema, possibly in an instance set aside just for your own purposes.

Listing 4-11. Creating the staging table

```
USE PBMResults

CREATE TABLE [dbo].[PolicyHistory_staging](
        [PolicyHistoryID] [int] IDENTITY(1,1) NOT NULL,
        [EvalServer] [nvarchar](100) NULL,
        [EvalDateTime] [datetime] NULL,
        [EvalPolicy] [nvarchar](max) NULL,
        [EvalResults] [xml] NULL,
 CONSTRAINT [PK_PolicyHistory_staging] PRIMARY KEY CLUSTERED
(
        [PolicyHistoryID] ASC
)WITH (PAD_INDEX  = OFF, STATISTICS_NORECOMPUTE  = OFF, IGNORE_DUP_KEY = OFF, ALLOW_ROW_LOCKS
= ON, ALLOW_PAGE_LOCKS  = ON) ON [PRIMARY]
) ON [PRIMARY]

GO

ALTER TABLE [dbo].[PolicyHistory_staging] ADD  CONSTRAINT [DF_PolicyHistory_EvalDateTime]
DEFAULT (getdate()) FOR [EvalDateTime]
GO
```

■ **Note**: The section uses a new empty database called **PBMResults**. If you do not have a database in which you would like to store this information, you can create a new one.

Loading Policy Evaluation History

Now that you've created the staging table, you can populate it with the XML results from policies you evaluated using PowerShell. Listing 4-12 shows how to load results from an XML file into the table.

Listing 4-12. Populating the PolicyHistory_staging table

```
$TargetServer = "TESTLAB01\BENCHDBS04"
$OutputXML = "C:\PowerShell\EvaluationDetails\AutoShrink.xml"
$PolicyName = "Database Auto Shrink"
$ServerInstance = "TESTLAB01\BENCHDBS04"
$Database = "PBMResults"

Set-Location "C:\Program Files\Microsoft SQL Server\100\Tools\Policies\DatabaseEngine\1033"
Invoke-PolicyEvaluation -Policy "Database Auto Shrink.xml" -TargetServer $TargetServer -
OutputXML > $OutputXML

$PolicyResult = Get-Content $OutputXML;

$EvalResults = $PolicyResult -replace "'", "''"

$QueryText = "INSERT INTO PolicyHistory_staging (EvalServer, EvalPolicy, EvalResults)
                VALUES(N'$TargetServer', N'$PolicyName', N'$EvalResults')"

Invoke-Sqlcmd -ServerInstance $ServerInstance -Database $Database -Query $QueryText
```

Edit the code in Listing 4-12 for your environment:

- **$TargetServer** is the SQL Server instance that you would like to run this policy against.

- **$OutputXML** is the path to where you want to store the XML file.

- **$PolicyName** is the name of the policy you want to evaluate.

- **$ServerInstance** is the name of the instance that contains the **PolicyHistory_staging** table.

- **$Database** is the name of the database that contains the **PolicyHistory_staging** table.

Save the code as Example4-10.ps1.

Querying the History

You've created and loaded the staging table. Now comes the payoff. You can query that table using standard SQL. This ability gives you virtually unlimited flexibility and power in reporting and analyzing your results. Figure 4-12 shows a very simple query and the results.

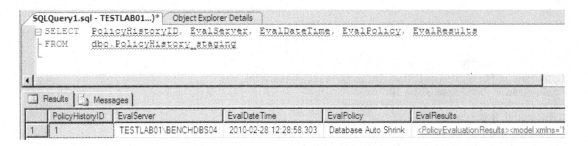

Figure 4-12. Data in PolicyHistory_staging table from Example 4-10.ps1

The information from the XML file is now stored in the table that was created in Listing 4-11, but the information is still not in a format that is easy to consume. You can make things easier by creating a view to "shred" the XML and pull out the information that you want to see. Listing 4-13 shows the definition for such a view.

Listing 4-13. Creating the vw_PolicyResults view

```
CREATE VIEW [dbo].[vw_PolicyResults] AS

WITH XMLNAMESPACES ('http://schemas.microsoft.com/sqlserver/DMF/2007/08' AS XMLNS)
SELECT  EvalServer, EvalDateTime, EvalPolicy,
                ResultNodes.NodeDetails.value('(../XMLNS:TargetQueryExpression)[1]',
'nvarchar(150)') AS EvaluatedObject,
                (CASE
                        WHEN
                                ResultNodes.NodeDetails.value('(../XMLNS:Result)[1]',
'nvarchar(150)')= 'FALSE' AND
                                NodeDetails.value('(../XMLNS:Exception)[1]', 'nvarchar(max)')
= ''
                        THEN 0
                        WHEN ResultNodes.NodeDetails.value('(../XMLNS:Result)[1]',
'nvarchar(150)')= 'FALSE' AND
                                NodeDetails.value('(../XMLNS:Exception)[1]',
'nvarchar(max)')<> ''
                                THEN 99
                        ELSE 1
                END) AS PolicyResult
FROM    dbo.PolicyHistory_staging CROSS APPLY
                EvalResults.nodes('
                        declare default element namespace
"http://schemas.microsoft.com/sqlserver/DMF/2007/08";
                        //TargetQueryExpression') AS ResultNodes(NodeDetails)

GO
```

The view created in Listing 4-13 lets you get at the individual bits of data by shredding the XML and presenting the data elements in columns with the following, easily referenced names:

- **`EvalServer`**: The instance that the policy was evaluated against
- **`EvalDateTime`**: The date/time of the policy evaluation
- **`EvalPolicy`**: The name of the policy that was evaluated
- **`EvaluatedObject`**: The name of the object that the policy was evaluation against
- **`PolicyResult`**: A pass (`1`)/fail (`0`) indicator

Query the view, and the results should look like those in Figure 4-13. Now you can easily query, analyze, and report on your policy evaluations.

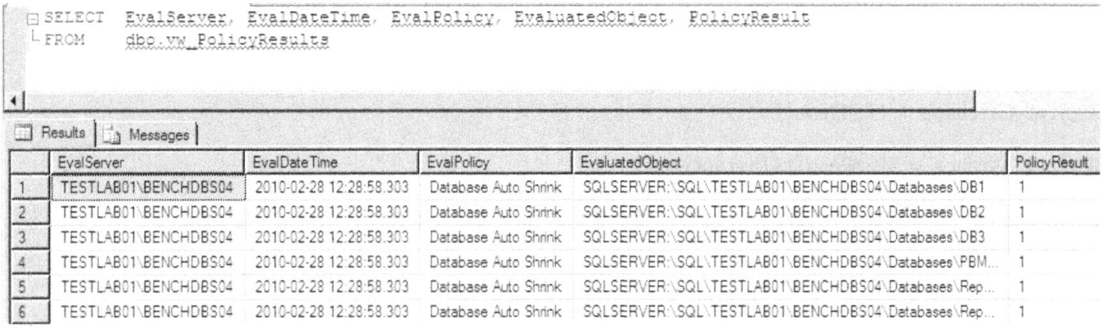

```
SELECT  EvalServer, EvalDateTime, EvalPolicy, EvaluatedObject, PolicyResult
FROM    dbo.vw_PolicyResults
```

	EvalServer	EvalDateTime	EvalPolicy	EvaluatedObject	PolicyResult
1	TESTLAB01\BENCHDBS04	2010-02-28 12:28:58.303	Database Auto Shrink	SQLSERVER:\SQL\TESTLAB01\BENCHDBS04\Databases\DB1	1
2	TESTLAB01\BENCHDBS04	2010-02-28 12:28:58.303	Database Auto Shrink	SQLSERVER:\SQL\TESTLAB01\BENCHDBS04\Databases\DB2	1
3	TESTLAB01\BENCHDBS04	2010-02-28 12:28:58.303	Database Auto Shrink	SQLSERVER:\SQL\TESTLAB01\BENCHDBS04\Databases\DB3	1
4	TESTLAB01\BENCHDBS04	2010-02-28 12:28:58.303	Database Auto Shrink	SQLSERVER:\SQL\TESTLAB01\BENCHDBS04\Databases\PBM...	1
5	TESTLAB01\BENCHDBS04	2010-02-28 12:28:58.303	Database Auto Shrink	SQLSERVER:\SQL\TESTLAB01\BENCHDBS04\Databases\Rep...	1
6	TESTLAB01\BENCHDBS04	2010-02-28 12:28:58.303	Database Auto Shrink	SQLSERVER:\SQL\TESTLAB01\BENCHDBS04\Databases\Rep...	1

Figure 4-13. Data from the vw_PolicyResults view

Evaluating Against a Central Management Server

In the previous sections, we've taken a simple PowerShell script, built upon it, and shown all the pieces needed in order to create a powerful script that can evaluate single or multiple policies against an instance of SQL Server. We've also demonstrated how to store and query the results. In this section, we will demonstrate how to use a Central Management Server (introduced in Chapter 3) to evaluate a group of policies against of group of SQL Server instances and store the results in the **`PolicyHistory_Staging`** table. The procedure is as follows:

1. Identify a category of policies to execute.
2. Identify a Central Management Server.
3. Identify instances controlled by that server.
4. Evaluate the policies from step 1 against the instances in step 3.

Listing 4-14 shows how to evaluate a category against a set of instances controlled by a Central Management Server.

■ **Note**: You must install SQL Server 2008 Cumulative Update 3 in order to run Listing 4-14.

Listing 4-14. Evaluating a category of policies against a Central Management Server group of instances

```
function PopulateStagingTable($ServerVariable, $DBVariable, $EvalServer, $EvalPolicy,
$EvalResults)
{
    $EvalResults = $EvalResults -replace "'", "''"
    $EvalPolicy = $EvalPolicy -replace "'", "''"

    $QueryText = "INSERT INTO PolicyHistory_staging (EvalServer, EvalPolicy, EvalResults)
                VALUES(N'$EvalServer', '$EvalPolicy', N'$EvalResults')"

    Invoke-Sqlcmd -ServerInstance $ServerVariable -Database $DBVariable -Query $QueryText
}

$PBMResultsInstance = "TESTLAB01\BENCHDBS04"
$HistoryDatabase = "PBMResults"

$PolicyInstance = $PBMResultsInstance

$CMSGroup = 'SQLSERVER:\SQLRegistration\Central Management Server Group\' + (Encode-SqlName
$PolicyInstance) + '\AllServers\'

$PolicyOutputLocation = "C:\PowerShell\EvaluationDetails\"

$PolicyCategory = "Microsoft Best Practices: Maintenance"

$PolicyStoreConnection = new-object
Microsoft.SqlServer.Management.Sdk.Sfc.SqlStoreConnection("server=$PolicyInstance;Trusted_Conn
ection=true");
$PolicyStore = new-object
Microsoft.SqlServer.Management.DMF.PolicyStore($PolicyStoreConnection);

$InstanceListFromCMS = dir $CMSGroup -recurse | where-object { $_.Mode.Equals("-") } | select-
object Name -Unique

del C:\PowerShell\EvaluationDetails\*

foreach ($InstanceName in $InstanceListFromCMS)
{

        foreach ($Policy in $PolicyStore.Policies)
    {

        if ($Policy.PolicyCategory -eq $PolicyCategory)
        {

            $PolicyNameFriendly = (Encode-SqlName $Policy.Name)
            $InstanceNameFriendly = (Encode-SqlName $InstanceName.Name)
```

```
$OutputFile = $PolicyOutputLocation + ("{0}_{1}.xml" -f $InstanceNameFriendly,
$PolicyNameFriendly);


Invoke-PolicyEvaluation -Policy $policy -TargetServerName $InstanceName.Name -OutputXML >
$OutputFile;


        $PolicyResult = Get-Content $OutputFile;
          PopulateStagingTable $PBMResultsInstance $HistoryDatabase $InstanceName.Name
$Policy.Name $PolicyResult;
      }
   }
}
```

Edit the code in Listing 4-14 for your environment:

- **$PBMResultsInstance** is the name of the instance that contains the **PolicyHistory_staging** table.

- **$HistoryDatabase** is the name of the database that contains the **PolicyHistory_staging** table.

- **$PolicyInstanc**e is the name of the instance that contains your policies.

- **$CMSGroup** is the path to the Central Management Server group you want to evaluate the policies against.

- **$PolicyOutputLocation** is the path to where you want to store the XML files that are output from the policy evaluation and imported into the database.

- **$PolicyCategory** is the group of policies that you want to evaluate.

Save the code as Example4-11.ps1. Then query the **vw_PolicyResults** view for only the failed evaluations. Your results should look similar to those in Figure 4-15 (assuming that you have some databases that fail the policies being checked).

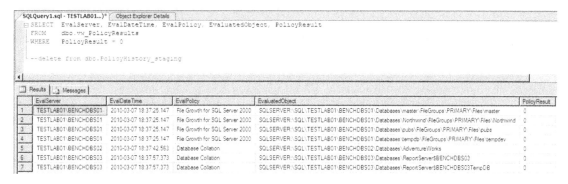

Figure 4-15. Data from the vw_PolicyResults view from Example 4-11.ps1

Summary

In this chapter, we've shown you how to build a very powerful PowerShell script that helps bridge the gap from what is currently available with Policy-Based Management in SQL Server 2008 to what may arrive in a future release—the ability to automate and store the results of multiple policy evaluations against multiple instances (and versions) of SQL Server.

Through multiple Central Management Server groups and multiple policy categories, you can set up any number of jobs and combinations that suit your requirements. Storing this information in a database allows you to track both successful and failed evaluations. That database provides you with an excellent central location for reporting on the health of your SQL Server environment based on policies that are defined as Microsoft best practices, and also on custom policies that you've created for your environment and business needs.

CHAPTER 5

■■■

Receiving Alerts for Policy Violations

One of the benefits of using Policy-Based Management is that it eases the administration effort required to manage and control all of the servers in your environment. If you need to continuously check your servers for policy violations, you are just redirecting your administrative efforts. You still have the benefits of managing by intent, but you haven't removed the mundane tasks from your daily routine. Luckily, you can take advantage of several components within SQL Server to receive automatic notifications when policy violations occur, so you can focus on more important things—like where you're going for lunch. With the proper configuration of Database Mail, operators, and alerts, you will know exactly when policy violations occur, and can even trigger events based on those violations.

Configuring Database Mail

In order to receive alert notifications when policy violations occur, you first need to configure Database Mail. You also need to create an operator and enable SQL Server Agent to use Database Mail. This and the next few sections will walk you through the prerequisites needed for the "Creating Alerts" section later in this chapter.

Setting Up Database Mail

You can use the GUI to configure Database Mail, but it is easier to create a T-SQL script you can have on hand whenever you need it. Using a T-SQL script also guarantees you have the same configuration on all of your servers.

First, you should make sure that you have Database Mail enabled. You can do this by using the **sp_configure** stored procedure, as follows:

```
sp_configure 'show advanced options', 1;
GO
RECONFIGURE;
GO
sp_configure 'Database Mail XPs', 1;
GO
RECONFIGURE
GO
```

You also need to make sure Service Broker is enabled for the **msdb** database. Database Mail depends on Service Broker to deliver e-mail messages. If Service Broker is not enabled, your mail messages will queue, but they will not be delivered. You can run the following query to determine whether Service Broker is enabled:

```
SELECT is_broker_enabled FROM sys.databases WHERE name = 'msdb'
```

If Service Broker is disabled, you can enable it by running the following **ALTER DATABASE** command. Enabling Service Broker requires a database lock. You will need to stop SQL Server Agent before running the **ALTER DATABASE** command so that Service Broker can acquire the appropriate lock.

```
ALTER DATABASE msdb SET ENABLE_BROKER
```

Now you need to add a Database Mail profile. You can do this by using the **sysmail_add_profile_sp** stored procedure. The following code adds a profile named DBA Mail Profile:

```
EXEC msdb.dbo.sysmail_add_profile_sp
     @profile_name = 'DBA Mail Profile',
     @description = 'Profile used by the database administrator to send email.'
```

You can use the **sysmail_add_account_sp** to create the mail accounts. The following code will create a mail account named DBA Mail Account:

```
EXEC msdb.dbo.sysmail_add_account_sp
     @account_name = 'DBA Mail Account',
     @description = 'Profile used by the database administrator to send email.',
     @email_address = 'DBA@somecompany.com',
     @display_name =  'KEN-PC\SQL2K8',
     @mailserver_name =  'KEN-PC'
```

■ **Tip** It is a good idea to get together with your e-mail administrator and create an e-mail group, such as DBASupport@SomeCompany.com, so alerts will be sent to multiple recipients when violations occur.

Once you have created a profile and an account, you need to associate the account with the profile by using the **sysmail_add_profileaccount_sp** stored procedure. The following code binds the DBA Mail Account to the DBA Mail Profile with a priority (sequence number) of 1. If you add multiple accounts with the same priority, Database Mail will randomly choose the account that sends the mail.

```
EXEC msdb.dbo.sysmail_add_profileaccount_sp
     @profile_name = 'DBA Mail Profile',
     @account_name = 'DBA Mail Account',
     @sequence_number = 1
```

The final script is shown in Listing 5-1. You can change the script to suit your organization by adding multiple accounts or changing parameters to the correct values. By using the **@@ServerName** function in the display name, each server will be able to send e-mail using its own name. You will also need to change the **@mailserver_name** parameter to the name of your mail server.

Listing 5-1. Database Mail setup script

```
--MAKE SURE TO STOP SQL SERVER AGENT BEFORE RUNNING THIS SCRIPT!
USE msdb
GO

--Enable Database Mail
sp_configure 'show advanced options', 1;
GO
RECONFIGURE;
GO
sp_configure 'Database Mail XPs', 1;
GO
RECONFIGURE
GO

--Enable Service Broker
ALTER DATABASE msdb SET ENABLE_BROKER

--Add the profile
EXEC msdb.dbo.sysmail_add_profile_sp
     @profile_name = 'DBA Mail Profile',
     @description = 'Profile used by the database administrator to send email.'

--Add the account
EXEC msdb.dbo.sysmail_add_account_sp
     @account_name = 'DBA Mail Account',
     @description = 'Profile used by the database administrator to send email.',
     @email_address = 'DBA@somecompany.com',
     @display_name =  (Select @@ServerName),
     @mailserver_name =  'KEN-PC'

--Associate the account with the profile
EXEC msdb.dbo.sysmail_add_profileaccount_sp
     @profile_name = 'DBA Mail Profile',
     @account_name = 'DBA Mail Account',
     @sequence_number = 1

Print 'Don't Forget To Restart SQL Server Agent!'
```

As you can see, creating a Database Mail script is a far more efficient way to set up Database Mail across multiple servers.

Testing Database Mail

Once you have set up Database Mail, you can make sure it is properly configured by sending a test e-mail message, either by using the GUI or by running a T-SQL script.

To send a test e-mail message using SQL Server Management Studio, right-click Database Mail (located under the Management node) and select Send Test E-Mail from the context menu. In the Send

Test E-Mail dialog box, enter the recipient's e-mail address in the To text box, and optionally, text for the subject and body, as shown in Figure 5-1. Then click the Send Test E-Mail button to test the e-mail functionality. If you do not receive an e-mail message, you can check the error logs by right-clicking Database Mail and selecting View Database Mail Log from the context menu.

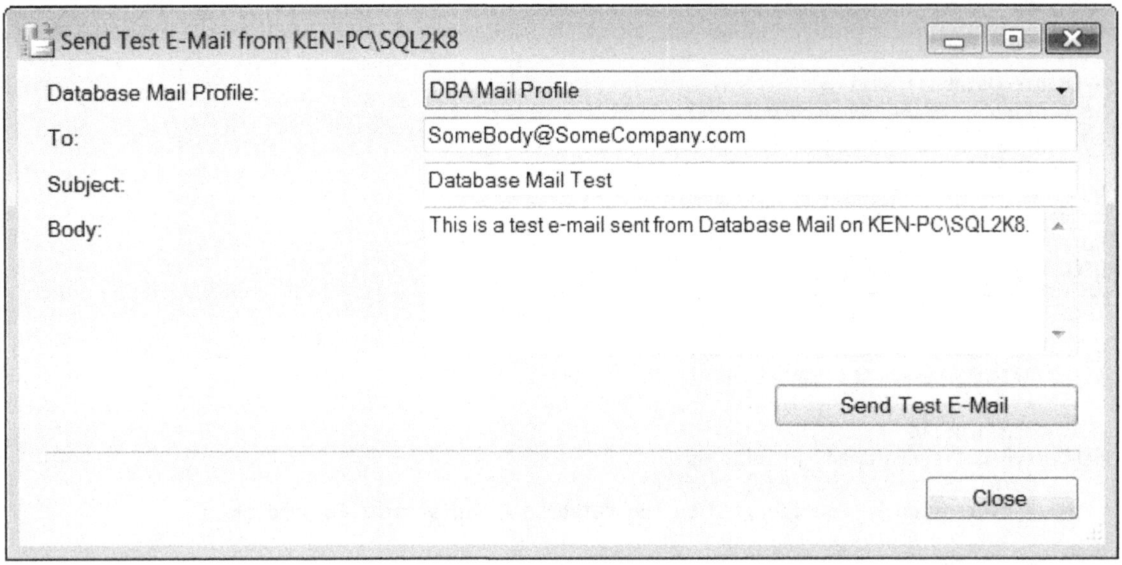

Figure 5-1. *Send Test E-Mail dialog box*

Alternatively, you can use T-SQL to send a test e-mail message, and then check the system tables for success or failure. The T-SQL script in Listing 5-2 will send a basic message, with a subject and a body. You can add multiple recipients by using a semicolon as a separator. If the statement is executed successfully, you will see the output "Mail queued" in the Messages pane.

Listing 5-2. T-SQL script to send an e-mail message

```
--Basic email
EXEC msdb.dbo.sp_send_dbmail
@recipients='Somebody@SomeCompany.com', --[ ; ...n ]
@subject = 'Basic Database Mail Sample',
@body= 'This is a test email.',
@profile_name = 'DBA Email Profile'
```

Once you have sent an e-mail, you can use the **sysmail_allitems** view to see all the items that have been processed using Database Mail, as shown in the following query:

```
SELECT * FROM msdb.dbo.sysmail_allitems
```

You may find a few other views useful as well. For example, the **sysmail_faileditems** view shows only failed messages, **sysmail_usentitems** shows only unsent messages, and **sysmail_sentitems** shows only sent messages.

Cleaning Up Database Mail History

Database Mail keeps a copy of every e-mail message that is sent, along with several event log entries in the **msdb** database. Over time, this buildup of sent mail can cause excessive growth in the **msdb** database. Two stored procedures allow you to purge mail history in order to keep the **msdb** database at a manageable size:

- You can use the **sysmail_delete_mailitems_sp** stored procedure to delete e-mail messages older than a specified date or all e-mail messages with a certain status.

- You can use the **sysmail_delete_log_sp** stored procedure to delete Database Mail logs older than a specified date or all Database Mail logs for a certain event type.

If you execute the sysmail_**delete_mailitems_sp** stored procedure without supplying any parameters, all e-mail messages will be deleted. Following is the complete syntax:

```
sysmail_delete_mailitems_sp
 [ [ @sent_before = ] 'sent_before' ] -- '1/1/2009'
 [ , [ @sent_status = ] 'sent_status' ] -- sent, unsent, retrying, failed
```

If you execute the **sysmail_delete_log_sp** stored procedure without supplying any parameters, all Database Mail log entries will be deleted. The complete syntax is as follows:

```
sysmail_delete_log_sp
 [ [ @logged_before = ] 'logged_before' ] --'1/1/2009'

[, [ @event_type = ] 'event_type' ] --success, warning, error, informational
```

You should incorporate both of these cleanup stored procedures into your regular maintenance routines. Come up with an acceptable retention policy for Database Mail, and then execute the cleanup stored procedures accordingly. Figure 5-2 shows a sample job that will delete all mail history older than 30 days.

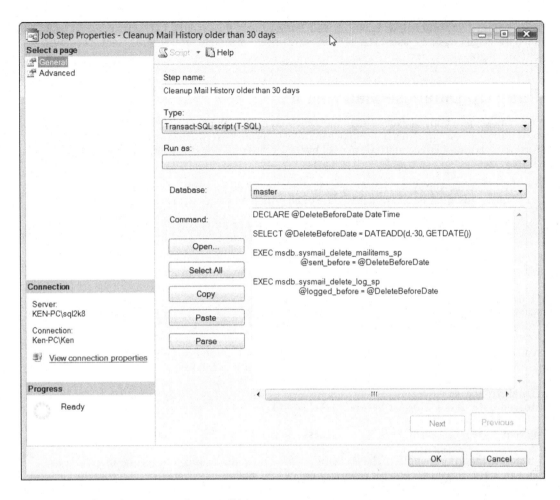

Figure 5-2. Job to clean up Database Mail history

You can create the job shown in Figure 5-2, which will run every Sunday at 4:00 AM, by running the T-SQL script in Listing 5-3.

Listing 5-3. T-SQL script to create a Database Mail cleanup job

```
USE [msdb]
GO

/****** Object:  Job [DBA - CleanupMsdbMailHistory]    ******/
BEGIN TRANSACTION
DECLARE @ReturnCode INT
SELECT @ReturnCode = 0
```

```
/****** Object:  JobCategory [Database Maintenance]    ******/
IF NOT EXISTS (SELECT name
                            FROM msdb.dbo.syscategories
                            WHERE name=N'Database Maintenance' AND
                                        category_class=1)
BEGIN
  EXEC @ReturnCode = msdb.dbo.sp_add_category
            @class=N'JOB',
            @type=N'LOCAL',
            @name=N'Database Maintenance'

  IF (@@ERROR <> 0 OR @ReturnCode <> 0) GOTO QuitWithRollback
END

DECLARE @jobId BINARY(16)

EXEC @ReturnCode =  msdb.dbo.sp_add_job
            @job_name=N'DBA - CleanupMsdbMailHistory',
            @enabled=1,
            @notify_level_eventlog=2,
            @notify_level_email=2,
            @notify_level_netsend=0,
            @notify_level_page=0,
            @delete_level=0,
            @description=N'No description available.',
            @category_name=N'Database Maintenance',
            @owner_login_name=N'sa',
            @notify_email_operator_name=N'DBASupport',
            @job_id = @jobId OUTPUT

IF (@@ERROR <> 0 OR @ReturnCode <> 0) GOTO QuitWithRollback

/****** Object:  Step [Cleanup Mail History older than 30 days]    ******/
EXEC @ReturnCode = msdb.dbo.sp_add_jobstep
            @job_id=@jobId,
            @step_name=N'Cleanup Mail History older than 30 days',
            @step_id=1,
            @cmdexec_success_code=0,
            @on_success_action=1,
            @on_success_step_id=0,
            @on_fail_action=2,
            @on_fail_step_id=0,
            @retry_attempts=0,
            @retry_interval=1,
            @os_run_priority=0, @subsystem=N'TSQL',
            @command=N'DECLARE @DeleteBeforeDate DateTime
SELECT @DeleteBeforeDate = DATEADD(d,-30, GETDATE())
EXEC msdb..sysmail_delete_mailitems_sp @sent_before = @DeleteBeforeDate
EXEC msdb..sysmail_delete_log_sp @logged_before = @DeleteBeforeDate',
        @database_name=N'master',
        @output_file_name=N'',
        @flags=0
```

```
IF (@@ERROR <> 0 OR @ReturnCode <> 0) GOTO QuitWithRollback

EXEC @ReturnCode = msdb.dbo.sp_update_job
            @job_id = @jobId,
            @start_step_id = 1

IF (@@ERROR <> 0 OR @ReturnCode <> 0) GOTO QuitWithRollback

EXEC @ReturnCode = msdb.dbo.sp_add_jobschedule
            @job_id=@jobId,
            @name=N'CleanupMsdbMailHistory',
            @enabled=1,
            @freq_type=8,
            @freq_interval=1,
            @freq_subday_type=1,
            @freq_subday_interval=0,
            @freq_relative_interval=0,
            @freq_recurrence_factor=1,
            @active_start_date=20020103,
            @active_end_date=99991231,
            @active_start_time=40000,
            @active_end_time=235959,
            @schedule_uid=N'8e6a9641-4b58-49c6-931f-fbdaaca2ada5'

IF (@@ERROR <> 0 OR @ReturnCode <> 0) GOTO QuitWithRollback

EXEC @ReturnCode = msdb.dbo.sp_add_jobserver
            @job_id = @jobId,
            @server_name = N'(local)'

IF (@@ERROR <> 0 OR @ReturnCode <> 0) GOTO QuitWithRollback

COMMIT TRANSACTION

GOTO EndSave
QuitWithRollback:
    IF (@@TRANCOUNT > 0) ROLLBACK TRANSACTION
EndSave:

GO
```

Creating SQL Server Agent Operators

An operator consists of two basic pieces of information: a name used to identify the operator and the contact information used to notify the operator. You will use the operator you create in this section later in this chapter when you specify who needs to receive alert notifications for policy violations.

To add an operator using SQL Server Management Studio, expand SQL Server Agent in Object Explorer, right-click the Operators folder, and select New Operator from the context menu. In the New Operator dialog box, enter an operator name and e-mail address, as shown in Figure 5-3, and then click

OK. Although you can configure net send and pager information, these options are deprecated and will be removed in a future version of SQL Server, so you should avoid using them. The only information you should enter here is the name of the operator and the e-mail address that you will use to receive event notifications.

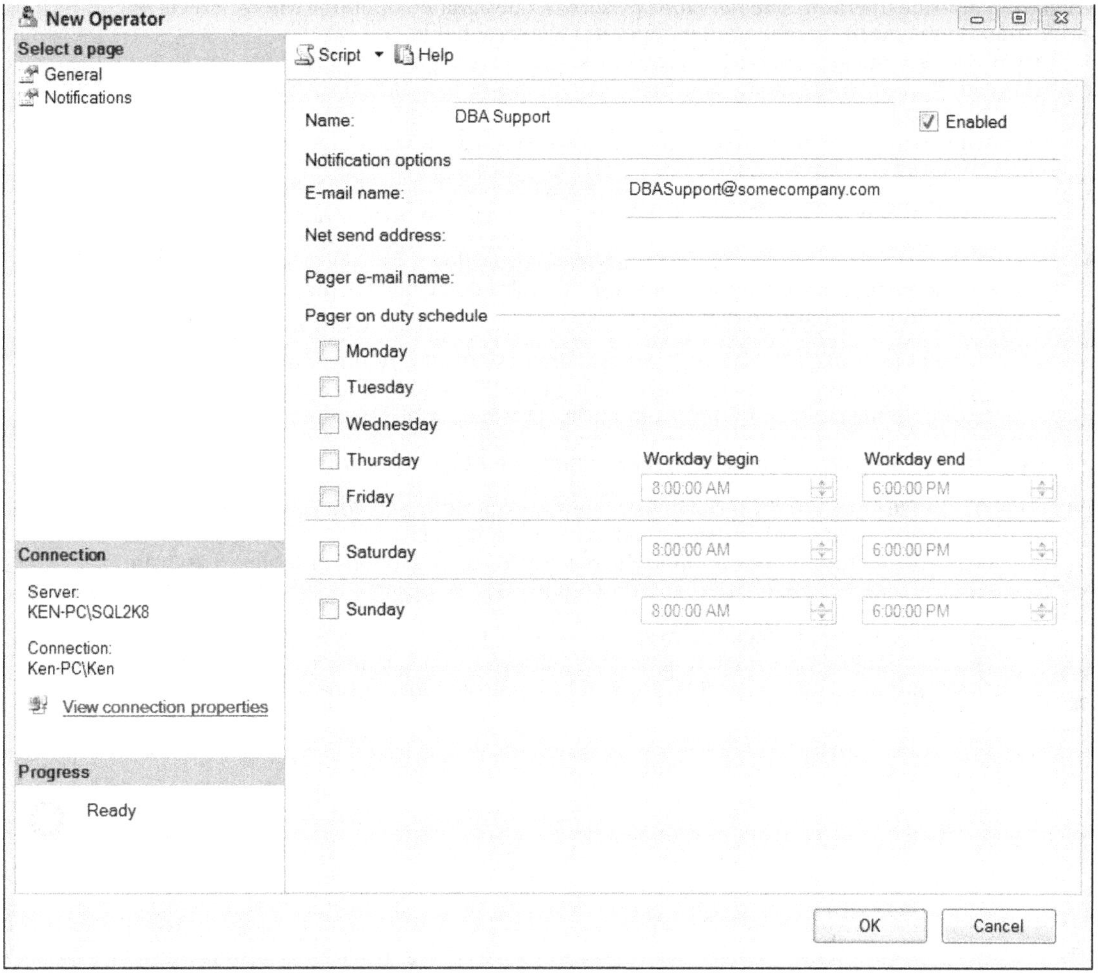

Figure 5-3. *New Operator dialog box*

You can also add an operator using the **sp_add_operator** procedure located in the **msdb** database. The following statement adds an operator named DBA Support and supplies an e-mail address as the contact information:

```
EXEC msdb.dbo.sp_add_operator
    @name='DBA Support',
    @email_address='DBASupport@somecompany.com'
```

Enabling SQL Server Agent Notifications

You must enable the alert system in SQL Server Agent before you can start receiving notifications. Once you have configured Database Mail and added an operator, you should enable the alert system and designate a fail-safe operator. The *fail-safe operator* is a designated operator who will receive notifications in the event that the primary operator is unreachable.

In SQL Server Management Studio, right-click SQL Server Agent and select properties from the context menu. This will bring up the SQL Server Agent Properties dialog box. Select the Alert System page.

You need to configure only a few settings on this page, as shown in Figure 5-4:

- In the Mail Session area, select Enable Mail Profile. This will allow you to select the mail system and profile that SQL Server Agent will use to send notifications.

- Select Database Mail from the Mail System drop-down list. SQL Mail is the other available mail system option; however, you should avoid SQL Mail because it will be removed in a future release.

- Select the profile SQL Server Agent will use to send alert notifications from the Mail Profile drop-down list. We are using the DBA Mail Profile option created earlier in the chapter, in the "Configuring Database Mail" section.

- In the Fail-Safe Operator area, select Enable Fail-Safe Operator.

- From the Operator drop-down list, select the operator that you want to receive notifications in case the designated operator is unreachable. SQL Server stores the fail-safe operator information in the registry in case the operator tables in **msdb** are unavailable. We are using an operator called DBA Support.

- Enable the E-mail check box to specify that the fail-safe operator will receive notifications using e-mail. (Remember that you should avoid the Pager and Net Send options, since they will no longer be supported in a future release.)

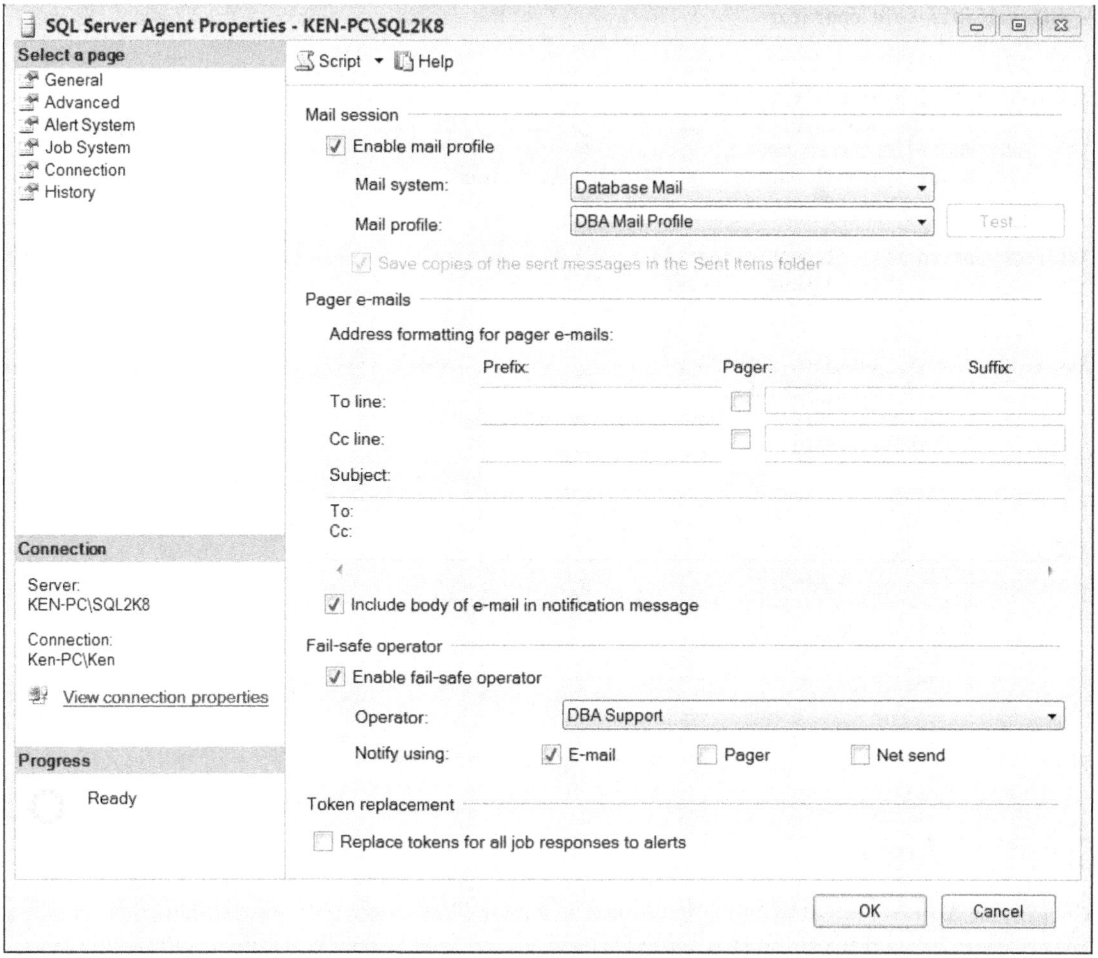

Figure 5-4. Alert System page of the SQL Server Agent Properties dialog box

Select OK to close the SQL Server Agent Properties dialog box. You must restart SQL Server Agent before the new settings will take effect.

You are now ready to start receiving automatic notifications from SQL Server Agent alerts and jobs.

In addition to the GUI, you can also use the script in Listing 5-4 to enable Database Mail in SQL Server Agent and set the fail-safe operator.

Listing 5-4. Script to enable Database Mail in SQL Server Agent

```
--MAKE SURE TO **START** SQL SERVER AGENT
--BEFORE RUNNING THIS SCRIPT!!!!!!!

--Enable SQL Server Agent to use Database Mail
```

119

```
-- and set fail-safe operator

EXEC master.dbo.sp_MSsetalertinfo
        @failsafeoperator=N'DBASupport', --Failsafe Operator
        @notificationmethod=1,
        @failsafeemailaddress = N'DBA@Somecompany.com'


EXEC msdb.dbo.sp_set_sqlagent_properties
        @email_save_in_sent_folder=1


EXEC master.dbo.xp_instance_regwrite
        N'HKEY_LOCAL_MACHINE',
        N'SOFTWARE\Microsoft\MSSQLServer\SQLServerAgent',
        N'UseDatabaseMail',
        N'REG_DWORD', 1


EXEC master.dbo.xp_instance_regwrite
        N'HKEY_LOCAL_MACHINE',
        N'SOFTWARE\Microsoft\MSSQLServer\SQLServerAgent',
        N'DatabaseMailProfile',
        N'REG_SZ',
        N'DBMailProfile'


 PRINT '***********Please Restart SQL Server Agent!************'
```

Creating Alerts

A SQL Server Agent alert is an automatic response to a predefined event. You can configure SQL Server Agent alerts to fire in response to SQL Server events, SQL Server performance counters, and Windows Management Instrumentation (WMI) events. Once an event has caused an alert to fire, you can respond to the alert by notifying operators of the event, or even by running a job after the event has occurred.

When a policy violation occurs, it raises a specific error number and writes the failure to the Windows event log. You can see a sample policy violation in Figure 5-5.

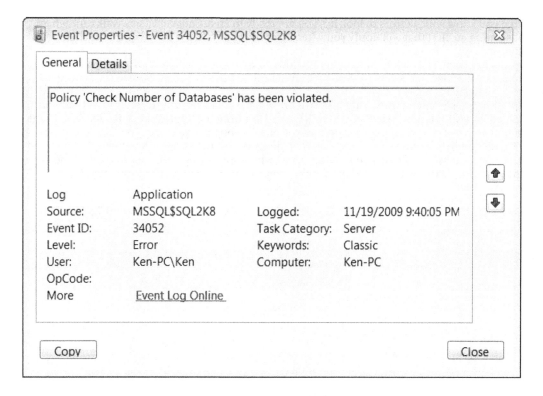

Figure 5-5. Policy violation shown in the Windows event log

As you can see in Figure 5-5, the policy Check Number of Databases has been violated and raised an event ID of 30452. You can create alerts that look for these specific events or error numbers, so you can respond by performing specific actions, such as sending e-mail.

■ **Note** No errors are raised for policies that are not enabled.

The following are the execution modes and the error numbers that are raised when a policy using the execution modes are violated:

- On change: prevent (automatic), 34050

- On change: prevent (on demand), 34051

- On schedule, 34052

- On change, 34053

Now that you know which errors to look for, you are ready to create an alert. Let's walk through an example of creating an alert that will notify you when error number 34052 is raised due to a scheduled policy violation.

To add an alert using SQL Server Management Studio, expand SQL Server Agent in Object Explorer, right-click the Alerts folder, and select New Alert from the context menu. This will open the New Alert dialog box.

Give the alert a descriptive name, and make sure the Enable check box is selected. We will call this alert **Scheduled Policy Violation**. Select SQL Server Event Alert from the Type drop-down list. The Event Alert Definition area will change depending on the type of alert you have selected. You can limit the alert to a specific database by selecting it from the Database name drop-down list; for this example, you should select <all databases>. We want to monitor errors with a specific error number, so select the Error number option to enable the text box, and then enter 34052. Figure 5-6 shows the completed General page for this example.

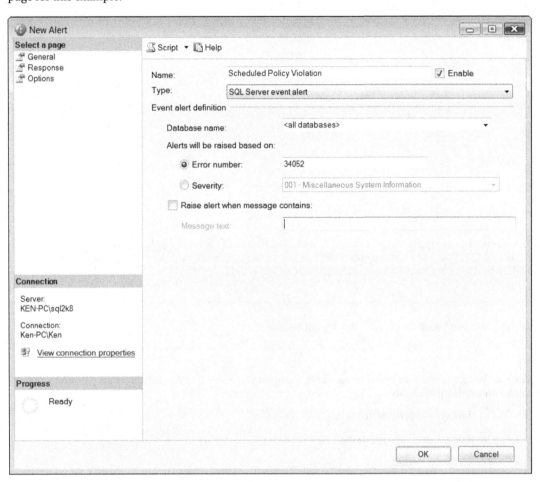

Figure 5-6. *General page of the New Alert dialog box*

Select the Response page to define the action that SQL Server Agent will perform when the event occurs. Here, you can choose to perform two actions in response to an event: execute a job and notify an operator of the event. You can select an existing job to run from the Execute Job drop-down list, or select the New Job button to open the New Job dialog box and create a new job. If you choose a job from the drop-down list and select the View Job button, SQL Server will display the Job Properties dialog box, which allows you to view and edit an existing job.

All of the existing operators are displayed in the Operator List area. Check the E-mail column for each operator you would like to receive a notification e-mail when the alert is triggered. (Again, the Pager and New Send options are deprecated, so you should avoid selecting them.) You can select the New Operator button to open the New Operator dialog box, or select the View Operator button to open the Operator Properties dialog box for the selected operator. We have chosen to notify the DBA Support operator we created earlier, as shown in Figure 5-7.

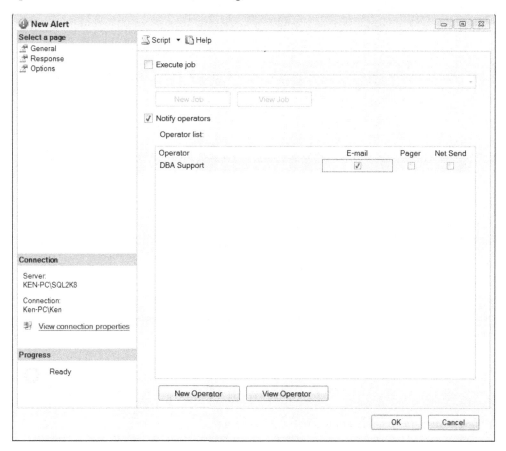

Figure 5-7. Response page of the New Alert dialog box

Select the Options page to make the final configurations to the new alert. Select the E-mail check box at the top of the Options section, as shown in Figure 5-8, so the error text for the event will be included in the e-mail that the operator receives. Optionally, you can enter text in the Additional Notification Message to Send text box, if you would like to send further information or instructions along with the error text to the operator. You can use the Delay Between Responses area to suspend additional responses for the alert for a specified amount of time. Adding a delay between responses is useful for error messages that may occur in rapid succession—no one wants to receive 100 e-mail messages in 5 minutes. Click OK to close the New Alert dialog box and create the alert.

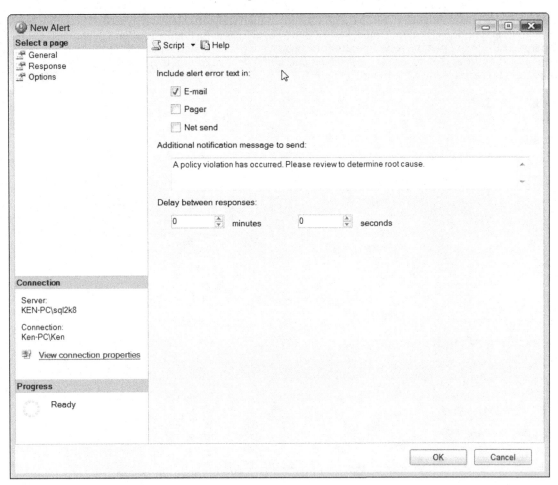

Figure 5-8. Options page of the New Alert dialog box

You can repeat this process for each alert you want to create on every SQL Server instance, or you can create a T-SQL script that you can run on all of your SQL Server instances. Not only will the T-SQL script in Listing 5-5 generate the same alert we just created for error number 34052 using SQL Server Management Studio, but it will also create the alerts for the remaining policy violation error numbers.

Listing 5-5. T-SQL script to create alerts for all policy violations

```
USE [msdb]
GO

EXEC msdb.dbo.sp_add_alert
    @name=N'Policy Violation: On change prevent automatic',
    @message_id=34050,
    @enabled=1,
    @include_event_description_in=1,
    @notification_message=N'A policy violation has occurred. Please review for root cause.'

GO

EXEC msdb.dbo.sp_add_notification
    @alert_name=N'Policy Violation: On change prevent automatic',
    @operator_name=N'DBA Support',
    @notification_method = 1

GO

EXEC msdb.dbo.sp_add_alert
    @name=N'Policy Violation: On change prevent on demand',
    @message_id=34051,
    @enabled=1,
    @include_event_description_in=1,
    @notification_message=N'A policy violation has occurred. Please review for root cause.'

GO

EXEC msdb.dbo.sp_add_notification
    @alert_name=N'Policy Violation: On change prevent on demand',
    @operator_name=N'DBA Support',
    @notification_method = 1

GO

EXEC msdb.dbo.sp_add_alert
    @name=N'Policy Violation: Scheduled',
    @message_id=34052,
    @enabled=1,
    @include_event_description_in=1,
    @notification_message=N'A policy violation has occurred. Please review for root cause.'

GO

EXEC msdb.dbo.sp_add_notification
    @alert_name=N'Policy Violation: Scheduled',
    @operator_name=N'DBA Support',
    @notification_method = 1
```

```
GO

EXEC msdb.dbo.sp_add_alert
    @name=N'Policy Violation: On change',
    @message_id=34053,
    @enabled=1,
    @include_event_description_in=1,
    @notification_message=N'A policy violation has occurred. Please review for root cause.'

GO

EXEC msdb.dbo.sp_add_notification
    @alert_name=N'Policy Violation: On change',
    @operator_name=N'DBA Support',
    @notification_method = 1

GO
```

Troubleshooting Policies

Once you have received an alert, you may need to figure out what cased the policy violation. While some policy failures are fairly self-explanatory, others may take a little more research to resolve. You also may need to do some general troubleshooting in order to find out why a policy is not acting as expected.

Viewing Policy History

The best way to review policy violations is by viewing the policy history. You can view policy history using the Log File Viewer. As with most tasks in SQL Server, there are multiple ways to launch the Log File Viewer. Also, the content of the Log File Viewer changes depending on the context in which it was launched.

You can view policy history in two general ways:

- View the history based on a policy.

- View the history based on an object.

We will walk you through both methods, beginning with the policy view.

Viewing History Based on Policies

The easiest way to view the execution history of a policy is to right-click a policy and select View History from the context menu. This will display the Log File Viewer with the execution history for the selected policy, as shown in Figure 5-9.

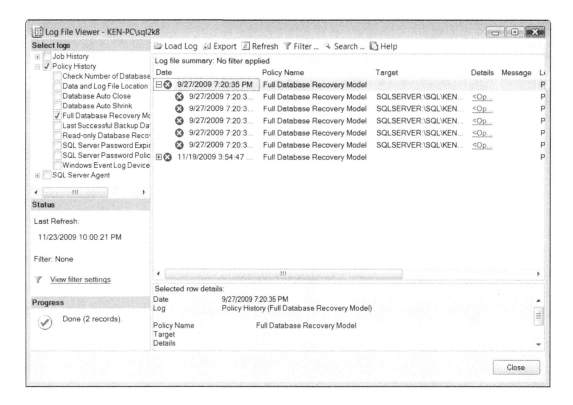

Figure 5-9. Log File Viewer with the execution history for the selected policy

Once you have launched the Log File Viewer, you can check and uncheck policies in the Select Logs list to display their history as well. However, if you want to see the history for all policies, it is easier to launch the Log File Viewer by right-clicking the Policy Management node or the Policies folder located under the Policy Management node and selecting View History from the context menu.

Viewing History Based on Objects

You can easily tell when an object has violated the policy by viewing the policy health state in SQL Server Management Studio. When an object (or any object in its hierarchical path) violates a policy, you will see a script icon with a red X beside the object, as shown in Figure 5-10. This can be an instance, database, table, and so on.

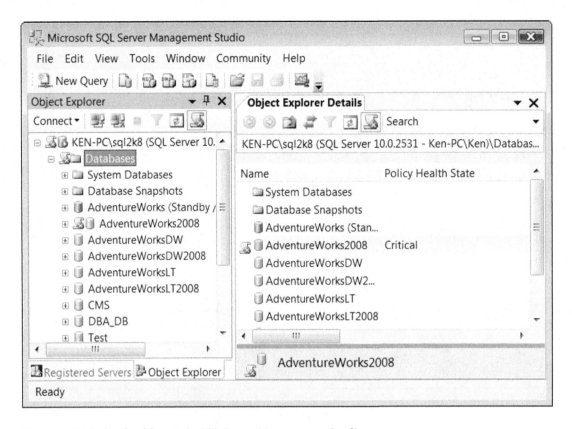

Figure 5-10. *Policy health state in SQL Server Management Studio*

In the example in Figure 5-10, you can see that the **AdventureWorks2008** database has violated a policy. Because the server instance is a parent object of the **AdventureWorks2008** database, the Policy Health State icon is displayed there as well. Finally, you see the icon on the Databases folder to help you pinpoint exactly where the policy violation occurred if you are just connecting to the instance. Basically, if you see an error at the instance level, just follow the path until you find the offending object.

In order to see which policies have failed for a given object, right-click the object and select Policies → View from the context menu to open the View Policies dialog box, as shown in Figure 5-11. You can identify the policy that has been violated by the script icon with the red X in the first column.

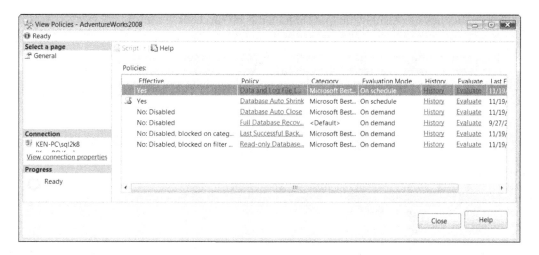

Figure 5-11. *View Policies dialog box*

The View Policies dialog box is also a good place to see which policies are effective on a specific object. You can see in Figure 5-11 that there are only two effective policies on the `AdventureWorks2008` database; the others are disabled, blocked on categories, or blocked on filters. You can also launch the Log File Viewer from here by selecting the History link, so you can see exactly why the policy failed. Finally, you can reevaluate the policy by selecting the Evaluate link.

General Troubleshooting

Sometimes you may need to do some general troubleshooting to figure out why a policy is not executing against a target or not working as expected. There are a handful of reasons why a policy may not be executing as expected, and all of them are fairly easy to figure out if you know where to look. The following is a checklist to help you track down general policy exceptions:

- The simplest and most common issue is that the policy is disabled. If a policy is not logging or executing against any targets, make sure it is enabled. Right-click the policy and selecting Enabled from the context menu.

- Make sure that the policy applies to the target in question. Right-click the object and select Policies → View from the context menu.

- Make sure the database subscribes to the category where the policy is located. Right-click the database and selecting Policies → Categories from the context menu.

- Check the policy to make sure the target is not excluded by a filter.

- When a policy is executed on schedule, SQL Server writes to the SQL Server Agent log in addition to the Windows event log. You can troubleshoot an on-schedule policy by reviewing the job history, just as you would for any other job in SQL Server Agent. However, a job does not fail just because a policy has been violated.

If the policy has successfully run (pass or fail), the job succeeds. If a job fails, it is due to a job execution error, not the results of a policy.

- Check for execution errors using the **syspolicy_policy_execution_history** and **syspolicy_policy_execution_history_details** system views. Listing 5-6 shows an example of a query that returns all policies with an exception, and Figure 5-12 shows its output.

Listing 5-6. Query to return policies with an exception message

```
SELECT sp.name,
       speh.exception_message
FROM msdb.dbo.syspolicy_policy_execution_history speh JOIN
    msdb.dbo.syspolicy_policies sp ON
        speh.policy_id = sp.policy_id
WHERE speh.exception_message <> ''
```

	name	exception_message
1	SQL Server Password Expiration	Property value 'PasswordExpirationEnabled' is not available.
2	SQL Server Password Policy	Property value 'PasswordPolicyEnforced' is not available.
3	Check Number of Databases	Invalid object name 'sys.databses'.

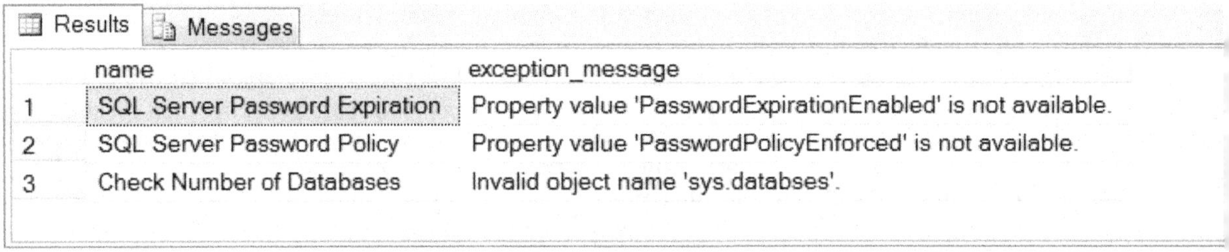

Figure 5-12. Output returned from Listing 5-6

Summary

In this chapter, we discussed ways to receive automatic notification when policy violations occur in your environment. First, we covered how to set up Database Mail, including testing and cleanup procedures you should be aware of once Database Mail has been configured. Next, we created an operator to receive notifications. Then we enabled notifications in SQL Server Agent and configured SQL Server Agent to use the operator we created. Next, we created alerts in SQL Server Agent to notify the operator when policies were violated. Finally, we discussed some ways to troubleshoot policies, including viewing policy history along with some general troubleshooting techniques.

In the next chapter, we will be exploring the internal architecture and system components of Policy-Based Management. Understanding the inner workings of Policy-Based Management can be a great asset when you need to go beyond the general troubleshooting routines described in this chapter.

CHAPTER 6

■ ■ ■

Policy-Based Management Internals

In this chapter, we will cover the basic makeup of the Policy-Based Management framework and its internal structures. Some of the objects that make up Policy-Based Management include system tables, views, and stored procedures. All these items are stored in the **msdb** system database and work together to provide the foundation for Policy-Based Management. Having a general knowledge of the internal structures that make up Policy-Based Management can help you when you're troubleshooting problems, as well as when you're automating tasks.

Policy-Based Management Properties

First, let's look at some of the basic properties for Policy-Based Management itself. You can get to a list of properties by right-clicking the Policy Management node under the Management folder and selecting Properties from the context menu. You will see the Policy Management Properties dialog box, as shown in Figure 6-1.

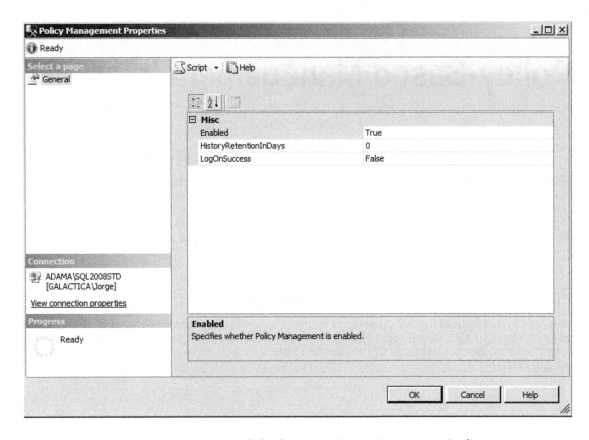

Figure 6-1. *Policy Management Properties dialog box in SQL Server Management Studio*

As you can see from Figure 6-1, only three properties are available at this level:

> *Enabled*: This specifies whether Policy-Based Management is enabled on the server, and it is True by default. You can set this property to False to disable the feature. Once Policy-Based Management is disabled, the icon on the Policy Management node changes to include a red arrow, so you can easily tell the state of Policy-Based Management. Disabling Policy-Based Management will also remove the policy health state indicator (red *X* icon) that is displayed by objects to indicate policy violations. However, you will need to refresh the instance in SQL Server Management Studio before the policy health state indicator is actually removed. You can still manually evaluate policies when Policy-Based Management is disabled, but the scheduled job will no longer write policy violations to the event log. Since no records are written to the event log, this also means you will not receive any alerts you have configured for those violations.

■ Note: You can also enable and disable Policy-Based Management from the context menu that appears when you right-click the Policy Management node.

HistoryRetentionInDays: Specifies the number of days the server keeps policy evaluation history in its tables. By default, this option is set to 0, which means historical evaluation data is not automatically removed from the table in the **msdb** database. You may want to change the value for this property to retain history for a reasonable length of time, such as 30 days, in order to avoid unnecessarily bloating the size of the **msdb** database. However, your auditing requirements may dictate the amount of history you need to retain. The cleanup job is handled by a scheduled job under the SQL Server Agent called **syspolicy_purge_history**, which runs every day at 2:00 AM, by default. This cleanup job is created automatically when you install SQL Server 2008.

LogOnSuccess: Specifies whether Policy-Based Management logs successful policy evaluations. By default, only failed evaluations are logged to the **syspolicy_policy_execution_history_details_internal** table. Logging successful evaluations can be useful if you are doing any reporting on the current state of a policy. If only failed evaluations are logged, you will not know if the policy is still in a failed state or if it has met the requirements in a subsequent evaluation.

Alternatively, you can query the **syspolicy_configuration** view in the **msdb** database to determine your currently configured values using the query in Listing 6-1.

Listing 6-1. Query to determine the current property settings for Policy-Based Management

```
SELECT CAST(serverproperty(N'Servername') AS sysname) AS [Name],
            CAST((SELECT current_value
                    FROM msdb.dbo.syspolicy_configuration
                    WHERE name = 'Enabled')
                AS bit) AS [Enabled],
            CAST((SELECT current_value
                    FROM msdb.dbo.syspolicy_configuration
                    WHERE name = 'HistoryRetentionInDays')
                AS int) AS [HistoryRetentionInDays],
            CAST((SELECT current_value
                    FROM msdb.dbo.syspolicy_configuration
                    WHERE name = 'LogOnSuccess')
                AS bit) AS [LogOnSuccess]
```

There is one row in the **syspolicy_configuration** view that you don't see in the Policy Management Properties dialog box: the globally unique identifier (GUID) of the job that actually cleans up the policy history. You can join this GUID to the **sysjobs** table to find out other information about the purge history job, as shown in Listing 6-2.

Listing 6-2. Query to view information about the purge history job

```
SELECT sc.name AS PropertyName,
       job_id,
       sj.name AS JobName,
       [enabled]
FROM msdb.dbo.syspolicy_configuration sc JOIN
     msdb.dbo.sysjobs sj ON
     CAST(current_value as uniqueidentifier) = sj.job_id
WHERE sc.name = 'PurgeHistoryJobGuid'
```

▪ **Note:** An interesting thing about these Policy-Based Management properties is that there is no facet to manage them. For example, you couldn't create a policy that ensured that HistoryRetentionInDays was always set to 30 without using a custom SQL script. There is an active suggestion on Microsoft Connect to add a facet for these properties (https://connect.microsoft.com/SQLServer/feedback/details/419574/pbm-facet-policy-management). It looks like the suggestion is on the radar for SQL Server 11. If you think this would be a valuable addition, make sure to visit this page to vote.

Policy-Based Management Architecture

The architecture of Policy-Based Management is composed of many different components within SQL Server. In addition, completely different components may be used depending on the policy evaluation mode: On Demand, On Change: Prevent, On Change: Log Only, or On Schedule. Here, we will look at the architecture used by each evaluation mode.

Keep in mind that the configuration settings and historical information about Policy-Based Management are housed in the **msdb** database. In addition, even though you can evaluate a policy directly from the file system, the only way you can evaluate a policy is On Demand, unless it is stored in the **msdb** database.

On Demand

On Demand is the simplest form of evaluation and lays the foundation for the remaining evaluation modes. Policy-Based Management is built on top of SQL Server Management Objects (SMO), a collection of objects used when programming to interact with SQL Server. When you evaluate a policy, the Policy Engine checks the current state of an object, or target, using SMO against the desired state you have defined by the conditions of your policy. This behavior is true for the remaining evaluation modes as well.

■ **Note**: SQL Server 2000, 2005, and 2008, support SMO, which is why Policy-Based Management works with all of these versions as well. However, Policy-Based Management also takes advantage of some new features in SQL Server 2008, which is why you have limited functionality with prior versions.

On Change: Prevent

When using the On Change: Prevent mode, SQL Server takes advantage of Data Definition Language (DDL) triggers to actually prevent changes from occurring if they violate a policy. Since these changes must be prevented before the changes are committed, the Policy Engine uses a Common Language Runtime (CLR) wrapper so it can handle the process within a transaction.

The complete process for On Change: Prevent is as follows:

- Database Engine Eventing sends DDL events synchronously to the Policy Event Handler.

- The Policy Event Handler invokes the Policy Engine, which evaluates the policy.

- If the policy fails, the change is committed; otherwise, the change is rolled back.

To increase performance, the Policy Event Handler is listening for only events that coincide with enabled policies. If you don't have any policies enabled, the Policy Event Handler will not be listening for any events. Furthermore, if all of your enabled policies are using the Server facet, the Policy Event Handler will be listening for only server events.

On Change: Log Only

Since policy violations only need to be logged (not prevented) when using the On Change: Log Only mode, Policy-Based Management can take advantage of asynchronous processing. This asynchronous processing is performed by using trace events in conjunction with Service Broker.

The complete process for On Change: Log Only is as follows:

- Database Engine Eventing sends trace events asynchronously to a Service Broker queue.

- Service Broker sends the events to the Policy Event Handler.

- The Policy Event Handler invokes the Policy Engine, which evaluates the policy.

- If the policy fails, the event is logged.

On Schedule

When using the On Schedule mode, Policy-Based Management uses the SQL Server Agent and PowerShell to execute policies at a given time. Since these policies are executed outside the Database Engine, Policy-Based Management uses PowerShell, rather than CLR, as a wrapper for the Policy Engine.

When you schedule a policy, a SQL Server Agent job is automatically created with two steps. The first step checks to see if the Policy-Based Management is enabled using the function fn_syspolicy_is_automation_enabled (shown in Listing 6-3). If Policy-Based Management is enabled, the job proceeds to the next step, which uses PowerShell to invoke the Policy Engine and evaluate the policy.

Listing 6-3. Function used to determine if Policy-Based Management is enabled

```
CREATE FUNCTION fn_syspolicy_is_automation_enabled()
RETURNS bit
AS
BEGIN
    DECLARE @ret bit;
    SELECT @ret = CONVERT(bit, current_value)
        FROM msdb.dbo.syspolicy_configuration
        WHERE name = 'Enabled'

    RETURN @ret;
END
```

Notice that the function in Listing 6-3 uses the **syspolicy_configuration** view we discussed in the Properties section earlier in the chapter.

You can create your own job in SQL Server that uses the function in Listing 6-3 to make sure Policy-Based Management is enabled using the script in Listing 6-4. If the job fails, you could send an alert notification informing you that Policy-Based Management is disabled.

Listing 6-4. Script to see if Policy-Based Management is enabled

```
IF (msdb.dbo.fn_syspolicy_is_automation_enabled() != 1)
        BEGIN
            RAISERROR(34022, 16, 1)
        END
```

Policy-Based Management Security Issues

Security for Policy-Based Management centers around two elements:

> **PolicyAdministratorRole**: A database role that allows those holding it to create and edit policies.

> **##MS_PolicyTsqlExecutionLogin##**: A proxy login used by Policy-Based Management when you schedule a policy that makes use of the **ExecuteSQL()** function. By default, the proxy login has very little access. You'll need to grant the necessary login access to execute the SQL that you schedule.

The role gives you control over who can define and edit policies. The login gives you control over SQL statements that those policies execute.

When you manually execute a policy, any SQL executed via the **ExecuteSQL()** function executes under your own username. It is as if you had logged in and executed that SQL. But when a policy execution is triggered by a schedule, any SQL gets executed under the proxy login. Thus, you should take the following into account when using **ExecuteSQL()**:

- Grant no unnecessary access to **##MS_PolicyTsqlExecutionLogin##**.

- Any access you grant to **##MS_PolicyTsqlExecutionLogin##** is effectively available to any user holding the **PolicyAdministratorRole**.

- When you create a policy to execute manually, be sure that your own login has the necessary privileges and roles to execute the SQL for that policy.

- When you create a policy to execute on schedule, you'll need to grant needed access to the **##MS_PolicyTsqlExecutionLogin##** user.

Remember that these concerns apply only when creating a policy that uses **ExecuteSQL()**. None of these issues apply to facet-based policies.

Whether or not you use **ExecuteSQL()** depends on the demands of your environment. If you do, be sure to keep strong control over the **PolicyAdministratorRole**. Know who has the role and why. Do not give the role out gratuitously. Likewise, take care in granting access to the **##MS_PolicyTsqlExecutionLogin##** user. Realize that any access granted to the user is effectively granted to any other user holding the rule.

■ **Tip**: Keep an eye out for new facets in upcoming releases of SQL Server. It is likely that policies that can now be enforced only through calls to **ExecuteSQL()** will in the future be enforceable through facets. As Microsoft updates SQL Server from release to release, watch for opportunities to convert SQL-based policies into facet-based policies. Each opportunity to convert is a potential opportunity to revoke access by the **##MS_PolicyTsqlExecutionLogin##** user, thus enhancing your overall security.

You may also notice another login called **##MS_PolicyEventProcessingLogin##**. This login is used by server-level DDL events, as well as by the activation procedure **sp_syspolicy_events_reader**, which is used to process messages in the Service Broker-called **syspolicy_event_queue**. This login is used only internally, and you should not need to manage any permissions pertaining to it.

Policy-Based Management Tables and Views

To see how Policy-Based Management is organized, we will look at its table structure within the **msdb** database, and then at some of the views that use these tables, which will give you a better understanding of how Policy-Based Management uses the tables internally.

Tables

Figure 6-2 illustrates how the tables in the **msdb** database relate to each other.

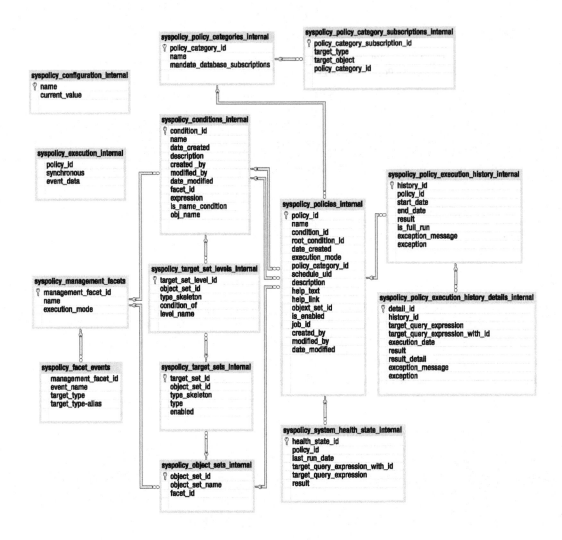

Figure 6-2. Policy-Based Management entity relationship diagram

You may not ever need to query the tables, but it's good to know that they exist, and to have some idea of the possibilities that they offer.

Contents of System Policy Tables

Following is a list of the tables shown in Figure 6-2, with brief descriptions of what each contains.

> `syspolicy_conditions_internal`: Contains all conditions existing on the server. These conditions can also be viewed via SQL Server Management Studio, from the Conditions folder under Policy Management. The table contains information such

as condition ID, creation date, description, created by, date last modified, and expression. The expression column holds the XML structure of the condition itself.

syspolicy_configuration_internal: Contains all of the properties for the Policy-Based Management configuration. These are the same properties you saw in the SQL Server Management Studio Policy Management Properties dialog box (Figure 6-1) earlier in the chapter.

syspolicy_execution_internal: Holds temporary data used to evaluate a policy. DDL triggers call the **sp_syspolicy_dispatch_event** stored procedure, which in turn inserts the event data into this table. You will probably never see any data in this table, because it is deleted at the end of each process.

syspolicy_facet_events: Contains the various event names and target types associated with a particular policy's triggered action. For example, a policy that enforces naming standards when creating new stored procedures would have a **management_facet_id** of **61**, which associates with the event **CREATE_PROCEDURE** and target type **PROCEDURE**, as shown in Figure 6-3.

syspolicy_management_facets: Contains a listing of all the facets exposed. This table includes the ID for the facet, the facet name, and the execution mode that facet is able to utilize.

syspolicy_object_sets_internal: Contains a listing of relationships between existing conditions and their related facets.

syspolicy_policies_internal: Contains detailed information on policies existing on the server. Useful information available in this table includes the policy name, condition ID associated with the policy, creation date, policy category ID, policy description, **is_enabled** flag, created/modified dates, and created by.

syspolicy_policy_categories_internal: Contains a listing of category groups for policies. The **mandate_database_subscriptions** column tells you which policy categories automatically force policy subscription to all databases. A value of **1** (the default) means all databases on the server subscribe to policies within this category. A value of **0** means the category is not mandated, and so a policy administrator (or someone with database owner rights on the database) can choose to subscribe to a category of policies for a given database.

syspolicy_policy_category_subscriptions_internal: Contains databases that explicitly subscribe to a given policy. By default, created policies are mandated to all databases. If a category is not mandated and has explicit subscribers to its category, then that information is kept in this table. Data kept includes target type for the policy, the name of the database (**target_object**) subscribing to the category, and the category ID.

syspolicy_policy_execution_history_details_internal: Contains detailed results from policy evaluations that have resulted in a failed policy state. If you wish to see detailed results from *all* policy evaluations, you must change the LogOnSuccess value to True from within the Policy Management properties. Details include the target of the executed policy (**target_query_expression**), the target expression with ID, execution date, Boolean value of the result (**0** for success and **1** for failure), result detail in XML format, and any exception messages.

syspolicy_policy_execution_history_internal: Contains information similar to the previous table, only result details are limited. The information in this table includes policy ID, start and end date of the execution, Boolean result of the execution (**0** for success and **1** for failure), and any exception messages.

syspolicy_system_health_state_internal: Contains information about the current health state for failed targets. This table is populated only when the policy is enabled. If the table contains data and you disable the policy, the data for that policy is removed immediately.

syspolicy_target_set_levels_internal: Specifies the levels a given policy targets, such as file, file group, stored procedure, or database.

syspolicy_target_sets_internal: Specifies the target type of a given policy and whether that policy set is enabled.

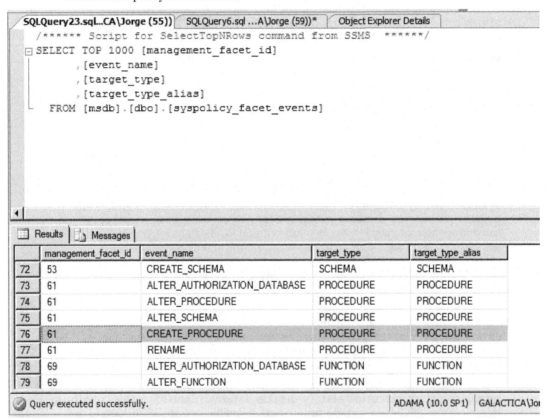

Figure 6-3. Sample data held in the syspolicy_facet_events table

Checking for New Tables

Since Policy-Based Management is a new feature, you never know when new tables will be added to the **msdb** database. You can get a listing of all the Policy-Based Management tables, including the creation date, using the query in Listing 6-5.

Listing 6-5. Query to get a listing of the Policy-Based Management tables

```
SELECT *
FROM msdb.sys.tables
WHERE name LIKE 'syspolicy%'
ORDER BY name
```

Views

Policy-Based Management also has a series of system views used by several internal operations. Many of these views simply query the base table directly; others provide additional logic. By creating views that query the base table, it is easy for Microsoft to create an abstraction layer between the code and the database. It is easy to add logic to a view to handle certain situations, such as always returning disabled for SQL Server Express edition, without needing to change application code.

The views described in this section allow you to query useful information without the need to know the relationships of the underlying tables. Note that querying the system policy views requires membership in the **PolicyAdministratorRole** in the **msdb** database.

■ **Note**: Currently, some of the views discussed here are documented in SQL Server Books Online (four are not). Two of those that are discussed in the documentation are named incorrectly there.

---

syspolicy_conditions

The **syspolicy_conditions** view displays one row for each condition and allows you to determine who created or last changed a condition. You can see by the following definition that the view joins the **syspolicy_conditions_internal** table with the **syspolicy_management_facets** table to display the facet name as well.

```
SELECT c.condition_id,
            c.name,
            c.date_created,
            c.description,
            c.created_by,
            c.modified_by,
            c.date_modified,
            c.is_name_condition,
            mf.name AS facet,
            c.expression,
            c.obj_name
```

```
FROM [dbo].[syspolicy_conditions_internal] c LEFT OUTER JOIN
        [dbo].[syspolicy_management_facets] mf ON
                c.facet_id = mf.management_facet_id
```

syspolicy_configuration

syspolicy_configuration is an undocumented view. However, you can see by the following definition that it is just displaying the data from the **syspolicy_configuration_internal** table with one additional check. If the engine edition is 4, which is Express edition, then the view returns **0** for enabled, no matter what the actual value is in the table.

```
SELECT name,
    CASE WHEN name = N'Enabled' and
            SERVERPROPERTY('EngineEdition') = 4
        THEN 0
        ELSE current_value
    END AS current_value
FROM [dbo].[syspolicy_configuration_internal]
```

syspolicy_object_sets

syspolicy_object_sets is an undocumented view that correlates an object set such as **Database Auto Close_ObjectSet** to a facet such as **IDatabasePerformanceFacet**. The definition is a follows.

```
SELECT os.object_set_id,
            os.object_set_name,
            os.facet_id,
            facet.name as facet_name
FROM [dbo].[syspolicy_object_sets_internal] AS os INNER JOIN
        [dbo].[syspolicy_management_facets] AS facet ON
            os.facet_id = facet.management_facet_id
```

syspolicy_policies

Among other detailed information, the **syspolicy_policies** view allows you to determine if a policy is enabled and who created or changed any policy. As you can see by the following definition, this view is just a straightforward query from the **syspolicy_policies_internal** table.

```
SELECT policy_id,
            name,
            condition_id,
            root_condition_id,
            date_created,
            execution_mode,
            policy_category_id,
            schedule_uid,
            description,
            help_text,
```

```
                help_link,
                object_set_id,
                is_enabled,
                job_id,
                created_by,
                modified_by,
                date_modified
FROM [dbo].[syspolicy_policies_internal]
```

syspolicy_policy_categories

The **syspolicy_policy_categories** view is incorrectly named as **syspolicy_groups** in SQL Server Books Online. This view displays a list of groups within Policy-Based Management and also lets you see if a given policy is mandated as an explicit database subscription. As you can see by the following definition, this view is a simple query against the **syspolicy_policy_categories_internal** table.

```
SELECT policy_category_id,
                name,
                mandate_database_subscriptions
FROM [dbo].[syspolicy_policy_categories_internal]
```

syspolicy_policy_category_subscriptions

The **syspolicy_policy_category_subscriptions** view is incorrectly named in SQL Server Books Online as **syspolicy_policy_group_subscriptions**. This view shows the targets that are subscribed to policy categories. As you can see by the following definition, the view simply queries the **syspolicy_policy_category_subscriptions_internal** table.

```
SELECT policy_category_subscription_id,
                target_type,
                target_object,
                policy_category_id
FROM [dbo].[syspolicy_policy_category_subscriptions_internal]
```

syspolicy_policy_execution_history

The **syspolicy_policy_execution_history** view contains general historical information on policies, such as the date and time the policy tried to run, the time the policy completed running, success or failure result, and any exception messages that may have occurred during evaluation. The definition follows.

```
SELECT history_id,
                policy_id,
                start_date,
                end_date,
                result,
                exception_message,
                exception
FROM [dbo].[syspolicy_policy_execution_history_internal]
```

syspolicy_policy_execution_history_details

syspolicy_policy_execution_history_details provides a more detailed view of the execution history for a policy. When troubleshooting Policy-Based Management, this is the preferred view to query, as it shows which target and condition expression combinations failed and when they failed, with a review of related errors. The definition follows.

```
SELECT detail_id,
               history_id,
               target_query_expression,
               execution_date,
               result,
               result_detail,
               exception_message,
               exception
FROM [dbo].[syspolicy_policy_execution_history_details_internal]
```

syspolicy_system_health_state

The syspolicy_system_health_state view shows the most recent health state of a target query expression for each enabled policy in the instance. The definition follows.

```
SELECT health_state_id,
               policy_id,
               last_run_date,
               target_query_expression_with_id,
               target_query_expression,
               result
FROM [dbo].[syspolicy_system_health_state_internal]
```

syspolicy_target_set_levels

syspolicy_target_set_levels is an undocumented view that specifies the levels a given policy targets, such as file, file group, stored procedure, or database. The definition follows.

```
SELECT target_set_level_id,
               target_set_id,
               type_skeleton,
               condition_id,
               level_name
FROM [dbo].[syspolicy_target_set_levels_internal]
```

syspolicy_target_sets

syspolicy_target_sets is another undocumented view that specifies the target type of a given policy and whether that policy set is enabled. The definition follows.

```
SELECT target_set_id,
```

```
            object_set_id,
            type_skeleton,
            type,
            enabled
FROM [dbo].[syspolicy_target_sets_internal]
```

Combining Views

You can combine many of these views to provide useful information. Listing 6-6 shows a sample query that combines four views to display detailed information about policy failures.

Listing 6-6. Query to display detailed information about policy failures

```
SELECT sp.name AS Policy,
            sc.name AS Condition,
            spehd.target_query_expression,
            spehd.execution_date,
            spehd.exception_message,
            spehd.exception
FROM msdb.dbo.syspolicy_policies AS sp JOIN
        msdb.dbo.syspolicy_conditions AS sc
            ON sp.condition_id = sc.condition_id JOIN
        msdb.dbo.syspolicy_policy_execution_history AS speh
            ON sp.policy_id = speh.policy_id JOIN
        msdb.dbo.syspolicy_policy_execution_history_details AS spehd
            ON speh.history_id = spehd.history_id
WHERE spehd.result = 0
```

Figure 6-4 shows an example of the output of Listing 6-6.

	Policy	Condition	target_query_expression	execution_date	exception_message	exception
103	Check Number of Databases	Check Number of Databases	SQLSERVER:\SQL\KEN-PC\SQL2K8	2010-03-02 23:25:30.830	Invalid object name 'sys.databses'.	System.Data.SqlClient.Sql
104	Data and Log File Location	Data and Log Files on Sep..	SQLSERVER:\SQL\KEN-PC\SQL2K8\Databas..	2010-03-02 23:25:31.063		
105	Data and Log File Location	Data and Log Files on Sep..	SQLSERVER:\SQL\KEN-PC\SQL2K8\Databas..	2010-03-02 23:25:31.117		
106	Data and Log File Location	Data and Log Files on Sep..	SQLSERVER:\SQL\KEN-PC\SQL2K8\Databas..	2010-03-02 23:25:31.173		
107	Data and Log File Location	Data and Log Files on Sep..	SQLSERVER:\SQL\KEN-PC\SQL2K8\Databas..	2010-03-02 23:25:31.233		
108	Data and Log File Location	Data and Log Files on Sep..	SQLSERVER:\SQL\KEN-PC\SQL2K8\Databas..	2010-03-02 23:25:31.283		
109	Data and Log File Location	Data and Log Files on Sep..	SQLSERVER:\SQL\KEN-PC\SQL2K8\Databas..	2010-03-02 23:25:31.340		
110	Data and Log File Location	Data and Log Files on Sep..	SQLSERVER:\SQL\KEN-PC\SQL2K8\Databas..	2010-03-02 23:25:31.410		
111	Data and Log File Location	Data and Log Files on Sep	SQLSERVER:\SQL\KEN-PC\SQL2K8\Databas..	2010-03-02 23:25:31.460		
112	Database Auto Shrink	Auto Shrink Disabled	SQLSERVER:\SQL\KEN-PC\SQL2K8\Databas..	2010-03-02 23:25:32.027		
113	Public Not Granted Server Per..	Public Server Role Has No...	SQLSERVER:\SQL\KEN-PC\SQL2K8	2010-03-02 23:25:34.800		
114	SQL Server Login Mode	Windows Authentication M...	SQLSERVER:\SQL\KEN-PC\SQL2K8	2010-03-02 23:25:36.223		
115	SQL Server Password Expiration	Password Expiration Enabled	SQLSERVER:\SQL\KEN-PC\SQL2K8\Logins\#..	2010-03-02 23:25:37.427		
116	SQL Server Password Expiration	Password Expiration Enabled	SQLSERVER:\SQL\KEN-PC\SQL2K8\Logins\#..	2010-03-02 23:25:37.433		
117	SQL Server Password Expiration	Password Expiration Enabled	SQLSERVER:\SQL\KEN-PC\SQL2K8\Logins\B..	2010-03-02 23:25:37.473	Property value 'PasswordExpirationEnabled' is not available.	Microsoft.SqlServer.Mana
118	SQL Server Password Policy	Password Policy Enforced	SQLSERVER:\SQL\KEN-PC\SQL2K8\Logins\B..	2010-03-02 23:25:37.590	Property value 'PasswordPolicyEnforced' is not available.	Microsoft.SqlServer.Mana
119	SQL Server Service Account	SQL Server Service Account	SQLSERVER:\SQL\KEN-PC\SQL2K8	2010-03-02 23:25:37.750		

Figure 6-4. Sample output returned by running the query in Listing 6-6

Checking for New Views

As with the Policy-Based Management tables, SQL Server may add new Policy-Based Management views to the **msdb** database at any time. You can get a listing of all the Policy-Based Management views, including the creation date, using the query in Listing 6-7.

Listing 6-7. Query to get a listing of the Policy-Based Management views

```
SELECT *
FROM msdb.sys.views
WHERE name LIKE 'syspolicy%'
ORDER BY name
```

Stored Procedures

As a DBA, you might want to take advantage of certain features without being restricted to using the GUI, or you may need to be able to use functionality via scripting for automation purposes. Taking advantage of the existing logic in stored procedures is a big help in the scripting process.

There are 43 Policy-Based Management stored procedures in the **dbo** schema and 5 in the **sys** schema, so we will not cover individual stored procedures in this section. However, we will show you how to find these stored procedures and provide an example of using them for scripting purposes.

You can run the query in Listing 6-8 to return all the stored procedures used by Policy-Based Management.

Listing 6-8. Query to return Policy-Based Management stored procedures

```
SELECT SCHEMA_NAME(schema_id) AS SchemaName,
       *
FROM msdb.sys.all_objects
WHERE type = 'P' AND
      name like 'sp_syspolicy%'
ORDER BY name
```

The query in Listing 6-8 should return 48 rows if you are using SQL Server 2008 Service Pack 1. If you want to view the definitions of any of these stored procedures, you can use **sp_helptext** followed by the procedure name. For example, **sp_helptext 'sp_syspolicy_rename_policy_category'** will return the definition for the **sp_syspolicy_rename_policy_category** stored procedure, as shown in Figure 6-5.

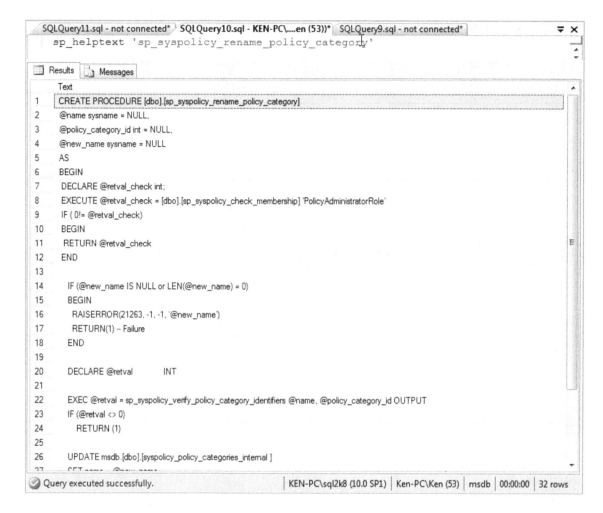

Figure 6-5. *Stored procedure definition returned by using sp_helptext*

Now let's say you wanted to rename a category on one of your servers. No big deal, right? Just go into SQL Server Management Studio and rename the category. But suppose you need to repeat this 50 or even 100 times (depending on the number of servers you have). The scripting option is starting to sound a little better. If you have all your servers set up using a Central Management Server, you can just run that script on your Central Management Server groups, greatly reducing the time it takes to do a simple maintenance task. You could script the task by using the following statement:

```
EXEC msdb.dbo.sp_syspolicy_rename_policy_category
     @name=N'OldPolicyName',
     @new_name=N'NewPolicyName'
```

■ **Tip:** It is a good idea to perform an action on a contained environment and capture the events that occur using SQL Server Profiler. By using SQL Server Profiler, you can capture the exact chain of events Microsoft uses to perform the same action in order to make sure your scripts cover those same actions.

Summary

In this chapter, we looked at the properties you can configure for Policy-Based Management itself, including whether it is enabled, the amount of history retained, and the type of logging being performed. Next, we covered the architecture of Policy-Based Management and how it differs by evaluation mode. Then we took a look at some security considerations related to Policy-Based Management. Finally, we covered the physical database objects used by Policy-Based Management, including tables, views, and stored procedures. The more knowledge you have about the way Policy-Based Management works internally, the more you can customize it to fit your environment.

CHAPTER 7

■ ■ ■

Practical Uses of Policy-Based Management

Like any feature, Policy-Based Management is useful only if it can help you in solving real-world problems. In this chapter, we'll show you how you can benefit from using specific policies in your SQL Server environment. First, we'll present a sample list of checks commonly performed by DBAs. Then we'll look at custom and predefined policies that will perform those checks for you automatically.

A DBA Checklist

Every DBA has a list of items to check on a daily, weekly, and monthly basis. For example, you may want to ensure the following conditions are true for each of your servers:

- Databases have sufficient free space.
- Transaction logs were backed up.
- SQL Server Agent is running.
- All SQL Server Agent jobs have notification on failure.
- Data purity checking is enabled.
- No databases have autoclose enabled.
- No databases have autoshrink enabled.
- Each database has had a full backup taken in the last 24 hours.
- Backup and data file locations are on different disks.

Of course, some of these checks might be irrelevant to you, depending on your situation. For example, if you're the only DBA, then you can be self-policing on some tasks, such as making sure that you never create a database with autoclose or autoshrink enabled. But even so, automation can work in your favor as a second line of defense. By automating checks that you would not otherwise perform on a consistent basis, you give yourself an additional layer of security.

By using the best practice policies defined by Microsoft and supplementing them with your own custom policies, you can optimize and centralize some (if not all) of your check list requirements. In this way, Policy-Based Management makes your job easier. In the remainder of this chapter, we will look at policies to handle the items on our sample check list.

Custom Policies

Creating custom policies allows you build on the best practice policies that are provided from Microsoft and develop a more comprehensive view of your environment. By tapping into the available facets and their properties, you can create your own conditions and policies to evaluate the SQL Server instances in your system. Here, we'll present several custom policies that we've found helpful. You're free to take them as is, or to modify them to suit your own needs and environment.

■ **NOTE:** All of the policies in this chapter use a custom category called `AutoEvaluate Policy`. You can create the new category by running the following script.

```
Declare @policy_category_id int
EXEC msdb.dbo.sp_syspolicy_add_policy_category
        @name=N'AutoEvaluatePolicy',
        @policy_category_id=@policy_category_id OUTPUT,
      @mandate_database_subscriptions=True
Select @policy_category_id
```

Database Free Space

It is good practice to keep a handle on the size and amount of free space available in your databases and grow them manually; you should use the autogrow setting only as a safeguard. Frequent autogrow operations can lead to slow response times while the file is expanding, as well as heavily fragmented files.

If you want granular control over when your database files grow and by how much, a custom policy will provide the solution. The custom policy we describe in this section checks that the available space in the database is at least 10% of the total size of the database.

Here are the steps for creating a condition that will fail if it encounters a database that has less than 10% space free:

1. Create a new condition by right-clicking the Conditions folder under Policy Management and selecting New Condition from the context menu.

2. Give the condition a name, such as Database Has Less than 10 Pct Free Space.

3. Select Database from the Facet drop-down list.

4. Click the ellipsis next to the Field column to open the Advanced Edit dialog box.

5. Enter the following in the Advanced Edit dialog box, and then click OK.

```
Divide(@SpaceAvailable, Multiply(@Size,1024))
```

6. Select > from the Operator drop-down list.

7. Type 0.1 in the Value column.

8. Your condition should look like the one shown in Figure 7-1. Click OK to save the new condition.

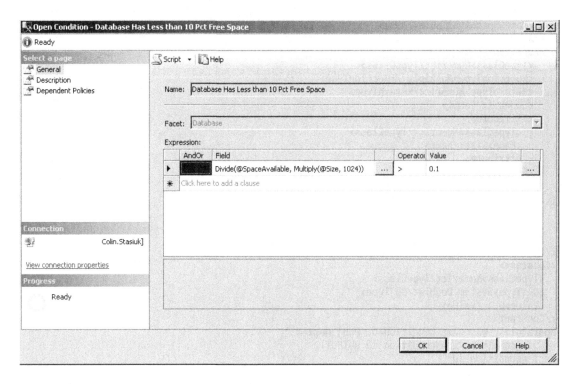

Figure 7-1. *Completed Database Has Less than 10 Pct Free Space condition*

Listing 7-1 shows the script to create the condition, and Listing 7-2 shows the script to create the policy.

Listing 7-1. Script to create the Database Free Space condition

```
Declare @condition_id int
EXEC msdb.dbo.sp_syspolicy_add_condition
        @name=N'Database Has Less than 10 Pct Free Space',
        @description=N'',
        @facet=N'Database',
        @expression=N'<Operator>
  <TypeClass>Bool</TypeClass>
  <OpType>GT</OpType>
  <Count>2</Count>
  <Function>
    <TypeClass>Numeric</TypeClass>
    <FunctionType>Divide</FunctionType>
    <ReturnType>Numeric</ReturnType>
    <Count>2</Count>
    <Attribute>
      <TypeClass>Numeric</TypeClass>
```

```
            <Name>SpaceAvailable</Name>
        </Attribute>
        <Function>
          <TypeClass>Numeric</TypeClass>
          <FunctionType>Multiply</FunctionType>
          <ReturnType>Numeric</ReturnType>
          <Count>2</Count>
          <Attribute>
            <TypeClass>Numeric</TypeClass>
            <Name>Size</Name>
          </Attribute>
          <Constant>
            <TypeClass>Numeric</TypeClass>
            <ObjType>System.Double</ObjType>
            <Value>1024</Value>
          </Constant>
        </Function>
      </Function>
      <Constant>
        <TypeClass>Numeric</TypeClass>
        <ObjType>System.Double</ObjType>
        <Value>0.2</Value>
      </Constant>
</Operator>', @is_name_condition=0, @obj_name=N'',
        @condition_id=@condition_id OUTPUT
Select @condition_id

GO
```

Listing 7-2. Script to create the Database Free Space policy

```
Declare @object_set_id int
EXEC msdb.dbo.sp_syspolicy_add_object_set
        @object_set_name=N'Database Has Less than 10 Pct Free Space_ObjectSet',
        @facet=N'Database',
        @object_set_id=@object_set_id OUTPUT
Select @object_set_id

Declare @target_set_id int
EXEC msdb.dbo.sp_syspolicy_add_target_set
        @object_set_name=N'Database Has Less than 10 Pct Free Space_ObjectSet',
        @type_skeleton=N'Server/Database', @type=N'DATABASE', @enabled=True,
        @target_set_id=@target_set_id OUTPUT
Select @target_set_id

EXEC msdb.dbo.sp_syspolicy_add_target_set_level
        @target_set_id=@target_set_id, @type_skeleton=N'Server/Database',
        @level_name=N'Database', @condition_name=N'', @target_set_level_id=0

GO
```

```
Declare @policy_id int
EXEC msdb.dbo.sp_syspolicy_add_policy
        @name=N'Database Has Less than 10 Pct Free Space',
        @condition_name=N'Database Has Less thean 10 Pct Free Space',
        @policy_category=N'AutoEvaluatePolicy', @description=N'', @help_text=N'',
        @help_link=N'', @schedule_uid=N'00000000-0000-0000-0000-000000000000',
        @execution_mode=0, @is_enabled=False, @policy_id=@policy_id OUTPUT,
        @root_condition_name=N'',
        @object_set=N'Database Has Less than 10 Pct Free Space_ObjectSet'
Select @policy_id


GO
```

Successful Transaction Log Backups

When you have a database in bulk logged or full recovery mode, you want to make sure to maintain and back up your transaction log as part of your normal maintenance. If you do not back up your transaction logs within a reasonable amount of time, the virtual log files (VLFs) that make up your transaction logs cannot be reused, and your transaction log file will continue to grow until you are out of disk space, causing unnecessary downtime. When you are using the simple recovery mode, you cannot perform transaction log backups, since the reuse of the VLFs is handled internally within SQL Server.

The custom policy presented in this section checks that all databases that are not in simple recovery mode have had a successful transaction log backup completed in the last 15 minutes.

Here are the steps to create a condition that looks for databases that have not had a successful transaction log backup within the last 15 minutes.

1. Create a new condition by right-clicking the Conditions folder under Policy Management and selecting New Condition from the context menu.

2. Give the condition a name, such as **Log Backup More than 15 Minutes Old.**

3. Select Database Maintenance from the Facet drop-down list.

4. Click the Field drop-down list and select @LastLogBackupDate.

5. Select > from the Operator drop-down list.

6. Enter the following in the Value column. You can enter the value directly or select the ellipsis to open the Advanced Edit dialog box.

```
DateAdd('minute', -15, GetDate())
```

7. Your condition should look like the one shown in Figure 7-2. Click OK to save the new condition.

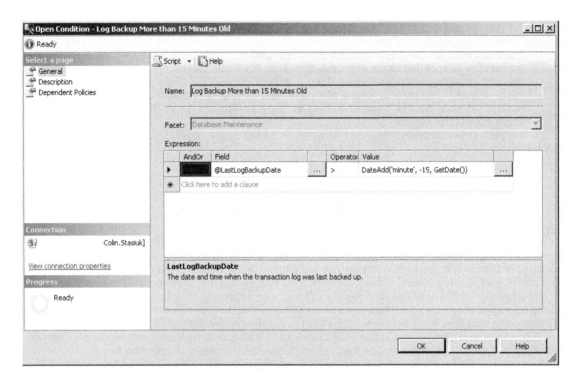

Figure 7-2. Completed Log Backup More than 15 Minutes Old condition

Next, you need to create a policy that limits the execution of the preceding condition to only databases that are not using the simple recovery mode. However, before you create the policy, you will need to create another condition that limits the execution targets for the policy. If you do not limit the execution, any database you have in simple mode will fail the condition, since you cannot back up their transaction logs.

Use the following steps to create the condition to limit the execution targets:

1. Create a new condition by right-clicking the Conditions folder under Policy Management and selecting New Condition from the context menu.

2. Give the condition a name, such as **Databases in Full or Bulk Logged**.

3. Select Database from the Facet drop-down list.

4. Click the Field drop-down list and select @RecoveryModel.

5. Select != from the Operator drop-down list.

6. Select Simple from the drop-down list in the Value column.

7. Your condition should look like the one shown in Figure 7-3. Click OK to save the new condition.

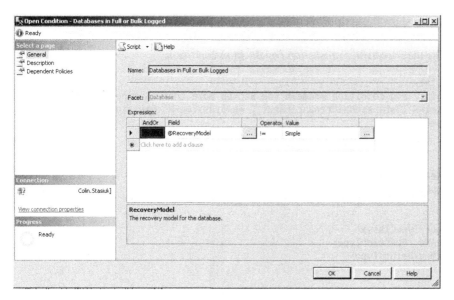

Figure 7-3. Completed Databases in Full or Bulk Logged condition

Now that you have both of the conditions you need, you can create the policy, as shown in Figure 7-4.

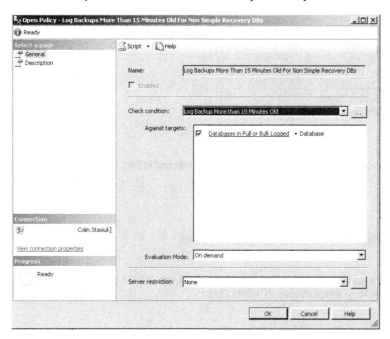

Figure 7-4. Completed Log Backups More than 15 Minutes Old for Non-Simple Recovery DBs policy

Listings 7-3, 7-4, and 7-5 show the scripts to create the conditions and the policy for this example.

Listing 7-3. Script to create the Successful Transaction Log Backups condition

```
Declare @condition_id int
EXEC msdb.dbo.sp_syspolicy_add_condition @name=N'Log Backup more than 15 minutes old',
@description=N'', @facet=N'IDatabaseMaintenanceFacet', @expression=N'<Operator>
  <TypeClass>Bool</TypeClass>
  <OpType>GT</OpType>
  <Count>2</Count>
  <Attribute>
    <TypeClass>DateTime</TypeClass>
    <Name>LastLogBackupDate</Name>
  </Attribute>
  <Function>
    <TypeClass>DateTime</TypeClass>
    <FunctionType>DateAdd</FunctionType>
    <ReturnType>DateTime</ReturnType>
    <Count>3</Count>
    <Constant>
      <TypeClass>String</TypeClass>
      <ObjType>System.String</ObjType>
      <Value>minute</Value>
    </Constant>
    <Constant>
      <TypeClass>Numeric</TypeClass>
      <ObjType>System.Double</ObjType>
      <Value>-15</Value>
    </Constant>
    <Function>
      <TypeClass>DateTime</TypeClass>
      <FunctionType>GetDate</FunctionType>
      <ReturnType>DateTime</ReturnType>
      <Count>0</Count>
    </Function>
  </Function>
</Operator>', @is_name_condition=0, @obj_name=N'', @condition_id=@condition_id OUTPUT
Select @condition_id

GO
```

Listing 7-4. Script to create the Databases in Full or Bulk Logged condition

```
Declare @condition_id int
EXEC msdb.dbo.sp_syspolicy_add_condition @name=N'Databases in Full or Bulk Logged',
@description=N'', @facet=N'Database', @expression=N'<Operator>
  <TypeClass>Bool</TypeClass>
  <OpType>NE</OpType>
  <Count>2</Count>
  <Attribute>
```

```
        <TypeClass>Numeric</TypeClass>
        <Name>RecoveryModel</Name>
    </Attribute>
    <Function>
        <TypeClass>Numeric</TypeClass>
        <FunctionType>Enum</FunctionType>
        <ReturnType>Numeric</ReturnType>
        <Count>2</Count>
        <Constant>
            <TypeClass>String</TypeClass>
            <ObjType>System.String</ObjType>
            <Value>Microsoft.SqlServer.Management.Smo.RecoveryModel</Value>
        </Constant>
        <Constant>
            <TypeClass>String</TypeClass>
            <ObjType>System.String</ObjType>
            <Value>Simple</Value>
        </Constant>
    </Function>
</Operator>', @is_name_condition=0, @obj_name=N'', @condition_id=@condition_id OUTPUT
Select @condition_id

GO
```

Listing 7-5. Script to create the Successful Transaction Log Backup policy

```
Declare @object_set_id int
EXEC msdb.dbo.sp_syspolicy_add_object_set
@object_set_name=N'Log Backups More than 15 minutes old for non Simple Recovery
DBs_ObjectSet', @facet=N'IDatabaseMaintenanceFacet', @object_set_id=@object_set_id OUTPUT
Select @object_set_id

Declare @target_set_id int
EXEC msdb.dbo.sp_syspolicy_add_target_set
@object_set_name=N'Log Backups More than 15 minutes old for non Simple Recovery
DBs_ObjectSet', @type_skeleton=N'Server/Database', @type=N'DATABASE', @enabled=True,
@target_set_id=@target_set_id OUTPUT
Select @target_set_id

EXEC msdb.dbo.sp_syspolicy_add_target_set_level @target_set_id=@target_set_id,
@type_skeleton=N'Server/Database', @level_name=N'Database', @condition_name=N'Databases in
Full or BulkLogged', @target_set_level_id=0

GO

Declare @policy_id int
EXEC msdb.dbo.sp_syspolicy_add_policy
@name=N'Log Backups More than 15 minutes old for non Simple Recovery DBs',
@condition_name=N'Log Backup more than 15 minutes old',
@policy_category=N'AutoEvaluatePolicy', @description=N'',
```

```
@help_text=N'', @help_link=N'',
@schedule_uid=N'00000000-0000-0000-0000-000000000000', @execution_mode=0, @is_enabled=False,
@policy_id=@policy_id OUTPUT,
@root_condition_name=N'',
@object_set=N'Log Backups More than 15 minutes old for non Simple Recovery DBs_ObjectSet'
Select @policy_id


GO
```

SQL Server Agent Is Running

As a DBA, you might have notifications enabled for failed jobs, and you might even have a job that sends you an e-mail message every time the SQL Server Agent is restarted. But what if the SQL Server Agent is stopped? No jobs are failing, because none are executing. And if the SQL Server Agent is stopped and not started again, you will not receive a notification that the Agent has restarted.

The custom policy presented in this section checks that the SQL Server Agent is running. This policy is an interesting one, because if you schedule this policy to execute, the SQL Server Agent must be running. You can use the PowerShell scripts in Chapter 4 to evaluate this policy against a group of instances and find the SQL Server Agent status of those instances.

You can use the following steps to create a condition that checks to make sure that SQL Server Agent is running:

1. Create a new condition by right-clicking the Conditions folder under Policy Management and selecting New Condition from the context menu.

2. Give the condition a name, such as **SQL Server Agent Is Running**.

3. Select Server from the Facet drop-down list.

4. Click the ellipsis next to the Field column to open the Advanced Edit dialog box.

5. Enter the following in the Advanced Edit dialog box, and then click OK.

```
ExecuteSql('numeric', 'SELECT COUNT(*)
                       FROM master.dbo.sysprocesses
                       WHERE program_name = N''SQLAgent - Generic Refresher''')
```

6. Select = from the Operator drop-down list.

7. Type 1 in the Value column.

8. Your condition should look like the one shown in Figure 7-5. Click OK to save the new condition.

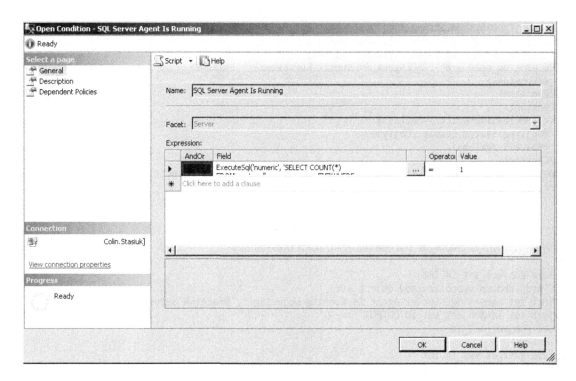

Figure 7-5. Completed SQL Server Agent Is Running condition

Listings 7-6 and 7-7 show the scripts to create the condition and the policy.

Listing 7-6. Script to create the SQL Server Agent Is Running condition

```
Declare @condition_id int
EXEC msdb.dbo.sp_syspolicy_add_condition @name=N'SQL Server Agent Is Running',
@description=N'', @facet=N'Server', @expression=N'<Operator>
  <TypeClass>Bool</TypeClass>
  <OpType>EQ</OpType>
  <Count>2</Count>
  <Function>
    <TypeClass>Numeric</TypeClass>
    <FunctionType>ExecuteSql</FunctionType>
    <ReturnType>Numeric</ReturnType>
    <Count>2</Count>
    <Constant>
      <TypeClass>String</TypeClass>
      <ObjType>System.String</ObjType>
      <Value>numeric</Value>
    </Constant>
    <Constant>
      <TypeClass>String</TypeClass>
```

159

```
      <ObjType>System.String</ObjType>
      <Value>SELECT COUNT(*) &lt;?char 13?&gt;
FROM master.dbo.sysprocesses &lt;?char 13?&gt;
WHERE program_name = N''''SQLAgent - Generic Refresher''''</Value>
    </Constant>
  </Function>
  <Constant>
    <TypeClass>Numeric</TypeClass>
    <ObjType>System.Double</ObjType>
    <Value>1</Value>
  </Constant>
</Operator>', @is_name_condition=0, @obj_name=N'', @condition_id=@condition_id OUTPUT
Select @condition_id

GO
```

Listing 7-7. Script to create the SQL Server Agent Is Running policy

```
Declare @object_set_id int
EXEC msdb.dbo.sp_syspolicy_add_object_set
@object_set_name=N'SQL Server Agent Is Running_ObjectSet', @facet=N'Server',
@object_set_id=@object_set_id OUTPUT
Select @object_set_id

Declare @target_set_id int
EXEC msdb.dbo.sp_syspolicy_add_target_set
@object_set_name=N'SQL Server Agent Is Running_ObjectSet', @type_skeleton=N'Server',
@type=N'SERVER', @enabled=True, @target_set_id=@target_set_id OUTPUT
Select @target_set_id

GO

Declare @policy_id int
EXEC msdb.dbo.sp_syspolicy_add_policy @name=N'SQL Server Agent Is Running',
@condition_name=N'SQL Server Agent Is Running', @policy_category=N'AutoEvaluatePolicy',
@description=N'', @help_text=N'', @help_link=N'',
@schedule_uid=N'00000000-0000-0000-0000-000000000000',
@execution_mode=0, @is_enabled=False, @policy_id=@policy_id OUTPUT,
 @root_condition_name=N'', @object_set=N'SQL Server Agent Is Running_ObjectSet'
Select @policy_id

GO
```

All SQL Server Agent Jobs Have Notification on Failure

If you do not have any job-monitoring tools in place, a job might fail, and you may never know. One way to avoid this is to configure jobs to alert you in the event of a failure. However, sometimes jobs may be created on your server without this failure notification. For example, some third-party applications may add jobs to your server as a part of their installation.

The custom script presented in this section checks that all SQL Server Agent jobs are set to notify you via e-mail if they fail.

Here are the steps to create the condition for this policy:

1. Create a new condition by right-clicking the Conditions folder under Policy Management and selecting New Condition from the context menu.

2. Give the condition a name, such as **SQL Agent Jobs with No Notification on Failure**.

3. Select Server from the Facet drop-down list.

4. Click the ellipsis next to the Field column to open the Advanced Edit dialog box.

5. Enter the following in the Advanced Edit dialog box, and then click OK.

```
ExecuteSql('numeric', 'SELECT COUNT(*)
                       FROM   msdb.dbo.sysjobs
                       WHERE  [enabled]  = 1 AND
                              notify_level_email NOT IN (1,2,3)')
```

6. Select = from the Operator drop-down list.

7. Type **0** in the Value column.

8. Your condition should look like the one shown in Figure 7-6. Click OK to save the new condition.

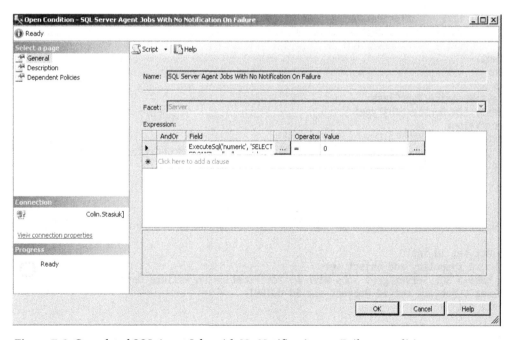

Figure 7-6. Completed SQL Agent Jobs with No Notification on Failure condition

Listings 7-8 and 7-9 show the scripts to create the condition and the policy for this check.

Listing 7-8. Script to create the All SQL Server Agent Jobs Have Notification on Failure condition

```
Declare @condition_id int
EXEC msdb.dbo.sp_syspolicy_add_condition
@name=N'SQL Server Agent Jobs With No Notification On Failure',
@description=N'', @facet=N'Server', @expression=N'<Operator>
  <TypeClass>Bool</TypeClass>
  <OpType>EQ</OpType>
  <Count>2</Count>
  <Function>
    <TypeClass>Numeric</TypeClass>
    <FunctionType>ExecuteSql</FunctionType>
    <ReturnType>Numeric</ReturnType>
    <Count>2</Count>
    <Constant>
      <TypeClass>String</TypeClass>
      <ObjType>System.String</ObjType>
      <Value>numeric</Value>
    </Constant>
    <Constant>
      <TypeClass>String</TypeClass>
      <ObjType>System.String</ObjType>
      <Value>SELECT     COUNT(*) &lt;?char 13?&gt;
FROM    msdb.dbo.sysjobs&lt;?char 13?&gt;
WHERE    name NOT LIKE ''''%TestDatabaseMail%'''' AND&lt;?char 13?&gt;
                [enabled]   = 1 AND&lt;?char 13?&gt;
                notify_level_email NOT IN (1,2,3)</Value>
    </Constant>
  </Function>
  <Constant>
    <TypeClass>Numeric</TypeClass>
    <ObjType>System.Double</ObjType>
    <Value>0</Value>
  </Constant>
</Operator>', @is_name_condition=0, @obj_name=N'', @condition_id=@condition_id OUTPUT
Select @condition_id

GO
```

Listing 7-9. Script to create the All SQL Server Agent Jobs Have Notification on Failure policy

```
Declare @object_set_id int
EXEC msdb.dbo.sp_syspolicy_add_object_set
@object_set_name=N'SQL ServerAgent Jobs With No Notification On Failure_ObjectSet',
@facet=N'Server', @object_set_id=@object_set_id OUTPUT
Select @object_set_id

Declare @target_set_id int
```

```
EXEC msdb.dbo.sp_syspolicy_add_target_set
@object_set_name=N'SQL ServerAgent Jobs With No Notification On Failure_ObjectSet',
@type_skeleton=N'Server', @type=N'SERVER', @enabled=True, @target_set_id=@target_set_id OUTPUT
Select @target_set_id

GO

Declare @policy_id int
EXEC msdb.dbo.sp_syspolicy_add_policy
@name=N'SQL Server Agent Jobs With No Notification On Failure',
@condition_name=N'SQL Server Agent Jobs With No Notification On Failure',
@policy_category=N'AutoEvaluatePolicy', @description=N'', @help_text=N'',
@help_link=N'', @schedule_uid=N'00000000-0000-0000-0000-000000000000',
@execution_mode=0, @is_enabled=False, @policy_id=@policy_id OUTPUT,
@root_condition_name=N'',
@object_set=N'SQL ServerAgent Jobs With No Notification On Failure_ObjectSet'
Select @policy_id

GO
```

Data Purity Flag Enabled

The **DBCC CHECKDB** command checks the integrity of the objects in a database and should be run on a regular basis. However, in databases created in versions prior to SQL Server 2005, this command does not check the integrity of the data in the columns. Adding the **DATA_PURITY** option causes the **CHECKDB** command to look for column values that are invalid or out of range. Any database that was created in SQL Server 2005 or later will include the **DATA_PURITY** check by default. However, if the database is being upgraded from an earlier version, you must run the command with the **DATA_PURITY** option at least once and fix any issues. Once the command has executed successfully and the issues have been resolved, an entry is made in the database header, and the **DATA_PURITY** option will be included by default as a part of the normal **CHECKDB** operation.

The custom policy presented in this section checks for databases that do not have the **DATA_PURITY** flag set in the database header.

Here are the steps to create a condition for this policy:

1. Create a new condition by right-clicking the Conditions folder under Policy Management and selecting New Condition from the context menu.

2. Give the condition a name, such as **Data Purity Flag Check**.

3. Select Database from the Facet drop-down list.

4. Click the ellipsis next to the Field column to open the Advanced Edit dialog box.

5. Enter the following in the Advanced Edit dialog box, and then click OK.

```
ExecuteSql('numeric', 'DBCC TRACEON (3604);

CREATE TABLE #DBCC (
ParentObject VARCHAR(255)
```

```
, [Object] VARCHAR(255)
, Field VARCHAR(255)
, [Value] VARCHAR(255)
)

INSERT INTO #DBCC EXECUTE (''DBCC DBINFO WITH TABLERESULTS'');
SELECT Value FROM #DBCC
WHERE Field = ''dbi_DBCCFlags''

DROP TABLE #DBCC')
```

6. Select != from the Operator drop-down list.

7. Type **0** in the Value column.

8. Your condition should look like the one shown in Figure 7-7. Click OK to save the new condition.

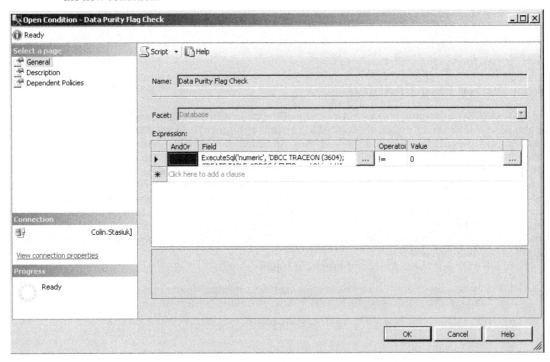

Figure 7-7. Completed Data Purity Flag Enabled condition

You can now create and evaluate a new policy that uses the preceding condition. Once you have identified the databases that do not have the **DATA_PURITY** flag enabled, you can correct them by running the following command:

```
DBCC CHECKDB ([DatabaseName]) WITH DATA_PURITY
```

Listings 7-10 and 7-11 show the scripts to create the condition and the policy for this example.

Listing 7-10. Script to create the Data Purity Flag Enabled condition

```
Declare @condition_id int
EXEC msdb.dbo.sp_syspolicy_add_condition @name=N'Data Purity Flag Check', @description=N'',
@facet=N'Database', @expression=N'<Operator>
  <TypeClass>Bool</TypeClass>
  <OpType>NE</OpType>
  <Count>2</Count>
  <Function>
    <TypeClass>Numeric</TypeClass>
    <FunctionType>ExecuteSql</FunctionType>
    <ReturnType>Numeric</ReturnType>
    <Count>2</Count>
    <Constant>
      <TypeClass>String</TypeClass>
      <ObjType>System.String</ObjType>
      <Value>numeric</Value>
    </Constant>
    <Constant>
      <TypeClass>String</TypeClass>
      <ObjType>System.String</ObjType>
      <Value>DBCC TRACEON (3604);&lt;?char 13?&gt;
CREATE TABLE #DBCC ( &lt;?char 13?&gt;
ParentObject VARCHAR(255)&lt;?char 13?&gt;
, [Object] VARCHAR(255)&lt;?char 13?&gt;
, Field VARCHAR(255)&lt;?char 13?&gt;
, [Value] VARCHAR(255) &lt;?char 13?&gt;
) &lt;?char 13?&gt;
&lt;?char 13?&gt;
INSERT INTO #DBCC EXECUTE ('''DBCC DBINFO WITH TABLERESULTS''');&lt;?char 13?&gt;
&lt;?char 13?&gt;
SELECT Value FROM #DBCC&lt;?char 13?&gt;
WHERE Field = '''dbi_DBCCFlags'''&lt;?char 13?&gt;
&lt;?char 13?&gt;
DROP TABLE #DBCC</Value>
    </Constant>
  </Function>
  <Constant>
    <TypeClass>Numeric</TypeClass>
    <ObjType>System.Double</ObjType>
    <Value>0</Value>
  </Constant>
</Operator>', @is_name_condition=0, @obj_name=N'', @condition_id=@condition_id OUTPUT
Select @condition_id

GO
```

Listing 7-11. Script to create the Data Purity Flag Enabled policy

```
Declare @object_set_id int
EXEC msdb.dbo.sp_syspolicy_add_object_set
@object_set_name=N'Data Purity Flag Check_ObjectSet', @facet=N'Database',
@object_set_id=@object_set_id OUTPUT
Select @object_set_id

Declare @target_set_id int
EXEC msdb.dbo.sp_syspolicy_add_target_set
@object_set_name=N'Data Purity Flag Check_ObjectSet',
@type_skeleton=N'Server/Database', @type=N'DATABASE', @enabled=True,
@target_set_id=@target_set_id OUTPUT
Select @target_set_id

EXEC msdb.dbo.sp_syspolicy_add_target_set_level
@target_set_id=@target_set_id, @type_skeleton=N'Server/Database',
@level_name=N'Database', @condition_name=N'', @target_set_level_id=0


GO

Declare @policy_id int
EXEC msdb.dbo.sp_syspolicy_add_policy @name=N'Data Purity Flag Check',
@condition_name=N'Data Purity Flag Check', @policy_category=N'', @description=N'',
 @help_text=N'', @help_link=N'', @schedule_uid=N'00000000-0000-0000-0000-000000000000',
  @execution_mode=0, @is_enabled=False, @policy_id=@policy_id OUTPUT,
  @root_condition_name=N'', @object_set=N'Data Purity Flag Check_ObjectSet'
Select @policy_id


GO
```

Best Practices Policies

Four items remain from our sample checklist presented at the beginning of this chapter:

- No databases have autoclose enabled.

- No databases have autoshrink enabled.

- Each database has had a full backup taken in the last 24 hours.

- Backup and data file locations are on different disks.

■ **Note**: See Chapter 2 for details on importing the best practice policies that ship with SQL Server 2008. By default, these policies are located in C:\Program Files\Microsoft SQL Server\100\Tools\Policies\DatabaseEngine\1033.

These items can be addressed by using Microsoft's predefined best practice policies. The following best practice policies apply to these checks:

Database Auto Close: This policy checks that autoclose is not enabled on any databases. Having a database with autoclose enabled can cause significant performance issues due to the resources consumed by opening and closing the database after each connection.

Database Auto Shrink: This policy checks that autoshrink is not enabled on any databases. Having a database with autoshrink enabled can cause significant performance issues due to the physical fragmentation that is the result of the autoshrink process.

Last Successful Backup Date: This policy checks whether all the databases have had a successful full backup within the time frame defined by the Safe Last Backup Date condition (the default value is within the last 24 hours).

Backup and Data File Location: This policy checks to make sure that the backup files are not located on the same device as the data files. This is a best practice to reduce I/O contention during backups and increase availability in the event of a drive failure. This policy will go through the `msdb.dbo.backupset` and `msdb.dbo.backupmediafamily` tables, and if there is a backup row in these tables from when the backup file is on the same device as the data file, this policy will fail.

Some of these policies might work for you and your environment as is, while others might need to be copied and tweaked for your specific situation or environment. In order to see the expressions used against the facets for the conditions, you will need to view the properties of the condition through SQL Server Management Studio. For example, to see the condition for the Database Auto Shrink policy, right-click the condition called Auto Shrink Disabled and select Properties, as shown in Figure 7-8.

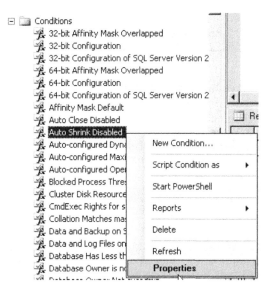

Figure 7-8. *Choosing to view the properties of a condition*

In the Open Condition dialog box, shown in Figure 7-9, you can see that the Database Performance facet is used for this condition, and the field @AutoShrink is set to False. When this condition is evaluated using the Database Auto Shrink policy, if a database has the AutoShrink property set to true, the policy will fail. From the Open Condition dialog box, you can make changes or tweak the condition to meet the needs of your environment.

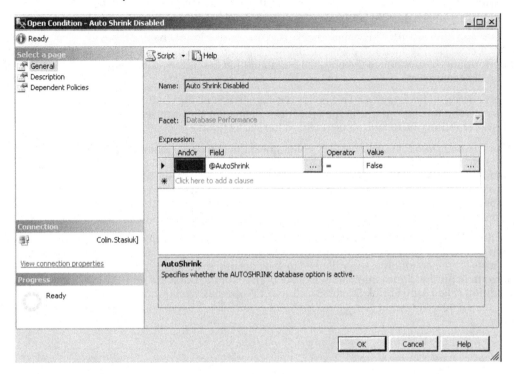

Figure 7-9. The condition for the Database Auto Shrink policy

In addition to the policies we have discussed in this chapter, you may want to review other best practice polices to see if they pertain to your environment. You can query the `syspolicy_policies_internal` table in the `msdb` database to see descriptions of all of the policies, as well as access help links to provide you with even more information about why you may or may not want to implement each policy.

Summary

In this chapter, we've shown you some realistic applications for Policy-Based Management, using both custom and predefined policies. As with any feature, it is important to understand how the Microsoft-provided policies are built, to avoid any false positives (or negatives). We suggest that you start small with a couple policies that you understand and build your Policy-Based Management implementation from there.

CHAPTER 8

■ ■ ■

Reporting

In Chapter 6, we explored some of the internal structures of Policy-Based Management, and you even learned how to query those pieces to extract useful information about policies and their executions. While this chapter focuses on the Enterprise Policy Management (EPM) Framework, having the knowledge of those internal structures allows you to create your own custom reports to meet your needs.

The EPM Framework is a free reporting solution developed by Lara Rubbelke, Dmitri Tchikatilov, and Tom Davidson. The EPM Framework helps extend Policy-Based Management to all versions of SQL Server in an enterprise (SQL Server 2000 and higher). The EPM Framework accomplishes this by utilizing PowerShell to evaluate your policies against your target servers. The EPM Framework reports the state of the specified targets against the policies, collects that information in a centralized management data warehouse, and displays your aggregated results through a series of Reporting Services reports. The EPM Framework is available as a free download from CodePlex (`http://epmframework.codeplex.com/`).

EPM Framework Prerequisites

In order to run the EPM Framework in your environment, you must have an instance of SQL Server 2008. To evaluate policies against previous versions of SQL Server, your SQL Server 2008 instance must be Service Pack 1 Cumulative Update 3 or higher.

Your SQL Server 2008 instance will be used as the Central Management Server, and it will execute PowerShell scripts. You can also use your SQL Server 2008 instance to store a management database and policy history table to archive policy evaluation results.

In addition to having an instance of SQL Server 2008, you will also need to make sure you have SQL Server 2008 Reporting Services configured in native mode in order to view the reports.

■ **Note:** Configuring the EPM Framework can be complicated, especially if you do not already have all the prerequisites installed on your server. You can refer to the documentation for the EPM Framework project (version 3.0 at time of this writing) at `http://epmframework.codeplex.com/releases/view/28621` for additional information. If you need more information about setting up SQL Server 2008 Reporting Services, you can pick up a copy of *Pro SQL Server 2008 Reporting Services* by Rodney Landrum, Shawn McGehee, and Walter J. Voytek II (Apress, 2008).

Setting Up the EPM Framework

Once all the major pieces (Reporting Services and your Central Management Server) are in place, and you've downloaded the project source files, there are three major EPM Framework components to set up and configure:

> *Setup script:* This is a T-SQL script that creates the necessary SQL objects such as tables, indexes, functions, views, and stored procedures used by the EPM Framework.

> *PowerShell script:* This script is the meat of the project, in that it is the means by which you evaluate policies against your enterprise. The script also contains the code that updates your Management Data Warehouse (MDW) database with policy evaluation history. This history is used by the EPM Framework to reflect policy evaluation trending reports.

> *Reporting Services reports:* The EPM Framework comes bundled with a Visual Studio solution file that contains five reports and a shared data source file.

We'll review each of these components in the following sections.

The Setup Script

The setup script creates the database objects necessary for the EPM Framework. You must run this script in SQLCMD Mode. To do this, in SQL Server Management Studio, select Query from the menu bar, and then select SQLCMD Mode.

Once SQLCMD mode is active, you will notice that the items prefaced with a colon in the script become highlighted in gray. This highlighting is helpful because it points out the two variables you will need to change in this script: **ServerName** and **ManagementDatabase**, as shown in Figure 8-1. The server name you supply here is the name of the server you have configured in your environment to be the Central Management Server. The management database is the name of the database that the EPM Framework will use to house historical information on your policy evaluations. If you specify a database that does not exist yet, the script will create it for you.

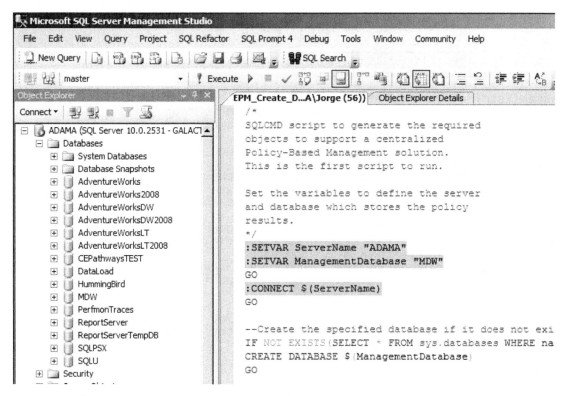

Figure 8-1. *The setup script in SQLCMD mode. Specify your Central Management Server and your Management Data Warehouse database in the script.*

▪ **Note:** The amount of information contained in the management database will vary depending on the amount of information you collect, as well as on the amount of history you keep. You need to make sure to size the disk space to meet your collection needs if you are creating the database ahead of time. Note that policy evaluation history is different from the history kept in `msdb`, as described in Chapter 6.

The PowerShell Script

The next step is to modify the PowerShell script. To do so, right-click the script file (EPM_EnterpriseEvaluation_3.0.0.ps1), and select Edit to open the file in Notepad, as shown in Figure 8-2. (You may use any text editor to edit the file.) Notice the highlighted values in the figure. These are the ones you should change to suit your environment.

```
# Evaluate specific Policies against a Server List
# Uses the Invoke-PolicyEvaluation Cmdlet

param([string]$ConfigurationGroup=$(Throw `
"Paramater missing: -ConfigurationGroup ConfigGroup"), `
[string]$PolicyCategoryFilter=$(Throw "Parameter missing: `
-PolicyCategoryFilter Category"), `
[string]$EvalMode=$(Throw "Parameter missing: -EvalMode EvalMode"))

# Parameter -ConfigurationGroup specifies the
# Central Management Server group to evaluate
# Parameter -PolicyCategoryFilter specifies the
# category of policies to evaluate
# Parameter -EvalMode accepts "Check" to report policy
# results, "Configure" to reconfigure any violations

# Declare variables to define the central warehouse
# in which to write the output, store the policies
$CentralManagementServer = "ADAMA"
$HistoryDatabase = "MDW"
# Define the location to write the results of the
# policy evaluation.  Delete any files in the directory.
$ResultDir = "e:\Results\"
$ResultDirDel = $ResultDir + "*.xml"
Remove-Item -Path $ResultDirDel
# End of variables
```

Figure 8-2. There are three variables you should change in the PowerShell script.

The variables to change specify the Central Management Server (**$CentralManagementServer**), the history database (**$HistoryDatabase**), and the results directory (**$ResultDir**). The results directory is where the results of the policy evaluations will be held in XML format. The XML files are the finished result scripts, and they contain the results of all of the policies evaluated against the target servers.

The **ConfigurationGroup** is the first of three parameters you must pass to the script. This parameter supplies the list of servers you will be evaluating polices against. The script then iterates through the server groups from the Central Management Server that you specify in the parameter. For example, if you have server groups under your Central Management Server called Production, Test, and Development, and you wish to evaluate your policies only against the Production group, you should specify **-ConfigurationGroup "Production"** during script execution. If you wish to evaluate your policies against all of the groups at once, use **-ConfigurationGroup ""** (double quotes with no space between them) to specify execution against all groups.

Be aware that when you specify a group, the script will also automatically iterate through any subgroups. For example, if under your Production group you have additional groupings called 2000, 2005, and 2008 (see Figure 8-3), the policies will evaluate against any servers registered under those groups when you specify **"Production"** as the target group.

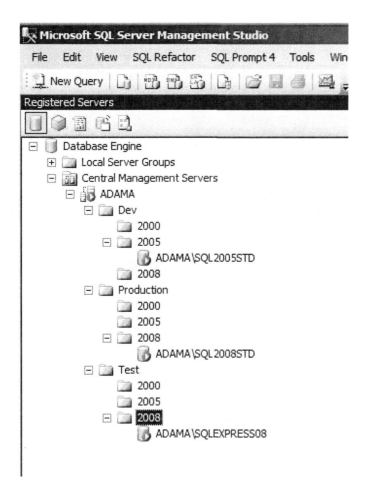

Figure 8-3. Example of server groupings and subgroupings on a Central Management Server

The next parameter, `PolicyCategoryFilter`, specifies which particular policies you wish to evaluate against your servers based on their categories. In Chapter 2, you learned how to categorize your policies. Here, you can take advantage of these logical groupings for policy evaluations. For example, suppose that you want to evaluate only the policies that pertain to maintenance that you've imported from Microsoft's collection of best practice policies. You would pass the parameter **–PolicyCategoryFilter** **"Microsoft Best Practices: Maintenance"**. You may also choose to evaluate all policies, from all categories, by passing the blank parameter of **–PolicyCategoryFilter ""**.

Be aware that the **–PolicyCategoryFilter** parameter is case-sensitive with respect to category names. The best way to make sure you specify each category name correctly is to open the Manage Policy Categories dialog box in SQL Server Management Studio (right-click the Policy Management node and select Manage Categories), highlight the category name, right-click it, and select Copy, as shown in Figure 8-4. This ensures you get the correct spelling and punctuation.

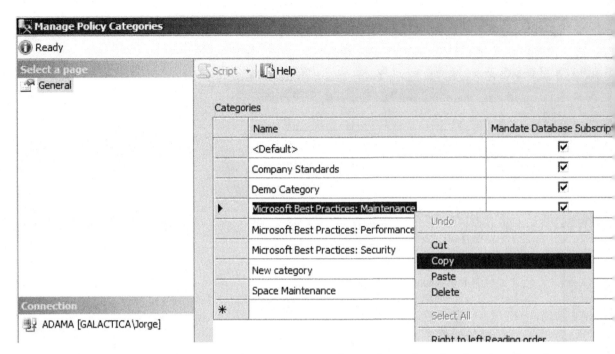

Figure 8-4. *Make sure you get the correct policy category name by copying and pasting the name from the Manage Policy Categories dialog box*

The final parameter passed, `EvalMode`, specifies the action the script will take when evaluating policies. This parameter accepts one of two values:

- Passing **"Configure"** tells the script that if a policy is violated, automatically reconfigure the option in question in order to bring the policy into compliance. If a policy cannot be automatically reconfigured, the script recognizes this and moves on, and does not attempt to reconfigure that particular option or setting.

- Your other option is to specify **"Check"**. This value tells the script to simply report the policy results and take no action.

The following example shows an invocation of the script, which is located in a folder called EPMF on the E: drive. We execute the script against the configuration group **"Production"** and evaluate all policies from all categories.

```
PS SQLSERVER:\SQL\ADAMA\DEFAULT> SL E:\EPMF
PS E:\EPMF> .\EPM_EnterpriseEvaluation_3.0.0.ps1 -ConfigurationGroup "Production" -
PolicyCategoryFilter "" -EvalMode "Check"
```

If you are going to run this script manually, you need to make sure you have the proper SQL Server providers loaded for PowerShell. If you launch PowerShell via SQL Server Management Studio (by right-clicking the instance and selecting Start PowerShell), these providers are automatically loaded for you. If you manually start a PowerShell instance outside SQL Server Management Studio and do not have the providers automatically loaded in your default profile, you can load them manually. See the MSDN article "Running SQL Server PowerShell" (`http://msdn.microsoft.com/en-us/library/cc281962.aspx`) for details.

Another potential issue to be aware of relates to automating the running of this script via the SQL Server Agent. When you launch a job step that uses PowerShell, it starts an individual instance of the **sqlps** process, which takes up approximately 20MB of memory. If you run large numbers of concurrent PowerShell job steps, you could adversely affect performance on that server. This warning is also covered in the MSDN "Running SQL Server PowerShell" article.

Reporting Services Reports

The EPM Framework comes with a prepackaged solution for the Microsoft Business Intelligence Developer Studio (BIDS). BIDS is an optional component you can install with SQL Server. You will need it in order to deploy the EPM Framework. The solution file is called PolicyReports.sln, and it is located in the Reporting folder from the EPMF zip file. Double-click the solution file to launch BIDS.

Once BIDS is open, you will see the Solution Explorer panel on the right side of your window. (If it does not appear, open the View menu and select Solution Explorer.) In the Solution Explorer panel, you will see all of the components of the solution. These include a shared data source (PolicyDW.rds), as well as all five of the reports available as part of the EPM Framework project.

The first piece you need to configure is the location of your report server. To do this, right-click the solution named PolicyReports and select the Properties option. This opens the PolicyReports Property Pages dialog box, as shown in Figure 8-5. Modify the value for the TargetServerURL property to point to the server you have configured for Reporting Services, and then click OK.

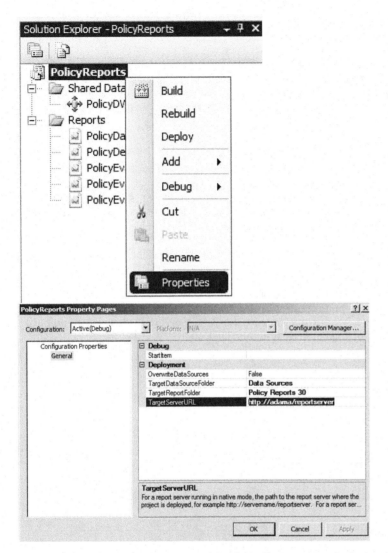

Figure 8-5. *Open the properties panel for the PolicyReports solution and change the TargetServerURL setting for your Reporting Services server.*

The next step is to modify the shared data source for these reports. The shared data source tells the reports where to locate the database that contains all of the historical data for the policy evaluations. This database is the same database you specified in the setup and PowerShell scripts described earlier. Right-click the PolicyDW.rds file and select Open. This opens the Shared Data Source Properties dialog box, as shown in Figure 8-6.

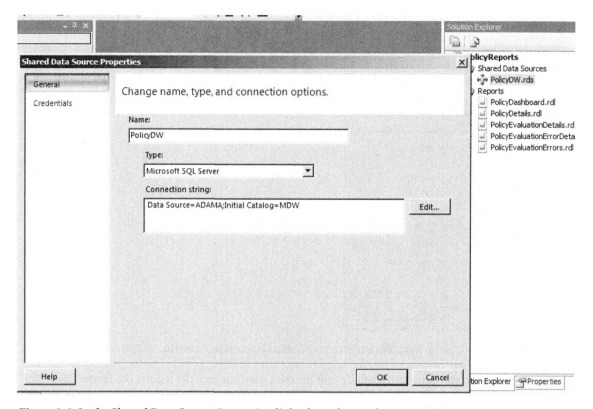

Figure 8-6. In the Shared Data Source Properties dialog box, change the connection string

Change your connection string to point to the correct SQL Server instance and database. You can either manually change the connection string or use the connection string editor to change it. Click the Edit button to open the connection string editor, as shown in Figure 8-7. From the editor, you can modify the server name, select the authentication method for the connection, select the database, and test the connection.

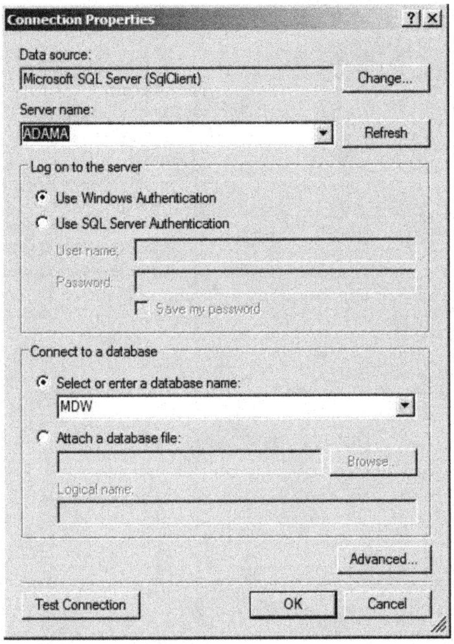

Figure 8-7, You can change your connection string in the Connection Properties dialog box.

Another option you may want to modify for the data source is how the reports use credentials. Click the Credentials option in the Shared Data Source Properties dialog box to display the dialog box shown in Figure 8-8. One option is Windows Authentication (integrated security), which is the default method. You may also wish to use a specified Active Directory user to run reports, prompt the reporting user for specific credentials, or choose to not use credentials at all.

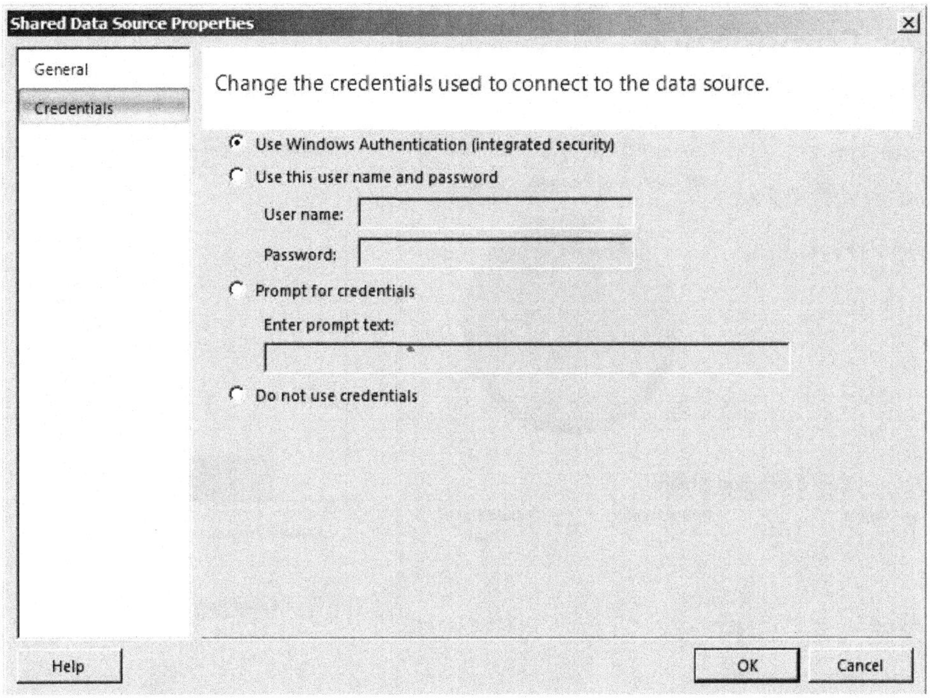

Figure 8-8. The Credentials option in the Shared Data Sources Properties dialog box

Now you are ready to deploy the project to your Reporting Services server. Right-click the project name (PolicyReports) and select Deploy from menu.

Viewing EPM Framework Reports

After you've deployed your PolicyReports project to your Reporting Services server, you can view your reports. Open your web browser and browse to **http://*yourservername*/reports**. When the Reporting Services home page appears, you will find a new folder located there called Policy Reports 30. Open that folder, and you will see the five reports you just deployed through BIDS. Click the report link for PolicyDashboard to open the Dashboard view for EPM Framework. You should see the Dashboard report shown in Figure 8-9.

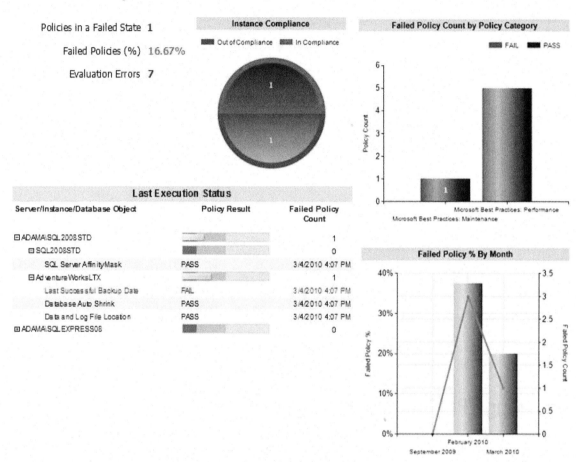

SQL Server Compliance
Current Enterprise State

Policies in a Failed State 1

Failed Policies (%) 16.67%

Evaluation Errors 7

Instance Compliance

■ Out of Compliance ■ In Compliance

Failed Policy Count by Policy Category

■ FAIL ■ PASS

Last Execution Status

Server/Instance/Database Object	Policy Result	Failed Policy Count	
⊟ ADAMA\SQL2008STD		1	
⊟ SQL2008STD		0	
SQL Server AffinityMask	PASS	3/4/2010 4:07 PM	
⊟ AdventureWorksLTX		1	
Last Successful Backup Date	FAIL	3/4/2010 4:07 PM	
Database Auto Shrink	PASS	3/4/2010 4:07 PM	
Data and Log File Location	PASS	3/4/2010 4:07 PM	
⊟ ADAMA\SQLEXPRESS08		0	

Failed Policy % By Month

Figure 8-9, *A view of the EPM Framework Dashboard report*

At a glance, you can see quite a bit of information about your policy evaluations. By default, the report uses the latest month of results, but you can modify the time frame using the drop-down menu. The report also shows the results for all server groups and all categories by default. You can modify these options through their respective drop-down menus.

The first portion of the report gives you the overall number of policies that are either in or out of compliance. It also displays this failure rate in percentage format. One of the great things about this Dashboard is that you are able to drill-through the reports for more details. For instance, if you click the number for Evaluation Errors, you are taken to a detailed report of any errors that were generated during the policy evaluations within the time period specified on the main Dashboard report.

The next portion of the report is the Failed Policy Count by Policy Category. Again, you see the number of policies that have either passed or failed. The graph breaks down those numbers based on the categorization of the policies. You can also drill-through by clicking a column, which takes you to the policy detail report for the category in question.

Beneath the Instance Compliance portion of the report is the Last Execution Status report, as shown in the example in Figure 8-10. This report lets you see all of the different servers that have policy evaluation history. You can expand each server selection by clicking the plus sign next to the server name. This shows the various databases within each server. Expanding the selection again lets you see the various policy evaluations and their results in detail. In addition to the aggregated numbers for failed policies, the report provides graphical data bars that show you, at a glance, the health state of your failed policies. The more failed policies you have within a server, the more color you will see within the bars. In addition, you can click any individual policy within a server to go to a detail page for that particular policy's execution.

Last Execution Status

Server/Instance/Database Object	Policy Result	Failed Policy Count
⊟ ADAMA\SQL2005STD		1
⊟ Test		1
Last Backup Date (legacy)	FAIL	3/8/2010 10:13 PM
⊞ ADAMA\SQL2008STD		2
⊟ ADAMA\SQLEXPRESS08		0
⊟ No Targets Found		0
Last Backup Date (legacy)	PASS	3/8/2010 10:13 PM
Data and Log File Location	PASS	3/4/2010 4:07 PM
Database Auto Shrink	PASS	9/15/2009 7:59 PM

Figure 8-10. The Last Execution Status portion of the EPM Framework Dashboard view. Here, you can see the various levels the graph bar shows in relation to failed policies.

The last piece of the Dashboard view is the Failed Policy Percentage (%) by Month display. This is another view of your overall policy evaluation health, grouped by month. Each column represents the policies evaluated that month. The height of the column represents the overall number of failures within that month, as well as that number represented by the overall percentage of policy evaluation results. A trend line overlaying the column lets you see how your policy evaluation health is either improving or declining by month. By clicking a column, you can drill-through to a detailed report of all the policies that month and their results. Within this report, you are also able to click any policy to drill-through to that policy's detail report.

Automating the EPM Framework

The EPM Framework comes with a PowerShell script that you must execute in order to evaluate policies against your target servers registered in your Central Management Server. You can see an example job used to execute the PowerShell script in Figure 8-11. By utilizing PowerShell in conjunction with the SQL Server Agent's ability to schedule scripted jobs, you can invoke the EPM Framework on a custom schedule and generate results to use in reporting trends. These reports can be used by yourself, your team, or your management to keep an eye on the health state of your SQL Server environment, to give you instant feedback on what needs attention and where.

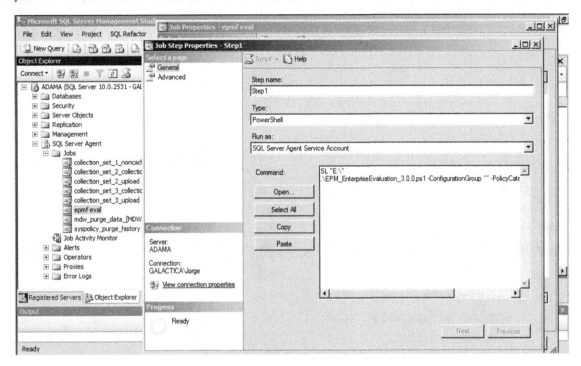

Figure 8-11. Creating a SQL Agent job to automate your PowerShell script execution for the EPM Framework

To create a new job, right-click the Jobs folder under the SQL Server Agent in SQL Server Management Studio and select New Job. Give the job a meaningful name. Next, click Steps in the left pane, and then click New to create a new job. In the New Job Step dialog box, click the Type drop-down and select PowerShell from the list. In the Run As drop-down list, you will see the SQL Server Agent Service Account option. This is a very important option to be aware of, because if the SQL Server Agent is not running as a domain account that has elevated rights on all of the target instances, your policy evaluations will not run correctly.

■ **Tip:** In order to avoid problems with the SQL Server Agent service account permissions, you can configure the job to run using a SQL Server Agent proxy. Allen White wrote a great article on how to accomplish this on his blog (`http://sqlblog.com/blogs/allen_white/archive/2008/05/06/use-a-sql-agent-proxy-for-special-tasks.aspx`).

Next, you need to supply the actual PowerShell script to run. In the command window, supply the following script invocation, replacing the sample parameter values as needed:

```
SL "C:\scripts"
.\EPM_EnterpriseEvaluation_3.0.0.ps1 -ConfigurationGroup
"Production" -PolicyCategoryFilter "" -EvalMode "Check"
```

The first key parameter to change is after `SL`. The `SL` command specifies the location of the folder in which the PowerShell script is located.

The next line, beginning with `.\EPM`, executes the PowerShell script. We pass the three PowerShell script parameters described earlier in the chapter, which specify the configuration group, category filter, and evaluation mode. The script executes against the Production server group and subgroups, evaluating all of the policies from any category. The script is running in Check mode, which means it will only report on policy evaluations and not attempt to make any changes.

Click OK to save the job step. Then click Schedules in the left pane and create a new schedule or pick from an existing schedule. Once you're finished setting up a schedule, click OK to save the job.

Summary

Using the EPM Framework, you can leverage the power of the Policy-Based Management feature set across your enterprise and get a clear overview of how your company is meeting (or not meeting) expected policy goals. You can execute policies on a scheduled basis and store results in a central database. You can draw on those results to generate reports showing historical trends and current status. The EPM Framework is almost a "must-have" if you're extending Policy-Based Management across a wide network of databases.

■ ■ ■

## CHAPTER 9

Enforcing Compliance

As the demand for data keeps growing, and security and compliance keep tightening, the role of the DBA has become an increasingly critical part of the organization. It is becoming more important for DBAs to have a good understanding of compliance, because they are the ones responsible for securing the data. Also, as compliance regulations continue to become more mainstream, the chances of working for a company that does not need to comply with these regulations is becoming more and more of a rarity.

SQL Server has made several enhancements to its feature set over the years to keep up with these growing compliance needs. As a part of these enhancements, in SQL Server 2008, you can use Policy-Based Management to ensure you have the proper server configuration and security settings in place, along with the appropriate encryption and auditing options for your environment.

While this chapter can help you maintain a secure environment, many auditors require specific configurations that will not be covered here. It is a good idea to document your existing procedures, processes, and policies. Then, when auditors show up, they can audit you based on your own documentation. Otherwise, the auditors are forced to get a best practices document from somewhere else, and you never know what you will end up having to conform to.

Compliance Overview

Before we dig into specific examples of how to enforce compliance, let's discuss why it is important and how it affects your organization. First, let's define *compliance*. According to mirriam-webster.com, compliance is "conformity in fulfilling official requirements." Other definitions of the term include words and phrases such as "obedience" and "yield readily to others." It's no surprise that compliance generally has a negative connotation associated with it. We don't know very many people who look forward to getting audited—whether it's for taxes or SQL Server systems.

Compliance is the last component of the increasingly popular term GRC, which stands for governance, risk management, and compliance. GRC is about identifying and assessing risks, developing policies to mitigate those risks, and ensuring that those policies are in place and enforced. If any of the components of GRC are not in place, each individual component is useless.

For example, let's say your company deals with a lot of financial information. Financial documents may be lying around the office. Your management has deemed it a risk to have office visitors such as vendors wandering around the building unattended. Therefore, management has put in place a policy that requires all office visitors to sign in, wear name tags, and always be attended by an employee. Up to this point, you have assessed a risk and implemented a policy. However, without the proper governance to audit the compliance with that policy, there is nothing to stop employees from letting visitors do as they please. The same theory holds true for your servers. While you can't always prevent users such as system administrators from accessing certain information, you can put controls in place to audit their activity and use Policy-Based Management to make sure those audits are being enforced.

Being the custodian of sensitive information, such as credit card numbers or personally identifiable information (PII), is not a task that can be taken lightly. Criminals would love to get their hands on that data, and in some cases, they do. According to the Privacy Rights Clearinghouse (`http://www.privacyrights.org/ar/ChronDataBreaches.htm`), there have been more than 300 million (and counting) records containing sensitive personal information involved in security breaches in the United States since January 2005. These breaches are due to hacking, stolen computers, dishonest employees, and so on.

A data breach not only has negative implications for the person whose data was compromised, but can also be devastating for the organization hosting that data. The bottom line is that policies and procedures need to be in place to protect you, the company you work for, and the sensitive information.

Compliance Regulations

In addition to having your own internal compliance standards, corporations are now expected to meet external regulations when dealing with certain kinds of data. The following are just a few of the regulations governing various types of organizations:

- Gramm-Leach-Bliley Act

- Sarbanes-Oxley Act

- Health Insurance Portability and Accountability Act

- Payment Card Industry Data Security Standard

The preceding list is by no means comprehensive. However, if you manage a database, chances are at least one or more of these regulations affect you. You may notice that many of the requirements of these regulations overlap, and a single database may fall into multiple categories.

Let's take a quick look at these four common regulations. Then we will use the rest of the chapter to discuss some of the ways you can use Policy-Based Management to help meet these regulations.

Gramm-Leach-Bliley Act

The Gramm-Leach-Bliley Act (GLBA) was introduced in 1999 to protect personal financial information stored by financial institutions such as banks, insurance companies, and securities firms, along with any other company that provides financial services or stores financial data. Compliance with GLBA is mandatory for any company holding financial data, meaning that policies and procedures must be in place to protect the information from malicious intent.

As organizations consolidate and combine products and services, much of your sought-after information is housed in one place. If unregulated, companies can use this information for financial gain by selling your data to other organizations, who might use it for marketing or sales opportunities, for example.

In order to adhere to GLBA, companies must meet the following criteria:

- Securely store personal financial data

- Inform customers of the policies and procedures used for sharing their financial data

- Provide customers the option to opt out of sharing their financial data with nonaffiliated companies

The Sarbanes-Oxley Act

The Sarbanes-Oxley Act (SOX) was enacted in 2002 due to the number of increasing corporate scandals costing investors billions of dollars. SOX applies only to publicly traded companies. The Enron accounting fraud scandal, which caused investors to lose nearly 11 billion dollars when the company filed bankruptcy in 2001, was a major contributing factor to the need for the SOX. Investors need to be assured that they are receiving accurate information on which to base their decisions about financial investments.

While SOX was primarily intended to ensure the accuracy of financial reporting, it requires publicly traded corporations to create and adhere to standard policies and procedures. You can use Policy-Based Management to help ensure those policies and procedures are not violated, and that your audits go as smoothly as possible.

SOX address issues such as the following:

- Protection of confidential information

- Access rights given to view confidential information

- Logging of events on systems that store confidential information

Health Insurance Portability and Accountability Act

The Health Insurance Portability and Accountability Act (HIPAA) was enacted in 1996 and primarily affects health-care providers handling patient information. HIPAA protects what is known as protected health information (PHI) and electronic protected health information (EPHI), which include any health records and payment information maintained by a health-care provider.

Prior to HIPAA, patient data was thought to be owned by the health-care provider, rather than by the patient, as it is today. HIPAA allows patients to request their data at any given time.

HIPAA addresses issues such as the following:

- Confidentiality of patient information

- Disaster recovery and availability of patient information

- Maintenance of proper audit trails on systems containing patient information

Payment Card Industry Data Security Standard

The Payment Card Industry Data Security Standard (PCI DSS) was introduced in 2004 to protect cardholder data and applies to any organization possessing credit card information. PCI DSS is a worldwide standard. Companies that do not comply with it can lose their ability to process credit card data and face substantial fines. Compliance is audited regularly, but can vary based on the amount of credit card data an organization handles.

Many new features introduced in SQL Server 2008 help you meet PCI DSS compliance. These include transparent data encryption, Extensible Key Management, and SQL Server Audit. You can use Policy-Based Management in conjunction with all of these new features to ensure compliance.

PCI DSS has 12 requirements, but only 6 of those requirements apply directly to SQL Server. The 12 requirements are grouped into six main objective categories, as follows (the requirements that can be directly addressed within SQL Server are preceded with an asterisk in this list):

Objective 1: Build and Maintain a Secure Network

1. Install and maintain a firewall configuration to protect cardholder data.

2. *Do not use vendor-supplied defaults for system passwords and other security parameters.

Objective 2: Protect Cardholder Data

3. *Protect stored cardholder data.

4. *Encrypt transmission of cardholder data across open, public networks.

Objective 3: Maintain a Vulnerability Management Program

5. Use and regularly update antivirus software on all systems commonly affected by malware.

6. Develop and maintain secure systems and applications.

Objective 4: Implement Strong Access Control Measures

7. *Restrict access to cardholder data by business need to know.

8. *Assign a unique ID to each person with computer access.

9. Restrict physical access to cardholder data.

Objective 5: Regularly Monitor and Test Networks

10. *Track and monitor all access to network resources and cardholder data.

11. Regularly test security systems and processes.

Objective 6: Maintain an Information Security Policy

12. Maintain a policy that addresses information security.

You can refer to these objectives as we discuss how to use Policy-Based Management to enforce them throughout the rest of the chapter.

Server Configuration

One of the first lines of defense in securing your system is to make sure you have to proper server configurations. You will need to change some configurations after you install SQL Server, such as the number of logs SQL Server keeps before the logs are recycled and the type of logins being audited (we will discuss the audit login configuration changes in the "Auditing" section later in this chapter). There are other configurations you need to change in order to ensure best practice standards are in place, such as the service account used by SQL Server as well as all of the options located under the Surface Area Configuration facet. Let's look at some of these configurations and see how you how you can use Policy-Based Management to make sure these configurations are enforced throughout your organization.

Service Account

When you install SQL Server, you are required to provide a service account for the SQL Server service. Ideally, the service account should be a domain account with as few permissions as possible. However, many times, you may find that the SQL Server service is running under the LocalSystem account. The LocalSystem account has far too many privileges to be a safe account for running the SQL Server service and is considered a security threat.

■ **Note** You should manage the SQL Server service account using the SQL Server Configuration Manager, not the Windows Services console.

The service account that SQL Server is using is stored in the registry. The script shown in Listing 9-1 determines whether SQL Server is running as a named instance and sets the registry location accordingly. Then it uses the **xp_regread** extended stored procedure to return the registry value. The catch here is that **xp_regread** may itself be on the list of procedures that you should avoid in your environment. If that is the case, you may be able to do a quick check of your existing environment, or you may be able to evaluate the policy during certain outages or maintenance windows.

Listing 9-1. Script to return the service account used by SQL Server

```
DECLARE @ServiceAccount TABLE
        (Value VARCHAR(50),
         Data VARCHAR(50))

DECLARE @RegistryLocation VARCHAR(200)

IF CHARINDEX('\',@@SERVERNAME)=0
  SET @RegistryLocation =
  'SYSTEM\CurrentControlSet\Services\MSSQLSERVER'
ELSE
  BEGIN
    SET @RegistryLocation =
    'SYSTEM\CurrentControlSet\Services\MSSQL$' +
    RIGHT(@@SERVERNAME,LEN(@@SERVERNAME)-
    CHARINDEX('\',@@SERVERNAME))
  END

INSERT INTO @ServiceAccount
EXEC master.dbo.xp_regread
     'HKEY_LOCAL_MACHINE' ,
     @RegistryLocation,
     'ObjectName'

SELECT TOP 1 Data AS ServiceAccount
FROM @ServiceAccount
```

You can use the **ExecuteSql()** function (introduced in Chapter 2) to create a condition that uses the script in Listing 9-1, as follows:

1. Create a new condition.

2. Click the ellipsis next to the Field column to open the Advanced Edit dialog box.

3. Use the **ExecuteSql**() function to insert the script from Listing 9-1. Note that you will need to replace all the single quotes with two single quotes before inserting the script. Also, we will be returning a string, so that will be the first parameter of the function. The following line of code shows a sample of the **ExecuteSql()** function used in the condition:

```
ExecuteSql('String', 'DECLARE @ServiceAccount TABLE … ')
```

4. Select != from the Operator drop-down list.

5. Type **LocalSystem** in the Value column.

6. Click OK to save the new condition.

■ **Tip** If you use a standard service account for SQL Server, it would be even more secure to set the remaining expression to = `'DomainName\ServiceAccount'`, instead of != `'LocalSystem'`.

You can now create a new policy that uses this condition, and will fail if SQL Server is running under the LocalSystem account.. Use the Server facet to create the policy, since the service account applies to the entire SQL Server instance. Figure 9-1 shows an example of the evaluation results for a SQL Server instance that is using the LocalSystem account.

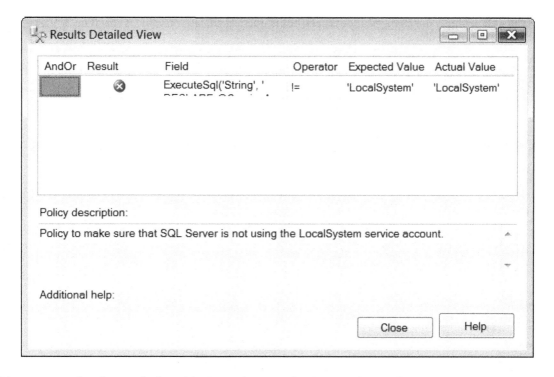

Figure 9-1. Evaluation results for a SQL Server instance that is using the LocalSystem account

Log Retention

Each time SQL Server is restarted, the old log file is renamed, and a new log file is created. By default, SQL Server keeps only six error logs. If you are having issues with your server and reboot the machine or recycle the SQL Server Service a few times, those six logs can become useless really fast. Most auditors will want you to increase the log retention to the maximum setting, which is 99.

■ **Note**: We have even heard of a case where an auditor suggested editing the registry to increase the number of logs beyond 99. While editing the registry to increase the number of error logs may work, anything above 99 is an unsupported setting that we do not recommend.

To configure the log retention for SQL Server, expand the Management node in Object Explorer, right-click the SQL Server Logs folder, and select Configure from the context menu. In the Configure SQL Server Error Logs dialog box, check the Limit the Number of Error Log Files before They Are Recycled check box to enable the Maximum Number of Error Log Files text box and enter **99**, as shown in Figure

9-2. Click OK to apply the changes. If the check box is unchecked, and no value is specified, SQL Server will keep six error log files.

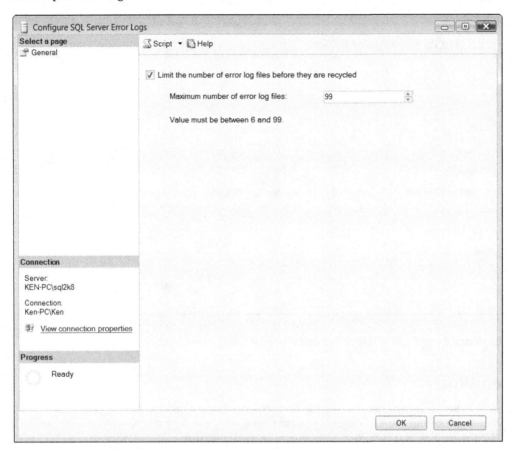

Figure 9-2. Configure SQL Server Error Logs dialog box

You can use the script in Listing 9-2 to return the number of error logs retained by SQL Server. First, the script checks the registry to find the value for the instance name you are using. The value that correlates to the instance name will be something like **MSSQL.1** or **MSSQL.2** for SQL Server 2005 and **MSSQL10.*InstanceName*** for SQL Server 2008. You need this value to reference the complete registry path used in the second part of the script to retrieve the number of error logs.

Listing 9-2. Script to return the number of error logs retained by SQL Server

```
DECLARE @RegValues TABLE(Value VARCHAR(50), Data VARCHAR(50))
DECLARE @RegPath VARCHAR(200)
DECLARE @ObjectName VARCHAR(50)
DECLARE @RegLocation VARCHAR(50)
```

```
--1. Get the location of the instance name in the registry
SET @RegPath = 'Software\Microsoft\Microsoft SQL Server\Instance Names\SQL\'

IF CHARINDEX('\',@@SERVERNAME) = 0
  --Not a named instance
  SET @ObjectName = 'MSSQLSERVER'
ELSE
  --Named instance
  SET @ObjectName = RIGHT(@@SERVERNAME,LEN(@@SERVERNAME) - CHARINDEX('\',@@SERVERNAME))

INSERT INTO @RegValues
EXEC master.dbo.xp_regread
    'HKEY_LOCAL_MACHINE',
    @RegPath,
    @ObjectName

SELECT @RegLocation = Data
FROM @RegValues

--2. Now get the number of error logs based on the location
SET @RegPath = 'Software\Microsoft\Microsoft SQL Server\' +
               @RegLocation + '\MSSQLServer'

SET @ObjectName = 'NumErrorLogs'

DELETE FROM @RegValues

INSERT INTO @RegValues
EXEC master.dbo.xp_regread
    'HKEY_LOCAL_MACHINE',
    @RegPath,
    @ObjectName

SELECT Data
FROM @RegValues
```

■ **Tip**: You should cycle your error logs on a regular basis (generally daily or weekly) using the **sp_cycle_errorlog** system stored procedure to keep the log files a manageable size. Executing the **sp_cycle_errorlog** command closes the current error log and creates a new one, just as a SQL Server restart does. Controlling the size of your error logs is especially important if you increase the number of error logs retained by SQL Server.

You can use the script in Listing 9-2 to create a condition using the **ExecuteSql()** function, in the same way as described for the script in Listing 9-1 for checking the service account. For this condition, the remaining expression after the **ExecuteSql()** function should read **= 99**.

Surface Area Configuration

By default, many features are disabled when you finish installing SQL Server, and you can use the Surface Area Configuration facet to make sure they stay that way. You should enable only the features needed by your application to reduce security threats. You can import four predefined Surface Area Configuration policies to help you secure your environment:

- Surface Area Configuration for Database Engine 2005 and 2000 Features

- Surface Area Configuration for Database Engine 2008 Features

- Surface Area Configuration for Service Broker Endpoints

- Surface Area Configuration for SOAP Endpoints

The following settings are controlled by the Surface Area Configuration for Database Engine 2008 Features policy (the default for all of these is False, so none of them are enabled by default):

- AdHocRemoteQueriesEnabled

- ClrIntegrationEnabled

- DatabaseMailEnabled

- OleAutomationEnabled

- RemoteDacEnabled

- ServiceBrokerEndpointActive

- SoapEndpointsEnabled

- SQLMailEnabled

- XPCmdShellEnabled

The settings controlled by the Surface Area Configuration for Database Engine 2005 and 2000 Features policy are the same, with the addition of **WebAssistantEnabled**, which was deprecated in SQL Server 2005. Each policy has a server restriction that prevents the policy from running against inappropriate versions of SQL Server.

You can change these values using the **sp_comfigure** system stored procedure or check their current values using the **sys.configurations** catalog view. For example, the script in Listing 9-3 will enable **xp_cmdshell** on your server.

Listing 9-3. Script to enable xp_cmdshell

```
EXEC sp_configure 'show advanced options', 1
GO
RECONFIGURE
GO
-- Enable xp_cmdshell
EXEC sp_configure 'xp_cmdshell', 1
GO
RECONFIGURE
GO
```

Since **xp_cmdshell** is considered an advanced option, you must first change the show advanced options setting to true using **sp_configure** before you can enable it. If someone enables a feature such as **xp_cmdshell**, which allows you to run external operating system commands, you can capture the event and raise an alert using the methods discussed in Chapter 5. Figure 9-3 shows the Windows event log with an alert that was raised due to enabling **xp_cmdshell** using the script in Listing 9-3.

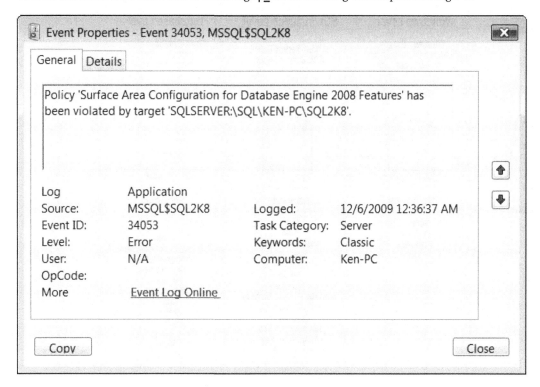

Figure 9-3. Error raised by enabling xp_cmdshell

Security

Tightening access to your servers by managing the appropriate security permissions is another important part of maintaining compliance. As a DBA, it is your job to make sure people can access only the objects they are supposed to access. You should always provide the minimum level of permissions users need in order to perform their tasks.

Figure 9-4 provides a good visual representation of the security features in SQL Server and how they relate to each other. You may find it helpful to refer back to Figure 9-4 throughout the remainder of this chapter.

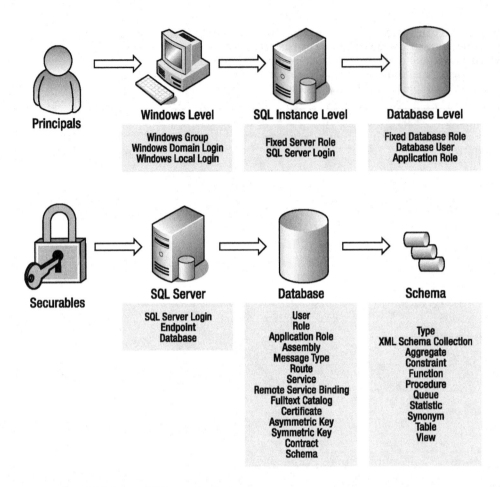

Figure 9-4. SQL Server 2008 security features

You can classify security objects as either principals or securables. A *principal* is an object that can request access to SQL Server. A *securable* is an object in SQL Server that you can protect by setting and managing permissions. In simple terms, principals try to access securables, but principals can access those securables only if you have granted them the appropriate permission to do so. You can implement a few policies to help you reduce security threats to those securables by limiting the use of administrative accounts. There are also several predefined security policies provided with the installation that you can import.

Administrative Accounts

You should be extremely mindful of who has administrative access to your SQL Server systems. While you must be cautious of all administrative accounts in your environment, two particular accounts pose more of a threat than the others do. Both Builtin\Administrators and sa (system administrator) are considered a security threat, and you should take extra measures to protect access using these accounts.

Removing the Builtin\Administrators Login

Prior to SQL Server 2008, by default, anyone who has administrative access to the server also has administrative access to SQL Server. This administrative access is given through a SQL Server login called Builtin\Administrators, which is mapped to the Windows Administrators group. The Builtin\Administrators login is not present in SQL Server 2008 unless someone specifically adds it.

If you are using SQL Server 2005, it is considered a best practice security measure to remove the Builtin\Administrators login. You can remove the login by running the following command:

```
DROP LOGIN [Builtin\Administrators]
```

■ **Caution** Before removing any administrative accounts in SQL Server, make sure you have alternative administrative access with other logins.

In order to make sure that you don't have any servers using the Builtin\Administrators login or to ensure that no one adds the login back once you remove it, you can create a policy that checks the **sys.serverprincipals** catalog view for the login name by using the query in Listing 9-4.

Listing 9-4. Query to check for the Builtin/Administrators login

```
SELECT COUNT(*)
FROM sys.server_principals
WHERE name = 'Builtin\Administrators'
```

Now that you have the query that checks for the existence of the login, it is easy to create a condition using the **ExecuteSql()** function, just as we did for the service account earlier in the chapter. Since we don't want any occurrences of the Builtin\Administrators account, for this condition the remaining expression after the **ExecuteSql()** function should read **= 0**.

Disabling the sa Login

It is considered bad practice to log in using the sa account, because the sa login has the highest permission set within SQL Server and also provides anonymity to the user who actually logs in. If you install SQL Server allowing only Windows authentication, the sa account is disabled; otherwise, it is enabled.

If you are using mixed-mode authentication, it is considered a best practice security measure to disable the sa login. You can disable the sa login by running the following command.

```
ALTER LOGIN sa DISABLE
```

■ **Caution** Before disabling the sa login, you should verify that it is not being used by your application connections or SQL Agent jobs.

You can create a policy that checks the **sys.serverprincipals** catalog view to make sure the sa login is disabled by using the query in Listing 9-5.

Listing 9-5. Query to make sure the sa login is disabled

```
SELECT COUNT(*)
FROM sys.server_principals
WHERE name = 'sa' AND
      disabled = 1
```

Again, after you have the query, you can create a condition using the **ExecuteSql()** function. And since we don't want any occurrences of an enabled sa account, for this condition, the remaining expression after the **ExecuteSql()** function should read **= 0**.

Best Practice Security Policies

Along with creating custom policies to secure you servers, you can import Microsoft best practice security policies to help protect your server. As explained in Chapter 2, when you import these policies, they will be in their own category called Microsoft Best Practices: Security.

The following are the best practice security policies provided by Microsoft, excluding the best practice policies related to encryption, which are listed later in the chapter:

CmdExec Rights Secured: This policy uses an underlying condition called CmdExec Rights for sysadmins Only and uses a server restriction called SQL Server Version 2000. It ensures that only sysadmins can run CmdExec and ActiveX script job steps in SQL Server 2000.

Guest Permissions: This policy uses an underlying condition called Has No Database Access that applies to all user databases, along with the model system database, and has no server restrictions. It is best practice to revoke access from the guest account in all databases except master and tempdb, if your applications are not using this account. You can disable the guest account on a database by running the command **REVOKE CONNECT FROM GUEST**.

Public Not Granted Server Permissions: This policy uses an underlying condition called Public Server Role Has No Granted Permissions and has no server restrictions. It ensures that server permission is not granted to the public role. Since every login you create has access to the public server role, if the public role has server permissions, every login will have server permissions as well.

SQL Server Login Mode: This policy uses an underlying condition called Windows Authentication Mode that checks to make sure the login mode is Windows integrated authentication and has no server restrictions. It is considered best practice to use Windows integrated authentication instead of mixed-mode authentication whenever possible. However, in real-world practice, using Windows integrated authentication only is rarely an option.

SQL Server Password Expiration: This policy uses an underlying condition called Password Expiration Enabled and uses a server restriction called SQL Server 2005 or a Later Version. This policy ensures that password expiration is enabled on all SQL Server logins. It is valid only on SQL Server 2005 or later, since password expiration is not an option in SQL Server 2000. The password expiration option is dependent on the enforce password policy option being enabled as well.

SQL Server Password Policy: This policy uses an underlying condition called Password Policy Enforced and uses a server restriction called SQL Server 2005 or a Later Version. This policy ensures that the password policy is enforced on all SQL Server logins. It is valid only on SQL Server 2005 or later, since enabling the password policy is not an option in SQL Server 2000. This policy uses the `NetValidatePasswordPolicy` API, which is available in Windows 2003 or later, to enforce password complexity.

Trustworthy Database: This policy uses an underlying condition called Database Owner Not sysadmin and uses a server restriction called SQL Server 2005 or a Later Version. This policy ensures that no login in the db_owner role has sysadmin privileges on databases where the Trustworthy property is enabled.

Encryption

Microsoft has made some key additions to encryption by introducing the new transparent data encryption and Extensible Key Management technologies. These new features are an integral part of meeting the growing compliance needs of the organization. Along with being able to use Policy-Based Management to help with these new features, some predefined policies can assist you with the features introduced in SQL Server 2005. If you will be using encryption in your environment, we highly recommend the book *Expert SQL Server 2008 Encryption* by Michael Coles and Rodney Landrum (Apress, 2009).

Transparent Data Encryption

Transparent data encryption enables the DBA to store the data, log, and backup files in a secure manner by automatically encrypting and decrypting the data as it is read from and written to the disk. The database uses a database encryption key, and without the correct certificate, the data files or the backups cannot be restored to another server. This process is implemented at the data layer and is transparent to front-end applications. This does not mean that the data is encrypted between the application and the server; only the pages containing the data on the server are encrypted.

You can create a policy for your databases that requires transparent data encryption, using the `EncryptionEnabled` property of the Database facet to ensure that it is enabled. As discussed in Chapter 2, you can create a policy by exporting the current state of an object. For example, you can right-click a database and select Facets from the context menu to display the View Facets dialog box. The example in Figure 9-5 shows this dialog box with the `EncryptionEnabled` property set to True for the `AdventureWorks2008` database.

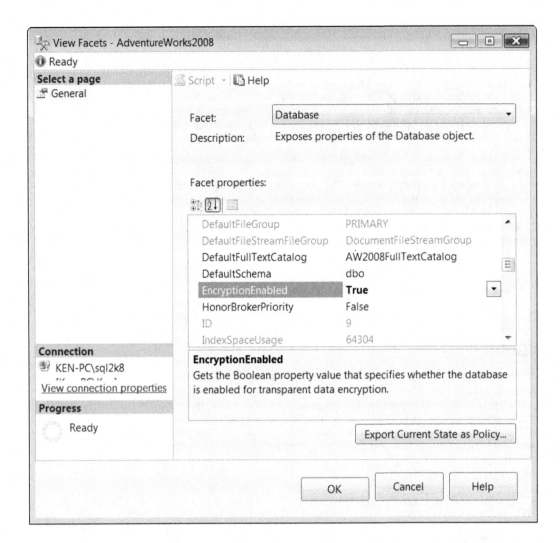

Figure 9-5. View Facets dialog box showing the Database facet with EncryptionEnabled set to True

In order to create a policy, you could click the Export Current State as Policy button, or you could just create a new policy using the **EncryptionEnabled** property.

■ **Note**: Keep in mind that if you export the current state of the database, you will create a policy that ensures all the database options remain the same, not just the property you enabled, such as **EncryptionEnabled** or **ExtensibleKeyManagementEnabled**.

Extensible Key Management

Extensible Key Management provides an enhanced method for managing encryption keys. It enables third-party software vendors to provide and manage keys by supporting hardware security module (HSM) products that can be registered and used with SQL Server. This provides many advantages, including the physical separation of data and keys. If you are using Extensible Key Management, you can ensure that it is enabled by using the **ExtensibleKeyManagementEnabled** property in the Server Configuration facet.

You can view the Server Configuration facet and all the properties it exposes by right-clicking the SQL Server instance and selecting Facets from the context menu. Once the View Facets dialog box is displayed, change the Facet option from Server to Server Configuration. You can see the **ExtensibleKeyManagementEnabled** property is set to True for the instance in the example in Figure 9-6.

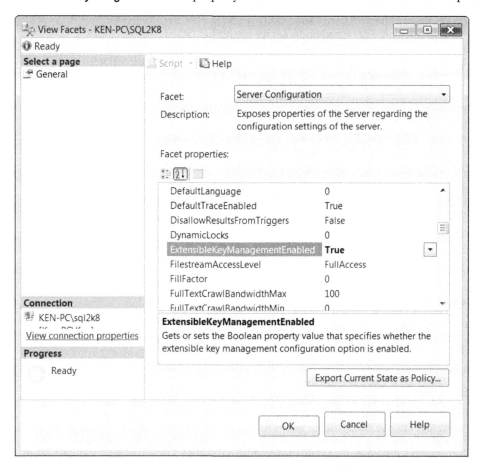

Figure 9-6. *View Facets dialog box showing the Server Configuration facet with the ExtensibleKeyManagementEnabled property set to True*

In order to create a policy, you could either click Export Current State as Policy or just create a new policy using the `ExtensibleKeyManagementEnabled` property.

Best Practice Encryption Policies

In addition to the best practice security policies listed in the "Best Practice Security Policies" section earlier in this chapter, you can import the following Microsoft best practice encryption policies:

Asymmetric Key Encryption Algorithm: This policy uses an underlying condition called RSA 1024 or RSA 2048 Encrypted and a server restriction called SQL Server 2005 or a Later Version. It ensures that every asymmetric key in every database has at least 1024-bit encryption.

Symmetric Key Encryption for User Databases: This policy uses an underlying condition called Strongly Encrypted and a server restriction called SQL Server 2005 or a Later Version. It checks to make sure every symmetric key that is less than 128 bytes in every database does not use the RC2 or RC4 encryption algorithm. If it is supported by your operating system, you should use AES 128-bit and above encryption; otherwise, you should use 3DES to create your symmetric keys.

Symmetric Key for master Database: This policy uses an underlying condition called Microsoft Service Master Key and a server restriction called SQL Server 2005 or a Later Version. It verifies that the symmetric key in the master database is the service master key and not a user-defined symmetric key.

Symmetric Key for System Databases: This policy uses an underlying condition called Fail For Any Symmetric Key and has a server restriction called SQL Server 2005 or a Later Version. It checks every system database except master to ensure there are no symmetric keys.

Auditing

Auditing your servers is a key part in maintaining compliance within your organization. An audit should provide the answers to the following questions:

- Who did something
- What they did
- How they did it
- When they did it

You must retain your audit logs for one year in order to meet PCI DSS compliance. You should review you audit criteria and choose exactly what needs to be audited, so that you do not end up with an overwhelming amount of information. In addition, audit trails must be tamperproof, meaning that the audit logs should be stored in a directory that is not accessible to the DBA. Once you have defined your audit criteria, you can use Policy-Based Management to help you enforce it.

SQL Server Audit

SQL Server Audit is a new feature in SQL Server 2008 that captures data for a specific group of server or database actions. Audits can be defined using event actions or action groups, which are a predefined set of actions. The following provide audit properties to help you ensure that your audits are not being tampered with:

1. *Server facet*: AuditLevel = All

2. *Audit facet: OnFailure* = Shutdown and Enabled = True

3. *Database Audit Specification*: Enabled = True

4. *Server Audit Specification*: Enabled = True

Many auditors require the OnFailure = Shutdown option in the Audit facet to ensure that no events can occur on your server without being captured by an audit. On the downside, if SQL Server cannot write to the audit destination you have defined, the SQL Server service will shut down, and you will be facing an outage. Therefore, you should be very cautious of the location and space allocated for your audit files.

Login Auditing

By default, when SQL Server is installed, it is configured to record only failed login attempts. Tracking failed login attempts allows you to identify unwanted login activity, but doesn't provide any information if the login is successful. But bad things usually happen on a server when people *can* log in, right? If you change the login auditing option to record both successful and failed logins, you can correlate actions on the server to successful logins.

To configure login auditing for SQL Server, right-click the instance name and select Properties from the context menu. In the Server Properties dialog box, select the Security page, and change the Login Auditing value from Failed Logins Only to Both Failed and Successful Logins, as shown in Figure 9-7. You can use the **LoginAuditLevel** property in the Server Audit facet to ensure that both successful and failed logins are being recorded on your servers.

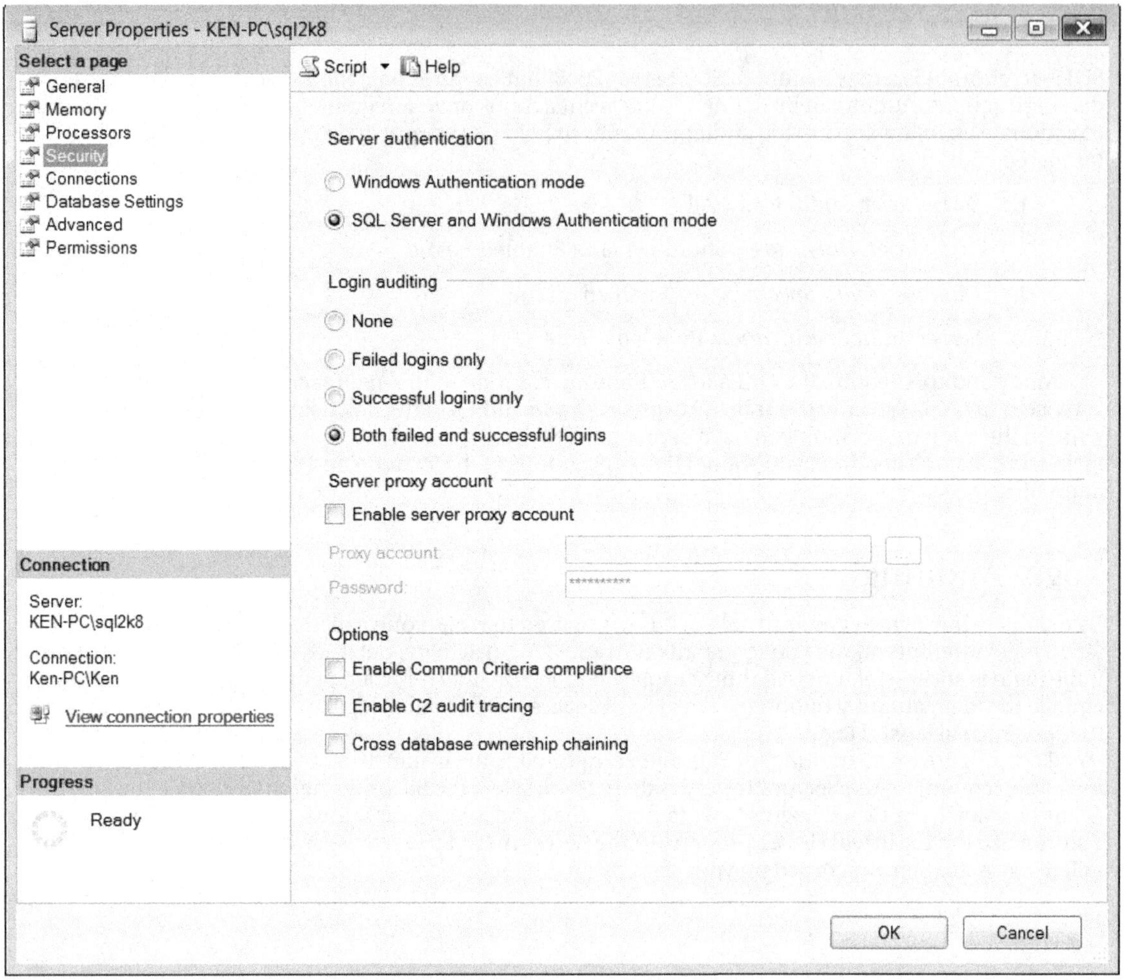

Figure 9-7. Security page of the Server Properties dialog box

Default Trace

When you install SQL Server 2005 or later, there is a lightweight trace running in the background, known as the *default trace*, that captures valuable information, such as server configuration changes and DDL statements. Although it is possible to remove the default trace, it is considered best practice to leave it in place. The benefits provided by the default trace far outweigh the performance gain you will receive by removing it.

You can view the trace files in the Log directory under your SQL Server installation folder, as shown in Figure 9-8.

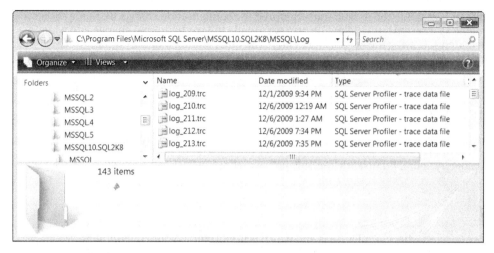

Figure 9-8. Default trace log file location

You can read the trace files by running this query:

```
SELECT * FROM fn_trace_gettable('c:\FilePath\FileName.trc', default)
```

Alternatively, you can simply open the .trc files using SQL Server Profiler, as shown in Figure 9-9.

EventClass	NTUserNa...	NTDomainNa...	HostName	ClientPro...	ApplicationName	LoginName	SPID	StartTime
ErrorLog	Ken	Ken-PC	KEN-PC	5520	Microsoft SQ...	Ken-PC\Ken	54	2009-12-06 00:36:09...
ErrorLog	Ken	Ken-PC	KEN-PC	5520	Microsoft SQ...	Ken-PC\Ken	54	2009-12-06 00:36:09...
Audit Server Alter Trace Event					Microsoft SQ...	sa	26	2009-12-06 00:36:20...
Audit Server Alter Trace Event					Microsoft SQ...	sa	26	2009-12-06 00:36:21...
Audit Server Alter Trace Event					Microsoft SQ...	sa	26	2009-12-06 00:36:21...
Audit Server Alter Trace Event					Microsoft SQ...	sa	26	2009-12-06 00:36:21...
ErrorLog	Ken	Ken-PC	KEN-PC	5520	Microsoft SQ...	Ken-PC\Ken	54	2009-12-06 00:36:36...
ErrorLog	Ken	Ken-PC	KEN-PC	5520	Microsoft SQ...	Ken-PC\Ken	54	2009-12-06 00:36:36...
Audit Server Alter Trace Event					Microsoft SQ...	##MS_PolicyEv...	26	2009-12-06 00:36:37...
Audit Server Alter Trace Event					Microsoft SQ...	##MS_PolicyEv...	26	2009-12-06 00:36:37...
ErrorLog	Ken	Ken-PC	KEN-PC	5520	Microsoft SQ...	Ken-PC\Ken	54	2009-12-06 00:36:41...
ErrorLog	Ken	Ken-PC	KEN-PC	5520	Microsoft SQ...	Ken-PC\Ken	54	2009-12-06 00:36:41...
Audit Server Alter Trace Event					Microsoft SQ...	##MS_PolicyEv...	26	2009-12-06 00:36:42...
Audit Server Alter Trace Event					Microsoft SQ...	##MS_PolicyEv...	26	2009-12-06 00:36:43...
Audit Server Alter Trace Event					Microsoft SQ...	##MS_PolicyEv...	26	2009-12-06 00:36:43...
Audit Server Alter Trace Event					Microsoft SQ...	##MS_PolicyEv...	26	2009-12-06 00:36:43...
Data File Auto Grow		Ken-PC	KEN-PC	5520	Microsoft SQ...	Ken-PC\Ken	52	2009-12-06 00:42:49...
Object:Created	Ken	Ken-PC	KEN-PC	5448	Microsoft SQ...	Ken-PC\Ken	52	2009-12-06 01:02:15...

```
2009-12-06 00:36:41.90 spid54     Configuration option 'xp_cmdshell' changed from 0 to 1. Run the RECONFIGURE statement to install.
```

Done.   Ln 57, Col 1   Rows: 302

Figure 9-9. Default trace sample data

205

As you can see in Figure 9-9, the default trace captured the configuration change we made earlier in the chapter to enable **xp_cmdshell**, including the user who made the configuration change and when it was made. Immediately following the **xp_cmdshell** entry is an entry stating that the Surface Area Configuration for Database Engine 2008 Features policy has been violated. Therefore, by reviewing the default trace, you can see exactly who made changes that caused certain policy violations.

Best Practice Audit Policy

You can import a predefined policy created by Microsoft called SQL Server Default Trace to ensure that the default trace is running on your server. The SQL Server Default Trace policy is in the Microsoft Best Practices: Audit category, and it is currently the only policy in that category.

Summary

In this chapter, we covered what compliance is and why it is important in your environment. We presented an overview of some of the most common regulations you will encounter. We then showed you several ways to integrate Policy-Based Management into your environment by creating policies to ensure that you have the proper server configuration options, as well as the best practice security in place. In addition, we showed you how you can use Policy-Based Management with some of the new encryption features, such as transparent data encryption and Extensible Key Management. Finally, we showed you how you can use policies along with auditing to guarantee that if someone tampers with your audits, you will know.

By no means is this chapter a comprehensive guide to maintaining compliance in your organization. You must work closely with your auditors to ensure your servers meet their requirements. However, we have shown you many different methods for using the new features in SQL Server 2008 along with Policy-Based Management to ensure that the process for meeting compliance is as painless as possible.

CHAPTER 10

■■■

Where to Go from Here

I am sure you know by now that being a DBA requires a huge skill set covering a wide spectrum of technologies. You also know that configuring and maintaining a stable and secure database environment takes a lot of planning and research. DBAs are expected to know a little about everything. But what makes being a DBA even harder is that technology is a fast-paced industry, with rapid advancements that seem to outdate things before you've even had a chance to learn them. The days are over when you learned a skill and then worked for several years before you needed to upgrade your skill set. You need to learn new things constantly and stay on top of the latest industry news in order to excel as a DBA.

Luckily, there is a plethora of resources to help you keep up with the latest technology and industry standards, including web sites, white papers, webcasts, podcasts, and even free training events. You should definitely take advantage of the knowledge and experience offered by others. If you have a question or an issue, chances are that you are not the first one to experience the problem, and there is already a well-documented solution on the Internet. You just need to know where to find it. This chapter lists resources that can help you with your planning and research, along with finding the answers to any questions or issues you may encounter along the way.

Upcoming Releases

At the time of this writing, the release of SQL Server 2008 Release 2 is just around the corner, and SQL Server 11 is in the works. From the looks of things, Policy-Based Management is going to stick around a while.

Microsoft's SQL Server Connect web site (`http://connect.microsoft.com/SQLServer`) allows you to collaborate with Microsoft employees and other members of the SQL Server community to provide feedback about SQL Server and submit ideas for the next release. If there is something you would like to see changed or added, or even if you just find a bug—in Policy-Based Management or elsewhere in SQL Server 2008—log in to this web site. The more votes an item receives on the SQL Server Connect web site, the more likely you are to see it added or fixed in the next release. If you do add something to the SQL Server Connect web site, make sure to advertise it.

SQL Server Web Sites

Following are some web sites that are useful when working with Policy-Based Management. They are good resources for anything you can imagine when working with SQL Server. Plenty of people frequent these web sites, and many are willing to answer any questions you may have.

- Professional Association for SQL Server (PASS): `http://www.sqlpass.org`

- SQL Server Central: `http://www.sqlservercentral.com`

- Simple-Talk: `http://www.simple-talk.com/sql`

- SQLServerPedia: `http://www.sqlserverpedia.com`

- MSSQLTips: `http://www.mssqltips.com`

- SQLTeam: `http://www.sqlteam.com`

- SQL Server Performance: `http://www.sql-server-performance.com`

- SQL Server Community: `http://www.sqlcommunity.com`

Blogs

The longer we have worked with SQL Server, the more we have found that blogs can be one of the most valuable sources of information on the Internet. Many of the people who post on blogs either had an issue they overcame or learned something interesting, and then published their findings for the world to see. This is the kind of information that you can't find in the product documentation.

In addition to an entire blog dedicated to Policy-Based Management maintained by many of the developers of the product, several other bloggers routinely post their experiences with Policy-Based Management. Many of the bloggers have a category you can use to filter on only the posts pertaining to Policy-Based Management.

The following are some blogs that contain useful Policy-Based Management information:

- MSDN Policy-Based Management: `http://blogs.msdn.com/sqlpbm/`

- Lara Rubbelke: `http://sqlblog.com/blogs/lara_rubbelke/archive/tags/Policy+Based+Management/default.aspx`

- Bob Beauchemin: `http://www.sqlskills.com/BLOGS/BOBB/category/Policy-Based-Management.aspx`

- Colin Stasiuk: `http://benchmarkitconsulting.com/tag/pbm/`

- Jorge Segarra: `http://sqlchicken.com/tag/policy-based-management/`

White Papers

White papers, sometimes referred to as technical articles, offer an in-depth look into a specific topic within SQL Server. There are several good white papers on Policy-Based Management. Also, some white papers that are not specifically targeted for Policy-Based Management are full of useful information when it comes to deploying Policy-Based Management in your environment.

The following are some white papers that contain information about Policy-Based Management information:

- SQL Server 2008 Policy-Based Management: `http://msdn.microsoft.com/en-us/library/dd938891.aspx`

- Enterprise Policy Management Framework with SQL Server 2008:
  `http://msdn.microsoft.com/en-us/library/dd542632.aspx`

- SQL Server 2008 Compliance Guide: `http://www.microsoft.com/downloads/details.aspx?FamilyId=6E1021DD-65B9-41C2-8385-438028F5ACC2&displaylang=en`

- Deploying SQL Server 2008 Based on Payment Card Industry Data Security Standards: `http://www.parentebeard.com/lib/pdf/Deploying_SQL_Server_2008_Based_on_PCI_DSS.pdf`

- Declarative Management in Microsoft SQL Server: `http://www.vldb.org/pvldb/2/vldb09-435.pdf`

Podcasts

Podcasts are another resource that many people often overlook. Podcasts are a great way to learn things while you are on the go. Several free podcasts are available for download.

■ **Note**: You can download some podcasts in both audio and video formats. However, we have downloaded the audio versions and didn't find a lot of value in listening to a demo. You really need to see what's going on.

Here are some sites where you can find podcasts related to SQL Server:

- The Voice of the DBA: `http://sqlservercentral.mevio.com`

- SSWUG: `http://www.sswug.org/media`

- SQL Down Under: `http://www.sqldownunder.com`

- Microsoft Events: `http://www.microsoft.com/events/podcasts`

- SQLServerPedia: `http://sqlserverpedia.com/wiki/SQL_Server_Tutorials`

- MidnightDBA: `http://midnightdba.itbookworm.com/`

Free Training Events

Always be on the lookout for free training events in your area. Here are some opportunities:

- Many times, Microsoft will come near your area with a road show to present some of the latest technology. Check out the events schedule at `http://www.msdnevents.com`.

- SQLSaturday is another way to get free training. SQLSaturday is a one-day training event packed full of sessions dealing with all aspects of SQL Server. These events are put on all around the country and are typically organized by the local area's user group(s). You can learn more at `http://www.sqlsaturday.com`.

- Find a local users group and get involved. Local users groups generally have monthly meetings with a one-hour session that covers various topics within SQL Server. A local users group is a good way to network with other SQL Server professionals in your area and learn something new in the process. See the listing of SQL Server users groups at **http://www.sqlpass.org/PASSChapters.aspx**.

Social Networking

There is a great SQL Server community out there. If you take advantage of the many social networking web sites, you have the expertise of some of the brightest minds in the business right at your fingertips.

Much of the SQL Server community has presence on web sites such as Facebook and LinkedIn, but Twitter seems to be the most active and fastest way to exchange information. In fact, as the result of a recent idea proposed by Aaron Nelson, you can add the hash tag #SQLHelp to any of your Twitter posts to make getting help even easier. You can read more about how #SQLHelp works on Brent Ozar's blog at **http://www.brentozar.com/archive/2009/12/i-need-sqlhelp/**.

■ **Tip**: To make social networking even easier, you can download an application such as TweetDeck (**http://tweetdeck.com**) to manage all your social networking web sites from a single interface.

You have a few options when you are looking for SQL Server people on Twitter:

- There is a good list on the SQLServerPedia wiki at **http://sqlserverpedia.com/wiki/Twitter**. Since SQLServerPedia is a wiki, all you need to do to add yourself to the list is sign in and edit the page.

- Use the WeFollow directory (**http://wefollow.com/**). You can search for keywords such as "SQL" and "SQLServer" to display everyone who has registered using the same keywords. You can add yourself to the WeFollow directory by supplying your location and up to five interests.

- Find someone who has categorized the people they follow and follow their list. Here are a few examples:

    1. **http://twitter.com/#/list/SQLChicken/sql-peeps**

    2. **http://twitter.com/#/list/peschkaj/sql-server-presenters**

    3. **http://twitter.com/#/list/SQLChicken/sql-user-group-leaders**

    4. **http://twitter.com/#/list/SQLRockstar/sql**

    5. **http://twitter.com/#/list/BrentO/sql-server**

Microsoft Support Options

Microsoft provides several support options, ranging from reading the documentation that comes with SQL Server to having your own personal support technician. You would be amazed at the number of people who are willing to help you solve your SQL Server issues free of cost, but you do need to know where to find those people.

■ **Tip**: We have actually seen three different answers (each one being correct) in response to a forum post, all within five minutes. However, you should still do your homework before posting to forums. Many times, a simple search in the right place will provide the answer to your question. In addition, you will receive a faster and more accurate response by providing a detailed explanation of your issue, including the things you have already tried to do to resolve the issue.

SQL Server Books Online

SQL Server Books Online is usually the first place we go when we have a quick question (especially about the certain syntax of a command). For example, if you cannot remember the exact syntax for the **ALTER TABLE** command, all you need to do is type **ALTER TABLE** in a query editor window, highlight the text, press F1, and voila, you are taken directly to the appropriate page in Books Online.

This context-sensitive help works in many other areas in SQL Server as well. For example, if you have the New Policy dialog box open and press F1, you will be taken to the page in Books Online that explains all of the new policy options.

You can view the web version of Books Online at **http://msdn.microsoft.com/en-us/library/ms130214.aspx**. However, to receive the context-sensitive help, we recommend that you install Books Online when you install SQL Server. Alternatively, you can download it from **http://www.microsoft.com/downloads/details.aspx?displaylang=en&FamilyID=765433f7-0983-4d7a-b628-0a98145bcb97** and install it separately.

Webcasts

Microsoft occasionally hosts webcasts on Policy-Based Management. These tend to last about an hour. Webcasts usually go pretty deep into a specific topic, sometimes with demonstrations and code samples.

Visit the Microsoft Events home page at **http://msevents.microsoft.com** to search for prerecorded or upcoming webcasts, as well as many other events.

The following are prerecorded webcasts that specifically cover Policy-Based Management:

- Simplify Management with Policy-Based Management:
  http://msevents.microsoft.com/CUI/WebCastEventDetails.aspx?EventID=1032369748&EventCategory=5&culture=en-US&CountryCode=US

- Governing Your Enterprise with Policy-Based Management:
  http://msevents.microsoft.com/CUI/WebCastEventDetails.aspx?EventID=1032402180&EventCategory=5&culture=en-US&CountryCode=US

- Using the New Policy-Based Management Framework in SQL Server 2008: `http://msevents.microsoft.com/CUI/WebCastEventDetails.aspx?EventID=1032360 211&EventCategory=5&culture=en-US&CountryCode=US`

SQL Server Troubleshooting and Support Resources

The SQL Server Troubleshooting and Support web site (`http://msdn.microsoft.com/en-us/sqlserver/bb895923.aspx`) is kind of like a support dashboard for SQL Server, providing you with a centralized support hub. This web site provides you with many important resources on a single web page, such as the following:

- Microsoft Knowledge Base search functionality

- Latest updates and service packs

- SQL Server forums

- Microsoft professional support

Microsoft Technical Communities

The Microsoft Technical Communities web site (`http://www.microsoft.com/communities/default.mspx`) provides several links that will connect you with other SQL Server users, including peers and Microsoft employees. The web site contains the following links:

- *Forums*: Directs you to forums that are hosted by Microsoft. Some of the best names in the business, both Microsoft and non-Microsoft employees, actively monitor these forums to answer your questions.

- *Blogs*: Allows you to search Microsoft Community blogs posted by Microsoft employees.

- *Technical Chats*: Allows you to view upcoming live chats hosted by Microsoft experts.

- *Newsgroups*: Allows you to post a question in one of the 2,000-plus newsgroups dedicated to Microsoft products.

- *Webcasts*: Allows you to search for an upcoming live webcast or pick from a wide selection of on-demand webcasts hosted by an industry specialist.

- *Find a Community Web Site*: Connects you with other web sites and resources, usually hosted by a SQL Server Most Valuable Professional (MVP).

- *User Groups*: Allows you to search for user groups in your area dedicated to your technology interests.

Paid Support

When all else fails, Microsoft offers several paid support options to help you with anything from researching implementation to assisting you in the event of a disaster. You can choose something as basic as per-incident support to an all-out enterprise support agreement. You can find the option that meets your needs on the Microsoft Support web site (`http://support.microsoft.com/default.aspx?scid=fh;EN-US;OfferProPhone`). The following are the Problem Resolution Services support options at the time of this writing:

- E-mail only support, $99 (one incident)

- Business hours telephone support, $259 (one incident)

- Business hours telephone support, $1,289 (five-pack of incidents)

- Business-critical after hours telephone support, $515 (one incident)

■ **Note**: Microsoft Problem Resolution Services business hours are Monday through Friday from 6:00 AM to 6:00 PM Pacific Standard Time.

The next level of support is Microsoft Advisory Services. Contacting Microsoft Advisory Services is like hiring an off-site consultant for a rate of $210 per hour. You enter a short-term agreement that allows you to work with the same technician. Microsoft Advisory Services support offers analyses and recommendations that go beyond the scope of Problem Resolution Services. You can use Microsoft Advisory Services with consultation pertaining to the following:

- Code reviews

- Installation and configuration technologies

- Performance tuning

- System management server deployments

- Migrations

For more information about Advisory Services, visit `http://support.microsoft.com/gp/advisoryservice`.

Finally, if you have enterprise support needs that go beyond Microsoft Services, you can visit the Enterprise Support web site (`http://www.microsoft.com/services/microsoftservices/srv_enterprise.mspx`).

Summary

There is a lot to learn about SQL Server, and there are also many ways you can learn it. In addition, you can provide feedback that can help shape the product. We discussed several ways you can stay up to date with what is going on in the SQL Server world, as well as find the information you need in order to get past any obstacles that come your way. You can take advantage of the many web sites dedicated to SQL Server, as well as blogs, white papers, and podcasts. You can reach out and interact with the community by attending a SQL Server event or leveraging one of the many social networking web sites. You can also take advantage of the support options offered by Microsoft, such as SQL Server Books Online, technical communities, and paid support.

You cannot be an expert in every area of SQL Server, but you may find that you are better in some areas than others. By interacting with the community and offering the knowledge you gain, you will receive the same benefits in return, often tenfold.

Microsoft SQL Server
Best Practice Policies

SQL Server 2008 ships with a number of "best practice" policies. These are policies created by Microsoft, ready for you to use. It's worth reviewing them, to see whether any of them apply to your environment.

Don't implement best practice policies blindly. They aren't absolute rules. Think of them more as strong suggestions. They are policies that tend to be useful, but you should carefully evaluate any policy before enabling it, to ensure that it's really a good fit in your environment.

This appendix contains descriptions of the best practice policies, as well as information about the conditions and facets used by these policies.

Best Practice Policy Descriptions

Listing A-1 shows a query that you can issue to get descriptions of the built-in policies

Listing A-1. Query against msdb database to return descriptions of best practice policies

```
SELECT   name, [description], help_link
FROM         msdb.dbo.syspolicy_policies_internal
ORDER BY     date_created, name
```

Table A-1 shows the output that you'll get from the query. You'll receive a list of short descriptions. Each description is associated with an HTML link that takes you to more in-depth information about the policy in question.

Table A-1. Best Practice Policies

Policy	Policy Description	HTML Link
Asymmetric Key Encryption Algorithm	Checks whether asymmetric keys were created with 1024-bit or better.	http://go.microsoft.com/fwlink/?LinkId=116370

Policy	Policy Description	HTML Link
Backup and Data File Location	Checks if database and the backups are on separate backup devices. If they are on the same backup device, and the device that contains the database fails, your backups will be unavailable. Also, putting the data and backups on separate devices optimizes the I/O performance for both the production use of the database and writing the backups.	http://go.microsoft.com/fwlink/?LinkId=116373
CmdExec Rights Secured	Checks that only members of the sysadmins fixed server role can execute CmdExec and ActiveX script job steps. Applies only to SQL Server 2000.	http://go.microsoft.com/fwlink/?LinkId=116363
Data and Log File Location	Checks whether data and log files are placed on separate logical drives. Placing both data and log files on the same drive can cause contention for that drive and result in poor performance. Placing the files on separate drives allows the I/O activity to occur at the same time for both the data and log files. The best practice is to specify separate drives for the data and log when you create a new database. To move files after the database is created, the database must be taken offline. Move the files by using one of the following methods: Restore the database from backup by using the **RESTORE DATABASE** statement with the **WITH MOVE** option. Detach and then reattach the database specifying separate locations for the data and log devices. Specify a new location by running the **ALTER DATABASE** statement with the **MODIFY FILE** option, and then restarting the instance of SQL Server.	http://go.microsoft.com/fwlink/?LinkId=116362

Policy	Policy Description	HTML Link
Database Auto Close	Checks that the **AUTO_ CLOSE** option is off for SQL Server Standard and Enterprise Editions. When set to on, this option can cause performance degradation on frequently accessed databases because of the increased overhead of opening and closing the database after each connection. **AUTO_CLOSE** also flushes the procedure cache after each connection.	`http://go.microsoft.com/fwlink/?LinkId=116338`
Database Auto Shrink	Checks that the **AUTO_SHRINK** option is off for user databases on SQL Server Standard and Enterprise Editions. Frequently shrinking and expanding a database can lead to poor performance because of physical fragmentation. Set the **AUTO_SHRINK** database option to OFF. If you know that the space that you are reclaiming will not be needed in the future, you can manually shrink the database.	`http://go.microsoft.com/fwlink/?LinkId=116337`

Policy	Policy Description	HTML Link
Database Collation	Looks for user-defined databases that have a collation different from the master or model databases. It is recommended that you not use this configuration because collation conflicts can occur that might prevent code from executing. For example, when a stored procedure joins one table to a temporary table, SQL Server might end the batch and return a collation conflict error if the collations of the user-defined database and the model database are different. This happens because temporary tables are created in **tempdb**, which obtains its collation based on that of the model database. If you experience collation conflict errors, consider one of the following solutions: Export the data from the user database and import it into new tables that have the same collation as the master and model databases. Rebuild the system databases to use a collation that matches the user database collation.Modify any stored procedures that join user tables to tables in **tempdb** to create the tables in **tempdb** by using the collation of the user database. To do this, add the **COLLATE database_default** clause to the column definitions of the temporary table. For example: **CREATE TABLE #temp1 (c1 int, c2 varchar(30) COLLATE database_default)**.	`http://go.microsoft.com/fwlink/?LinkId=116336`

Policy	Policy Description	HTML Link
Database Page Status	Checks whether the database has suspect database pages. A database page is set suspect by error 824. This error occurs when a logical consistency error is detected during a read operation, which frequently indicates data corruption caused by a faulty I/O subsystem component. When the SQL Server Database Engine detects a suspect page, the page ID is recorded in the **msdbo.dbo.suspect_pages** table. This is a severe error condition that threatens database integrity and must be corrected immediately. Best practices recommendations: Review the SQL Server error log for the details of the 824 error for this database. Complete a full database consistency check (**DBCC CHECKDB**). Implement the user actions defined in MSSQLSERVER_824.	`http://go.microsoft.com/fwlink/?LinkId=116379`
Database Page Verification	Checks if the **PAGE_VERIFY** database option is not set to **CHECKSUM** to provide a high level of data-file integrity. When **CHECKSUM** is enabled for the **PAGE_VERIFY** database option, the SQL Server Database Engine calculates a checksum over the contents of the whole page, and stores the value in the page header when a page is written to disk. When the page is read from disk, the checksum is recomputed and compared to the checksum value that is stored in the page header. This helps provide a high level of data-file integrity.	`http://go.microsoft.com/fwlink/?LinkId=116333`

Policy	Policy Description	HTML Link
File Growth for SQL Server 2000	Checks an instance of SQL Server 2000. Warns if the data file is 1 GB or larger, and is set to autogrow by a percentage, instead of growing by a fixed size. Growing a data file by a percentage can cause SQL Server performance problems because of progressively larger growth increments. For an instance of SQL Server 2000, set the **FILEGROWTH** (autogrow) value to a fixed size to avoid escalating performance problems.	`http://go.microsoft.com/fwlink/?LinkId=116378`
Guest Permissions	Checks if permission to access the database is enabled for guest user. Remove access to the guest user if it is not required. The guest user cannot be dropped, but a guest user account can be disabled by revoking its **CONNECT** permission. You do this by executing **REVOKE CONNECT FROM GUEST** from within any database other than master or tempdb.	`http://go.microsoft.com/fwlink/?LinkId=116354`

Policy	Policy Description	HTML Link
Last Successful Backup Date	Checks whether a database has recent backups. Scheduling regular backups is important for protecting your databases against data loss from a variety of failures. The appropriate frequency for backing up data depends on the recovery model of the database, on business requirements regarding potential data loss, and on how frequently the database is updated. In a frequently updated database, the amount of work-loss exposure increases relatively quickly between backups. The best practice is to perform backups frequently enough to protect databases against data loss. The simple recovery model and full recovery model both require data backups. The full recovery model also requires log backups, which should be taken more often than data backups. For either recovery model, you can supplement your full backups with differential backups to efficiently reduce the risk of data loss. For a database that uses the full recovery model, Microsoft recommends that you take frequent log backups. For a production database that contains critical data, log backups would typically be taken every 1 to 15 minutes. Note: The recommended method for scheduling backups is a database maintenance plan.	http://go.microsoft.com/fwlink/?LinkId=116361
Public Not Granted Server Permissions	Checks that the server permission is not granted to the Public role.	http://go.microsoft.com/fwlink/?LinkId=116364
Read-only Database Recovery Model	Checks whether the recovery model is set to simple for read-only databases.	http://go.microsoft.com/fwlink/?LinkId=116383

Policy	Policy Description	HTML Link
SQL Server 32-bit Affinity Mask Overlap	Checks an instance of SQL Server having processors that are assigned with both the affinity mask and the affinity I/O mask options. On a computer that has more than one processor, the affinity mask and the affinity I/O mask options are used to designate which CPUs are used by SQL Server. Enabling a CPU with both the affinity mask and the affinity I/O mask can slow performance by forcing the processor to be overused.	http://go.microsoft.com/fwlink/?LinkId=116381
SQL Server 64-bit Affinity Mask Overlap	Checks an instance of SQL Server having processors that are assigned with both the affinity64 mask and the affinity64 I/O mask options. On a computer that has more than one processor, the affinity64 mask and the affinity64 I/O mask options are used to designate which CPUs are used by SQL Server. Enabling a CPU with both the affinity64 mask and the affinity64 I/O mask can slow performance by forcing the processor to be overused.	http://go.microsoft.com/fwlink/?LinkId=116381
SQL Server Affinity Mask	Checks an instance of SQL Server for setting affinity mask to its default value of 0, since in most cases, the Microsoft Windows 2000 or Windows Server 2003 default affinity provides the best performance. Confirms whether the setting affinity mask of server is set to 0.	http://go.microsoft.com/fwlink/?LinkId=116357
SQL Server Blocked Process Threshold	Checks whether the blocked process threshold option is set lower than 5 and is not disabled (0). Setting the blocked process threshold option to a value from 1 to 4 can cause the deadlock monitor to run constantly. Values 1 to 4 should be used only for troubleshooting and never long term or in a production environment without the assistance of Microsoft Customer Service and Support.	http://go.microsoft.com/fwlink/?LinkId=116356

Policy	Policy Description	HTML Link
SQL Server Default Trace	Checks whether default trace is turned on to collect information about configuration and DDL changes to the instance of SQL Server. This information can be helpful for customers and Microsoft Technical Support when troubleshooting issues with the Database Engine.	http://go.microsoft.com/fwlink/?LinkId=116384
SQL Server Dynamic Locks	Checks whether the value of the locks option is the default setting of 0. This enables the Database Engine to allocate and deallocate lock structures dynamically, based on changing system requirements. If locks is nonzero, batch jobs will stop, and an out of locks error message will be generated when the value specified is exceeded.	http://go.microsoft.com/fwlink/?LinkId=116358
SQL Server I/O Affinity Mask For Non-enterprise SQL Servers	Checks that the I/O Affinity Mask is disabled for non-Enterprise editions.	http://go.microsoft.com/fwlink/?LinkId=116381
SQL Server Lightweight Pooling	Checks whether lightweight pooling is disabled on the server. Setting lightweight pooling to 1 causes SQL Server to switch to fiber mode scheduling. Fiber mode is intended for certain situations when the context switching of the UMS workers are the critical bottleneck in performance. Because this situation is unusual, fiber mode rarely enhances performance or scalability on the typical system.	http://go.microsoft.com/fwlink/?LinkId=116350

Policy	Policy Description	HTML Link
SQL Server Login Mode	Checks for Windows Authentication. When possible, Microsoft recommends using Windows Authentication. Windows Authentication uses Kerberos security protocol, provides password policy enforcement in terms of complexity validation for strong passwords (applies only to Windows Server 2003 and later), provides support for account lockout, and supports password expiration.	http://go.microsoft.com/fwlink/?LinkId=116369
SQL Server Max Degree of Parallelism	Checks the max degree of parallelism option for the optimal value to avoid unwanted resource consumption and performance degradation. The recommended value of this option is 8 or less. Setting this option to a larger value often results in unwanted resource consumption and performance degradation.	http://go.microsoft.com/fwlink/?LinkId=116335
SQL Server Max Worker Threads for 32-bit SQL Server 2000	Checks the max worker threads server option for potentially incorrect settings of an instance of SQL Server 2000 that is running on a 32-bit server. Setting the max worker threads option to a small value might prevent enough threads from servicing incoming client requests in a timely manner, and can lead to shortage of threads. Conversely, because each active thread consumes 512 KB on 32-bit servers, setting the option to a large value can waste address space.	http://go.microsoft.com/fwlink/?LinkId=116324

Policy	Policy Description	HTML Link
SQL Server Max Worker Threads for 64-bit SQL Server 2000	Checks the max worker threads server option for potentially incorrect settings of an instance of SQL Server 2000 that is running on a 64-bit server. Setting the max worker threads option to a small value might prevent enough threads from servicing incoming client requests in a timely manner, and can lead to shortage of threads. Conversely, because each active thread consumes up to 4 MB on 64-bit servers, setting the option to a large value can waste address space.	http://go.microsoft.com/fwlink/?LinkId=116324
SQL Server Max Worker Threads for SQL Server 2005 and above	Checks the max work threads server option for potentially incorrect settings of an instance of SQL Server 2005. Setting the max worker threads option to a nonzero value will prevent SQL Server from automatically determining the proper number of active worker threads based on user requests.	http://go.microsoft.com/fwlink/?LinkId=116324
SQL Server Network Packet Size	Checks whether for the value specified for network packet size server option is set to the optimal value of 8060 bytes. If the network packet size of any logged-in user is more than 8060 bytes, SQL Server performs different memory allocation operations. This can cause an increase in the process virtual address space that is not reserved for the buffer pool.	http://go.microsoft.com/fwlink/?LinkId=116360
SQL Server Open Objects for SQL Server 2000	Checks whether the open objects server option is set to 0, the optimal value on instances SQL Server 2000. Using a nonzero value can lead to errors when you are using SQL Server 2000. This value should not be changed from the default value of 0, unless you are working with Microsoft Customer Support Services to solve a specific problem.	http://go.microsoft.com/fwlink/?LinkId=116334

Policy	Policy Description	HTML Link
SQL Server Password Expiration	Checks whether enforce password expiration on SQL Server logins is enabled. Enforce password expiration should be enabled for all SQL Server logins.	http://go.microsoft.com/fwlink/?LinkId=116332
SQL Server Password Policy	Checks whether password policy enforcement on SQL Server logins is enabled. Password policy should be enforced for all SQL Server logins.	http://go.microsoft.com/fwlink/?LinkId=116331
SQL Server System Tables Updatable	Checks whether SQL Server 2000 system tables can be updated. We recommend that you do not allow system tables to be updated.	http://go.microsoft.com/fwlink/?LinkId=116352
Surface Area Configuration for Database Engine 2005 and 2000 Features	Checks for default surface area settings for Database Engine 2005 and 2000 features. Only the features required by your application should be enabled. Disabling unused features helps protect your server by reducing the surface area.	http://go.microsoft.com/fwlink/?LinkId=117322
Surface Area Configuration for Database Engine 2008 Features	Checks for default surface area settings for Database Engine 2008 features. Only the features required by your application should be enabled. Disabling unused features helps protect your server by reducing the surface area.	http://go.microsoft.com/fwlink/?LinkId=117323
Surface Area Configuration for Service Broker Endpoints	Checks for stopped Service Broker endpoint on the instance of SQL Server. Service Broker provides queuing and reliable messaging for the Database Engine. Service Broker uses a TCP endpoint for communication between instances of SQL Server. Enable Service Broker endpoint only if your applications use Service Broker to communicate between instances of SQL Server.	http://go.microsoft.com/fwlink/?LinkId=117326

Policy	Policy Description	HTML Link
Surface Area Configuration for SOAP Endpoints	Checks for disabled Simple Object Access Protocol (SOAP) endpoints on the instance of SQL Server. Native XML Web Services provide database access over HTTP by using SOAP messages. Enable HTTP endpoints only if your applications use them to communicate with the Database Engine.	http://go.microsoft.com/fwlink/?LinkId=117327
Symmetric Key Encryption for User Databases	Checks that symmetric keys with a length less than 128 bytes do not use the RC2 or RC4 encryption algorithm. The best practice recommendation is to use AES 128 bit and above to create symmetric keys for data encryption. If AES is not supported by the version of your operating system, use 3DES.	http://go.microsoft.com/fwlink/?LinkId=116328
Symmetric Key for master Database	Checks for user-created symmetric keys in the master database, which is not recommended. The master database contains the Master Symmetric key.	http://go.microsoft.com/fwlink/?LinkId=116329
Symmetric Key for System Databases	Checks for user-created symmetric keys in the **msdb**, **model**, and **tempdb** databases. This is not recommended. This recommendation does not apply to the **master** database.	http://go.microsoft.com/fwlink/?LinkId=116329
Trustworthy Database	Checks whether the dbo or a db_owner is assigned to a fixed server sysadmin role for databases where the trustworthy bit is set to on. Database users with the appropriate level of permissions can elevate privileges to the sysadmin role. In this role, the user can create and execute unsafe assemblies that compromise the system. The best practice is to turn off the trustworthy bit or change the dbo and db_owner to a fixed server role other than sysadmin.	http://go.microsoft.com/fwlink/?LinkId=116327

Policy	Policy Description	HTML Link
Windows Event Log Cluster Disk Resource Corruption Error	Detects SCSI host adapter configuration issues or a malfunctioning device error message in the system log. http://support.microsoft.com/kb/311081	http://go.microsoft.com/fwlink/?LinkId=116377
Windows Event Log Device Driver Control Error	Detects error event ID –11 in the system log. This error could be because of a corrupted device driver, a hardware problem, a malfunctioning device, poor cabling, or termination issues. http://support.microsoft.com/kb/259237 http://support.microsoft.com/kb/154690	http://go.microsoft.com/fwlink/?LinkId=116371
Windows Event Log Device Not Ready Error	Detects error messages in the system log that can be the result of SCSI host adapter configuration issues or related problems. http://support.microsoft.com/kb/259237 http://support.microsoft.com/kb/154690	http://go.microsoft.com/fwlink/?LinkId=116349
Windows Event Log Disk Defragmentation	Detects an error message in the system log that can result when the Windows 2000 disk defragmenter tool does not move a particular data element, and schedules Chkdsk.exe. In this condition, the error is a false positive. There is no loss of data, and the integrity of the data is not affected. http://support.microsoft.com/kb/885688 http://support.microsoft.com/kb/320866	http://go.microsoft.com/fwlink/?LinkId=116353
Windows Event Log Failed I/O Request Error	Detects a failed I/O request error message in the system log. This could be the result of a variety of things, including a firmware bug or faulty SCSI cables. http://support.microsoft.com/kb/311081 http://support.microsoft.com/kb/885688	http://go.microsoft.com/fwlink/?LinkId=116385

Policy	Policy Description	HTML Link
Windows Event Log I/O Delay Warning	Detects event ID 833 in the system log. This message indicates that SQL Server has issued a read or write request from disk, and that the request has taken longer than 15 seconds to return. This error is reported by SQL Server and indicates a problem with the disk I/O subsystem. Delays this long can severely limit the performance of your instance of SQL Server.	http://go.microsoft.com/fwlink/?LinkId=116375
Windows Event Log I/O Error During Hard Page Fault Error	Detects I/O error during hard page fault in system log. http://support.microsoft.com/kb/304415 http://support.microsoft.com/kb/305547	http://go.microsoft.com/fwlink/?LinkId=116355
Windows Event Log Read Retry Error	Detects error event ID 825 in the system log. This error message indicates that SQL Server could not read data from the disk on the first try. This message indicates a major problem with the disk I/O subsystem, not with SQL Server itself. However, the disk problem can cause data loss or database corruption if it is not resolved.	http://go.microsoft.com/fwlink/?LinkId=116339
Windows Event Log Storage System I/O Timeout Error	Detects error event ID –9 in the system log. This error indicates that I/O timeout has occurred within the storage system, as detected from the driver for the controller. http://support.microsoft.com/kb/259237 http://support.microsoft.com/kb/154690	http://go.microsoft.com/fwlink/?LinkId=116330
Windows Event Log System Failure Error	Detects error event ID 6008 in the system log. This error indicates an unexpected system shutdown. The system might be unstable and might not provide the stability and integrity that is required to host an instance of SQL Server. If it is known, you should address the root cause of the unexpected server restarts. Otherwise, move the instance of SQL Server to another computer.	http://go.microsoft.com/fwlink/?LinkId=116326

Best Practice Policy Conditions and Facets

You might also be interested in condition and facet information for the best practice policies. Listing A-2 shows a query that you can use to retrieve condition and facet details from the **msdb** database.

Listing A-2. Query against msdb database to return condition and facet information for best practice policies

```
SELECT   a.name AS 'Policy', c.name as 'Condition',
c.facet
FROM          msdb.dbo.syspolicy_policies_internal a INNER JOIN
              msdb.dbo.syspolicy_policies_internal b ON a.policy_id = b.policy_id INNER JOIN
              msdb.dbo.syspolicy_conditions c ON b.condition_id = c.condition_id
ORDER BY      a.Name
GO
```

Executing the query in Listing A-2 gives you the results shown in Table A-2.

Table A-2. Condition and Facet Details for Best Practice Policies

Policy	Condition	Condition Facet
Asymmetric Key Encryption Algorithm	RSA 1024 or RSA 2048 Encrypted	AsymmetricKey
Backup and Data File Location	Data and Backup on Separate Drive	IDatabaseMaintenanceFacet
CmdExec Rights Secured	CmdExec Rights for sysadmins Only	IServerSecurityFacet
Data and Log File Location	Data and Log Files on Separate Drives	IDatabasePerformanceFacet
Database Auto Close	Auto Close Disabled	IDatabasePerformanceFacet
Database Auto Shrink	Auto Shrink Disabled	IDatabasePerformanceFacet
Database Collation	Collation Matches master or model	IDatabasePerformanceFacet
Database Page Status	No Suspect Database Pages	IDatabaseMaintenanceFacet
Database Page Verification	Page Verify Checksum	IDatabaseMaintenanceFacet
File Growth for SQL Server 2000	Growth Type Not Percent	DataFile
Guest Permissions	Has No Database Access	User

Last Successful Backup Date	Safe Last Backup Date	IDatabaseMaintenanceFacet
Public Not Granted Server Permissions	Public Server Role Has No Granted Permissions	IServerSecurityFacet
Read-only Database Recovery Model	Recovery Model Simple	IDatabaseMaintenanceFacet
SQL Server 32-bit Affinity Mask Overlap	32-bit Affinity Mask Overlapped	IServerPerformanceFacet
SQL Server 64-bit Affinity Mask Overlap	64-bit Affinity Mask Overlapped	IServerPerformanceFacet
SQL Server Affinity Mask	Affinity Mask Default	IServerPerformanceFacet
SQL Server Blocked Process Threshold	Blocked Process Threshold Optimized	IServerPerformanceFacet
SQL Server Default Trace	Default Trace Enabled	IServerAuditFacet
SQL Server Dynamic Locks	Auto-configured Dynamic Locks	IServerPerformanceFacet
SQL Server I/O Affinity Mask For Non-enterprise SQL Servers	I/O Affinity Mask Disabled	IServerConfigurationFacet
SQL Server Lightweight Pooling	Lightweight Pooling Disabled	IServerPerformanceFacet
SQL Server Login Mode	Windows Authentication Mode	IServerSecurityFacet
SQL Server Max Degree of Parallelism	Maximum Degree of Parallelism Optimized	IServerPerformanceFacet
SQL Server Max Worker Threads for 32-bit SQL Server 2000	Maximum Worker Threads for 32-bit Configuration Optimized	IServerPerformanceFacet
SQL Server Max Worker Threads for 64-bit SQL Server 2000	Maximum Worker Threads for 64-bit Configuration Optimized	IServerPerformanceFacet
SQL Server Max Worker Threads for SQL Server 2005 and above	Auto-configured Maximum Worker Threads	IServerPerformanceFacet
SQL Server Network Packet Size	Network Packet Size Optimized	IServerPerformanceFacet
SQL Server Open Objects for SQL Server 2000	Auto-configured Open Objects	IServerPerformanceFacet

SQL Server Password Expiration	Password Expiration Enabled	ILoginOptions
SQL Server Password Policy	Password Policy Enforced	ILoginOptions
SQL Server System Tables Updatable	System Tables Do Not Allow Updates	IServerConfigurationFacet
Surface Area Configuration for Database Engine 2005 and 2000 Features	Surface Area Configuration for Database Engine 2005 and 2000 Features	ISurfaceAreaFacet
Surface Area Configuration for Database Engine 2008 Features	Surface Area Configuration for Database Engine 2008 Features	ISurfaceAreaFacet
Surface Area Configuration for Service Broker Endpoints	Endpoint Stopped	Endpoint
Surface Area Configuration for SOAP Endpoints	Endpoint Disabled	Endpoint
Symmetric Key Encryption for User Databases	Strongly Encrypted	SymmetricKey
Symmetric Key for master Database	Microsoft Service Master Key	SymmetricKey
Symmetric Key for System Databases	Fail For Any Symmetric Key	SymmetricKey
Trustworthy Database	Database Owner Not sysadmin	IDatabaseSecurityFacet
Windows Event Log Cluster Disk Resource Corruption Error	Cluster Disk Resource Corruption Error Check	Server
Windows Event Log Device Driver Control Error	Device Driver Control Error Check	Server
Windows Event Log Device Not Ready Error	Device Not Ready Error Check	Server
Windows Event Log Disk Defragmentation	Disk Defragmentation Resulting Data Corruption	Server
Windows Event Log Failed I/O Request Error	Failed I/O Request Check	Server

Windows Event Log I/O Delay Warning	I/O Delay Warning Check	Server
Windows Event Log I/O Error During Hard Page Fault Error	I/O Error During Hard Page Fault Error Check	Server
Windows Event Log Read Retry Error	Read Retry Error Check	Server
Windows Event Log Storage System I/O Timeout Error	Storage System I/O Timeout Error Check	Server
Windows Event Log System Failure Error	System Failure Error Check	Server

Index

■ C